WHAT DO THE STARS SAY ABOUT YOU IN 1995?

Whatever it is you seek—love, adventure, good health, or good fortune—Sydney Omarr has an astonishingly accurate forecast for every aspect of your life. For 18 exciting months from July 1994 to December 1995, you will learn:

- how to make your love connections strong and sexy
- how to fine-tune your life by coordinating your activities with the rhythms of the universe.
- how to use the Saturn sign to master a fear, phobia, or anxiety.
- how to use the moon and planets for prosperity
- how to relieve your stress and live a healthier life

So chart your very own star-studded course now—and make 1995 your best year ever!

SYDNEY OMARR'S DAY-BY-DAY ASTROLOGICAL GUIDE FOR TAURUS IN 1995

SYDNEY OMARR'S 1995 DAY-BY-DAY ASTROLOGICAL GUIDES
18 Months of Daily Horoscopes From
July 1994 to December 1995

Let America's most accurate astrologer show you what the signs of the zodiac and Pluto's welcome transit into Sagittarius will mean for you in 1995! Sydney Omarr gives you invaluable tips on your love life, your career, your health—and your all-round good fortune.

☐ **Capricorn**—December 22–January 19   (181166—$3.99)

☐ **Taurus**—April 20–May 20   (181131—$3.99)

☐ **Virgo**—August 23–September 22   (181123—$3.99)

☐ **Sagittarius**—November 22–December 21   (181239—$3.99)

☐ **Scorpio**—October 23–November 21   (181220—$3.99)

☐ **Aquarius**—January 20–February 18   (181174—$3.99)

☐ **Libra**—September 23–October 22   (181247—$3.99)

☐ **Leo**—July 23–August 22   (181212—$3.99)

☐ **Cancer**—June 21–July 22   (181190—$3.99)

☐ **Gemini**—May 21–June 20   (181158—$3.99)

☐ **Aries**—March 21–April 19   (181204—$3.99)

☐ **Pisces**—February 19–March 20   (181182—$3.99)

Buy them at your local bookstore or use this convenient coupon for ordering.

PENGUIN USA
P.O. Box 999 — Dept. #17109
Bergenfield, New Jersey 07621

Please send me the books I have checked above.
I am enclosing $_____ (please add $2.00 to cover postage and handling). Send check or money order (no cash or C.O.D.'s) or charge by Mastercard or VISA (with a $15.00 minimum). Prices and numbers are subject to change without notice.

Card #_____ Exp. Date _____
Signature_____
Name_____
Address_____
City _____ State _____ Zip Code _____

For faster service when ordering by credit card call **1-800-253-6476**

Allow a minimum of 4-6 weeks for delivery. This offer is subject to change without notice.

SYDNEY OMARR'S

DAY-BY-DAY ASTROLOGICAL GUIDE FOR

TAURUS

April 20–May 20

1995

A SIGNET BOOK

SIGNET
Published by the Penguin Group
Penguin Books USA Inc., 375 Hudson Street,
New York, New York 10014, U.S.A.
Penguin Books Ltd, 27 Wrights Lane,
London W8 5TZ, England
Penguin Books Australia Ltd, Ringwood,
Victoria, Australia
Penguin Books Canada Ltd, 10 Alcorn Avenue,
Toronto, Ontario, Canada M4V 3B2
Penguin Books (N.Z.) Ltd, 182–190 Wairau Road,
Auckland 10, New Zealand

Penguin Books Ltd, Registered Offices:
Harmondsworth, Middlesex, England

First published by Signet, an imprint of Dutton Signet,
a division of Penguin Books USA Inc.

First Printing, July, 1994
10 9 8 7 6 5 4 3 2 1

 REGISTERED TRADEMARK—MARCA REGISTRADA

Printed in the United States of America

Contents

INTRODUCTION

Setting the Stage for the New Century

There's a new feeling of anticipation in the air as we go to press. There's a new century ahead and we're rushing forward to meet it! Headlines in the business news at this writing tell the story: "American Rush to Funds That Invest Abroad" and "Bell Atlantic Takes a Big Step into Mexico." Globalism is here, marking the next step in our evolution as the year 2000 approaches. There is uncharted territory ahead, full of new kinds of experiences, thanks to the mushrooming progress of high technology. There are sure to be new people in our lives, perhaps introduced over a computer screen. In this year's atmosphere, when everyone's more optimistic, more in the mood for risk taking, there are fortunes to be made as well as potential disasters for the overly optimistic.

We're here to help you chart the future and make your dreams happen. Astrology can provide you with insight into the latest trends, help you know where the action is and how to take advantage of it. This book is designed to help you ride the crest of '95 and develop ideas that take full advantage of this year's potential by moving in harmony with the cosmic cycles. We'll tell you what's "in" this year, from what you'll be wearing to where the hot jobs are. We'll help you set up your daily agenda so you'll be doing the right thing at the right time.

The most valuable knowledge of all is self-knowledge, and here astrology has much to offer you. We take you through your sun sign and beyond, into the territory of eight other planets, to help you better know yourself and how you get along with others. Remember, astrology was one of the first techniques to give psychological insights, and it's still one of the best.

We'll give you basic information, so you'll know what astrology is all about. We'll tell you everything you need to know about your sun sign. And what's more, you can look up all your planets and find out how each contributes to your total personality. If you're interested in going deeper into astrology, there's a resource list where you can find computer programs, clubs, tapes, or classes to expand your knowledge and connect with fellow astrology buffs.

Many readers are fascinated by astrology's insights into their love lives. Sometimes the one you love is not the sign you thought you were supposed to get along best with. The fact is, our hearts don't always read horoscopes. Through our "love games," you might discover the sign you're *really* attracted to—it might come as a surprise! You'll find out how a tiny planet on the edge of the solar system can change our lifestyle and how it will color the next century.

The year 1995 marks a major shift in emphasis from the materialistic, sex-and-power issues of the eighties and early nineties to a higher vision of world unity. As the groundwork is laid for the new century, we'll be reborn on a new spiritual level, brought about by the movement of Pluto from Scorpio, where it has been transiting for the last ten years, into Sagittarius. You'll be able to understand this main event of 1995 and where it will affect your life, for we've devoted two chapters to this powerhouse planet.

Your daily forecasts will guide you with wise advice, lucky numbers and moon-sign positions, so you can plan your activities in harmony with the lunar and numeric cycles.

Let this guide help you set your personal stage for the next century and make 1995 the happiest, most productive, successful year ever—in both your personal and professional lives!

CHAPTER 1

What's "In" This Year

The year 1995 is sure to be full of breakthroughs. To help you plan ahead, here are some predictions about where we're heading and what we'll be doing and wearing in '95. These ideas are based on the movement of the distant, slow-moving planets, Uranus and Pluto, into different signs. When this happens, there is a major shift in mass consciousness that shows up throughout our lives. In April, Uranus, the planet of sudden changes, electricity, and high technology, moves into Aquarius, the sign it rules, marking a big push forward in technology. Though we have covered Pluto's move into Sagittarius elsewhere in the book, we'll also be considering some more specific ways it will influence our daily lives in this chapter. Jupiter's move into Sagittarius, the sign it rules, is another powerful factor that reinforces expansive new directions in Jupiter-ruled areas.

What You'll Be Wearing

Throw out those black clothes and buy some clothes in bright colors, especially the Sagittarius-influenced colors: purple, turquoise, and orange.

Clothes will have a strong ethnic look influenced by exotic cultures, especially those with a strong religious tradition. Fashion should also have the flavors of Spain and Latin America. Clothing styles at this writing are beginning to show a more monastic, religious look. This will increase; we may all be wearing updated versions of monk's garb or ecclesiastical robes.

Outdoor hunting, fishing, and forest gear is very important this year. We should be deeply into the environmentally conscious trend, with the use of natural fabrics and with motifs that proclaim ecology consciousness. We may be buying these in ecological themed stores and washing them in environmentally conscious laundromats.

Other inspirations could be the Renaissance look, inspired by fashions of the early sixteenth century. Horse themes will abound in prints and equestrian hunt-club looks.

Clothes and clothing advertisements will trade the current sexual emphasis for a more spiritual, visionary approach.

Look for revolutionary high-tech ways of selling clothes by television, CD, or computer mail. Home shopping networks will become more sophisticated. If you want to buy an Italian suit, for instance, you might be able to view the store's merchandise on your computer screen and place an order by fax. The merchandise would then arrive the next day by high-speed mail.

What Music You'll Be Playing

Music will be more cross-culture oriented. At this writing, Paul Simon and Sting have got the right message. Blends of many cultures will influence the arts, which will become a true melting pot. At the same time, many cultures will be trying to maintain the purity of their artistic tradition.

Look for new kinds of music that is more spiritually uplifting, if not actually promoting a specific religious message. The sexual content of the early nineties Pluto-in-Scorpio period should be deemphasized as we begin to look for a higher meaning in life.

The New Games Will Serve Many Purposes

Computer games will become more sophisticated and used as a means of teaching or preaching. Learning through creative play will become more important, as will games and recreational activities that bring people and families together. In this area, there will be many new multipurpose toys, which have an extra message besides that of play.

Portability Is a Key Word

"You *can* take it with you" is the motto this year, as Pluto and Jupiter in Sagittarius have us all up and running! Everything will be on wheels. You'll be able to pack up your office in a suitcase and roll it anywhere you like, with ever-smaller personal computers, fax modems, printers, and portable phones.

Global Communication Gets Easier

Thanks to computerized communication, via E-mail and computer bulletin boards, you'll be able to talk to someone in Australia or China more easily and inexpensively than ever. Perhaps there will be a computer that instantly translates your message into any language you wish.

With so much shopping by mail, home-delivery services will be expanded and central mail-processing systems like Fedex should thrive, becoming much more sophisticated.

What You'll Be Reading and How

Publishing, which is ruled by both Sagittarius and Jupiter, is in for a rapid sea change. Books will be visualized on computers or video disks; magazines will come in CD-ROM versions. Soon we'll be able to tap into a library anywhere in the world and log in the latest magazines on our home PCs. Imagine dialing a number and having your favorite magazine appear on your TV or computer screen!

Desktop publishing will make it possible for many new players to get into the publishing field. How about writing that novel on your computer and selling it via a worldwide computer bulletin board system instead of a bookstore?

Along with a new philosophical and spiritual emphasis in the kinds of books you'll be reading, look for new interpretations of ancient manuscripts. This is also happening in astrology, as scholars are reinterpreting many ancient writings in a more astrology-friendly light.

What You'll Be Driving

The year 1995 marks the beginning of an era of incredible global mobility. While some may choose to stay home and log onto a world communication network, others may investigate the new possibilities in long-distance travel, such as high-speed trains and planes, solar-powered vehicles, and many high-tech advances in automobiles

Individual mobility also takes new leaps. Possibly, the current trend in rollerblading is only the beginning of a trend toward individual movement that is fast and fun. High-speed water transport is another way to get where you're going in record time.

What You'll Be Doing

There's a good possibility that many of us will be going back to school, either to expand our personal interests or to keep up with the new technology. Both Pluto and Jupiter in Sagittarius, which rules higher education, will make this a prime area for creative development and profitable investment. Being an intellectual, a philosopher, or a theologian will be "in" this year, as the life of the higher mind is accented.

Studying via videotape, tapping into libraries with a computer, accessing many teachers easily on electronic bulletin boards open up many educational options to a wide market. It will be easier to learn than ever.

Where You'll Be Going

The trend toward more ecologically oriented vacations and resorts designed to enhance the environment will grow. So will action-oriented vacation places, which offer either physical diversion or a chance to improve mental skills. Spiritual retreats to ashram-like resorts and vacations with a religious emphasis, such as pilgrimages to sacred places, are hot now.

Since Sagittarius is the sign of the gambler, this too, is

an area of expansion, especially in underdeveloped countries and on Native American reservations.

Sagittarius-influenced places should be where the action is: Latin America, Madagascar, Singapore, Czechoslovakia, Spain, Hungary, Moravia, Australia. Within countries, important areas are Tuscany and Naples in Italy, Provence and Narbonne in France, Toronto in Canada, Nottingham and Sheffield in England, Cologne and Stuttgart in Germany. In the United States, there's Toledo, Seattle, Pennsylvania, the Mississippi River, and New Jersey.

Your Financial Life

When Jupiter, the sign of expansion, is strong in the sign of bankers, this should be prime time for investments. There should be a much more favorable atmosphere for taking risks. The danger is in overoptimism. However, after the past few years, this time should definitely be an upswing.

Your Love Life

Interracial, cross-cultural romance could be the new trend, as long-distance communications turn to matters of love and romance. There should be many new ways to meet people, as the "personals" expand to accessing worldwide databases of eligibles. You may be able to review photos or videos of potential romances, meet and network through computer or video parties, or meet each other over a video phone.

After the telephone sex of the Pluto in Scorpio period, it's possible that lovemaking will enter the high-tech realm of virtual reality. You may find yourself falling in love with a computer-designed mate.

Hot Careers

The sky's the limit in publishing now, especially for those with high-tech knowledge. Higher education, as well as all areas of the travel business, publicity, and advertising, should present new options.

Religion will be redefined, as more people seek out the spiritual life in new ways. Churches could be revitalized as forces in the community and as educational and recreational institutions. This should open up many new kinds of careers within the context of church or spiritual life.

The sign of the Centaur, Sagittarius has always been associated with hunting, hunters, and archery. It's anyone's guess how these might provide career opportunities now.

Banks and banking, the legal and judicial profession, and any professions involving foreign trade, such as the import–export business, should present many new kinds of opportunities. Look for new high-tech areas of these businesses for the best way to get in on the ground floor.

Sagittarius Personalities in the News

New Sagittarius stars will be coming to center stage, and some old favorites should be still in the news:

On TV, there's Phil Donahue, William F. Buckley, Lesley Stahl, Don Johnson, Susan Dey, Donna Mills, Robin Givens, Charlene Tilton, Richard Pryor, Morgan Brittany.

In film, there's Steven Speilberg, Woody Allen, Kim Basinger, Jeff and Beau Bridges, Liv Ullman, Jennifer Beals, Teri Garr, Tim Conway.

In music, there's Bette Midler, Tina Turner, Frank Sinatra, Sinead O'Connor, Dionne Warwick, Beethoven.

In sports, there's Chris Evert, Cathy Rigby, Suzy Chaffee, Katarina Witt.

In fashion, there's Gianni Versace and Thierry Mugler.

Mega-celebrities: J.F.K. Jr., Darryl Hannah, Caroline Kennedy Schlossberg, Jane Fonda, Tom Hayden, Strom Thurmond.

CHAPTER 2

The Big Switch—Pluto, the Power Planet, Enters Sagittarius

1995 is sure to be a year of changes, from Teenage Mutant Ninja Turtles to religious cartoons, from dirt bikes to the World Car, from movies about Dracula to those about angelic visitations. These are only a few possible manifestations of a powerful shift in energy that marks a turning point in the decade and points us toward the coming millenium.

We're talking about the power of Pluto. This tiny planet orbiting on the farthest reaches of our solar system moves into Sagittarius on January 17 until April 21, then retrogrades back into Scorpio to tie up loose ends and take care of unfinished business before it finally moves onward to Sagittarius for good on November 10. Those who are new to astrology may well wonder how a planet so far away that it has never been accurately mapped can affect our daily lives. Pluto is the mystery planet of the zodiac, one that can't be seen, but makes a powerful impact on mass consciousness.

We'll sense Pluto power in a subtle shift in the atmosphere. Things may seem to be looking up, after the chaos and confusion of the early nineties. Now we may feel it's safe to take more risks, as if a heavy cloud has lifted. Will the second half of this decade be the "Gay Nineties" of the twentieth century? Perhaps. There will definitely be a more optimistic feeling in the air.

Yet Pluto power is as shrouded in mystery as the planet itself. We're never quite sure what is in store. This is the planet of extremes, discovered at the same time as atomic energy, as the growth of extreme political movements and the rise of mass media. Astrologers associate Pluto with intense forces that lie dormant within collective systems and burst forth, like the invisible power of the atom—or like the planet's namesake, the legendary god of the underworld, who opened the earth and kidnapped the innocent maiden Persephone, precipitating a drama that resulted in the creation of the seasons. With Pluto, our lives are forced to evolve in important ways.

Discovered in 1930, Pluto has never been explored by a satellite like other planets. Scientists guess that it is about four thousand miles in diameter. We do know that Pluto has a large moon, almost a twin planet, and a very eccentric elliptical orbit, which means it spends a varying amount of time in each sign, as little as eleven years or as long as thirty-one years. It takes about 248 years to travel through the entire zodiac. Astrologers decided that Pluto had certain qualities, based on observation of its effects in horoscopes and on what was happening at the time of the planet's discovery. Therefore, some of the most important characteristics of Pluto are power, elimination, mass movements, collective phenomena, the media, mob psychology, atomic energy, sexuality, healing, recycling, the occult, and needs for control.

We've been feeling Pluto power throughout our lives on a personal and collective level, especially during the past eleven years, when Pluto has been traveling through Scorpio, the sign it rules. Like the underworld of the mythical god Pluto, this planet inspires fear of the unknown. Perhaps that is why, during this time, there was so much fascination with vampires (*Dracula*), the more sinister side of the occult (*Kiss of the Beast*), violent aberrations (*Silence of the Lambs*), or underworld organizations like the Mafia. But the purpose of Pluto is to transform in order to transcend. Just as in the transcendance of death there is immortality, Pluto forces one to evolve to the next stage by confronting the lessons of the sign it is passing through.

As Pluto slowly moves through a single zodiac sign, important transformational changes take place that impact the whole generation born during that time. Since 1984, Scorpio-type influences were all over our mass consciousness. In order to understand how Pluto works, let's look at the past dozen years.

In Scorpio, we see Pluto at its most potent. Scorpio is

the sign of sex, and nobody can deny that our lives were saturated with a hypersexual charge—from blatant sexuality in advertisements, to suggestive clothing (in the Scorpio noncolor, black), to S&M themes in fashion, to telephone sex, to readily available adults-only videos, to the proliferation of sexually oriented adult-entertainment clubs.

At the same time, there was the Plutonian emphasis on life or death—abortion issues, suicide, mercy killing, AIDS, and new strains of sexually transmitted diseases. The irony is that, at the same time as we were bombarded with all kinds of sexual titillation, we were also told that sex is dangerous—we must have "safe sex." Sexual issues were hot topics politically, as abortion attitudes and candidates' sex lives made headlines. Rape, sexual harassment, child sexual abuse, and incest made the rounds of media talk shows and tabloids, as deep secrets were exposed and publicly analyzed.

On another note, Pluto in Scorpio brought Scorpio media celebrities to prominence: Roseanne Arnold, Demi Moore, Whoopi Goldberg, Julia Roberts, Goldie Hawn, Jodie Foster, Dan Rather, and Kevin Kline, to name a few. These people transformed our ideas about what is acceptable in our mass media—whether it's a pregnant nude, a fat bluntly sexual comedienne, the first black woman to receive an Academy Award, or the female producer–star who calls the shots with studio honchos. Other stars with strong Pluto influences in their horoscope, such as Madonna and Michael Jackson, pushed the limits of what is acceptable behavior on and off screen.

In retrospect, it might be useful to examine what some of the events of this Pluto in Scorpio transit accomplished. For better or for worse, we're freer than we were at the beginning of the eighties. The AIDS epidemic forced us to confront our attitudes toward death and toward those with different sexual orientation, resulting in a new tolerance and understanding. When many prominent personalities, such as Arthur Ashe, Rudolf Nureyev, Rock Hudson, and Halston, died, everyone was touched. Transvestite trends like "voguing" and exposure in plays like *M. Butterfly* or in films like *The Crying Game* opened up more formerly hidden areas and moved American culture to new levels of acceptance.

We also had our own personal life-or-death issues

aroused with the transformation of the insurance and health-care industries. Many of us were involved in self-transformation via the New Age and human potential movements. Plastic surgery became more prevalent as celebrities resculpted bodies with liposuction, inflated lips, and lifted faces. Body building became another way to take control of our looks and transform them, as muscle-bound heroes in life-or-death action dramas like *The Terminator* and *Die Hard* became male ideals.

Power became a key word at this time, becoming an adjective to describe meals, as in "power lunches" or exercise, as in "power aerobics," computers, such as the Macintosh PowerBook or in the titles of omnipresent self-help books. The news stories headlined those who manipulated others to get power, such as David Koresh and the Branch Davidian cult or, more positively, corporate takeovers and leveraged buyouts that transformed or eliminated entire industries.

On the other hand, there were many teachers who were dedicated to empowering others, helping people free themselves from their own limitations so they can progress in their own development. And there were endless talk shows, where people who had experienced different forms of abuse or limitation shared their experiences with the public.

At this writing, as Pluto is winding up its stay in Scorpio, we are already seeing harbingers of change. The focus is gradually shifting to Sagittarius-ruled topics and trends in the mass culture. A fire sign, Sagittarius is ruled by Jupiter, the planet of expansion and optimism, which sounds like very good news. After a decade of black clothes and sexual allusions everywhere, we can expect the happier, brighter influence of Sagittarius. This will be amplified the first year, brought in with trumpets, when Jupiter joins Pluto in Sagittarius as well. (Coincidentally, 1995 is the year that the satellite Galileo is scheduled to rendezvous with Jupiter.) Perhaps, with this expansive shift in energy, cures will be found for the sexually transmitted diseases that have plagued us over the last decade.

Sagittarius is a sign concerned with the big picture and with how everything relates to everything else. It is the sign of wisdom, of philosophers, educators, teachers, priests, and gurus.

Sagittarius is connected to expansion through transportation. That means all kinds of new forms of transportation are possible—high-speed trains, automobiles powered by a new kind of fuel, different forms of air travel. Some astrologers are predicting more space travel (and possibly space visitors). Already, Ford is announcing a high-tech "World Car," which will be built and sold in the same form all over the world. An expensive and risky effort, this uniform global design is sure to characterize new marketing ventures in the late nineties, when open world trade will allow more contact between cultures than ever before. Historically, this was the time when Venice rose to world power, expanding its territory throughout the Mediterranean. In the 1750s, England became a major world power, gaining territory after winning the French and Indian War and establishing itself as a major force in India. In the thirteenth century, the Mongol empire, the largest in history, was at its height, spanning from the Siberian steppes to the Danube and the Arabian Sea. With the current world trade talks forging new relationships between governments, the result is sure to be an entirely different kind of international trade that transcends each country's individual concerns and ethnic biases.

Pluto pushes to extremes, so we'll see the extreme form of Sagittarius-ruled things. This sign is connected to higher education, philosophy, religion, and expansive thinking in general, and should be good for universities. We'll be much more concerned with the quality of education overall, and with educating our children to have higher aims and ideals. The mid-eighteenth century, a previous Pluto-in-Sagittarius time, was one of the great times for philosophy, when great philosophers challenged the prevailing religions and created the humanistic movements of the period. This was the time of Diderot, Rousseau, Hume, Voltaire, and the Encyclopedists, who foreshadowed the French Revolution. At an earlier time, the philosopher Thomas Aquinas attempted to reconcile reason with revelation in the mid-thirteenth century.

Religion is also Sagittarius territory, and with the planet of extremes activating religious and metaphysical issues, it's anyone's guess how this energy will manifest. Already we are experiencing edicts from the pope against sexual permissiveness, calling for a "higher vision," a new morality to guide youngsters who are without values. We will probably get the extremes of either side, with conservatives becoming more dogmatic and liberal metaphysical leaders also asserting themselves. Through the many spiritual and philosophical confrontations, we in the West must learn to deal with spiritual challenges as well as material ones. At this time, the West is apprehensive about dealing with the more spiritually oriented Islamic cultures, which should bring some interesting developments as this transit moves on. In previous years, Pluto in Sagittarius was the time of the Spanish Inquisition (early 1500s) and the Protestant Reformation.

In America, religious conservatives have been addressing Scorpio issues like abortion and homosexuality for the last decade. Now this sector of the Right is reaching out into education and other social arenas. The influence of religion on education and vice versa is sure to be a much-debated topic. So will the creation of values and ideals in our children, and motivating them to prepare for higher education.

Sagittarius influences several countries, and it is amazing how many are in the news at this writing, either as scenes of controversy (Dalmatia, Czechoslovakia, Hungary, Arabia), or as up-and-coming places (Australia, Chile, Provence in France, Spain, Singapore). With Hong Kong changing hands, it is possible that the headquarters of Far Eastern trade will now move to Singapore.

Sagittarius is the sign of optimism and risk taking. Expect a surge in gambling casinos, lotteries, and chance-taking ventures. The downside of this is that we must guard against overspending and too much risk taking without any practical grounding. It is very important that we understand how to manage money so it can do the most good.

This is one of the most animal-loving signs of the zodiac, so Pluto here should push our concern for animals to the limits. Expect animal-rights activism to hit a new high. Sports involving animals, especially horses, like racing, polo, horse shows, jumping, and rodeos should be superpopular.

As a sign that represents hunters, Sagittarius has an affinity for Native Americans. As we go to press, there is discussion about whether Native Americans should operate gambling casinos (also Sagittarius-ruled) on their reservations.

In the media, "global" is the key word, as networks go

worldwide via satellite. Expect more programming from foreign countries, with subtitles, and more CNN-type stations that give intensive round-the-globe reporting. Shopping via television will extend to worldwide shopping. You might be able to buy a suit made in Hong Kong or glassware directly from Italy via your television shopping channel. American television is already reaching out to viewers in different countries, especially with MTV Latino (Sagittarius rules Spain and strongly influences most Latin countries), its new Latin American TV network that will include twenty countries in the Caribbean and South America.

Sagittarius rules publishing, so it's no surprise that the very first book was printed in China in 576 A.D. under Pluto in Sagittarius. It's fascinating to speculate about how Pluto will transform the publishing business beyond recognition in the next twelve years. Perhaps future readers will buy this book on computer disk, complete with astrology programs to calculate their own charts. The whole field of desktop publishing has many ramifications for the publishing industry, as more players will be entering the industry and publishing on a smaller scale. At the same time, the way books are being sold is changing, with block-long book markets, cafes, and celebrity autograph signings revising our ideas of what a bookstore can and should be. Perhaps the bookstore–coffee house will become a new center of intellectual and philosophical discussion.

Will the printed word be conveyed by paper, by computer screen, by voice, or by "virtual reality," where you'll experience the contents via electronic simulation of reality? One thing's for sure—after this transit, publishing will take off in some exciting new directions.

On a deeper, evolutionary level, this is a time when those who have strongly held, inflexible beliefs and principles may realize that there are many different points of view that are equally valid. Over the past few years, there has been much dissolution of the boundaries between cultures, and now the actual cross-contact will begin, thanks to global media and new trade agreements. It is those cultures which are firmly grounded in traditional beliefs who will feel the transformational impact of other points of view, because it will be very difficult to remain isolated. The religious extremes that have caused wars in Czechoslovakia, the Middle East, and Ireland will no longer be able to operate as before. Thanks to the new global society, there will be much more exposure to other cultures, and mutual exchange of ideas and beliefs. And through these exchanges, we should be able to arrive at a more universal understanding and tolerance of each other's version of truth.

True, there will be many who will not want to risk their safe, established belief systems, or who will fiercely resist any challenges, as happened during the Spanish Inquisition. But the most positive way to use this transit is through an attitude of mutual sharing, realizing that differing belief systems have valuable insights to why we are here. By exposure to many diverse points of view through the new globalism of Pluto in Sagittarius, we should have a much better understanding of who we are as a world culture and what our higher purpose might be.

For each one of us, Pluto's passage through this sign of truth and high moral vision should bring us many experiences, though a clash of cultures, through philosophical discussions, and through unprecedented exposure to the rest of the world, which will force us to examine our own point of view. And by confronting our own belief systems, we should come closer to discovering an authentic individual personal truth for ourselves. Many of us will be shaken up and transformed; however, in doing so, we may also have a true experience of a higher power.

CHAPTER 3

Where's Pluto in Your Life?

With Pluto making the most waves this year, you'll want to know how it will affect your personal life and what kinds of happenings to expect. You don't need an astrologer to do this; you can make a very good estimate yourself, and learn some more about astrology while doing it. The object of this exercise will be to find the Sagittarius area of your astrological chart, which is where Pluto will be passing through.

First, you must find out your time of birth, preferably from your birth certificate or hospital records. Then, look up your rising sign in the chapter in this book.

Now you're ready to make an estimated astrological chart. We'll keep it as easy as possible. Draw a circle and divide it into twelve equal segments, like a clock. Write your rising sign down at the nine o'clock position, then list the other signs in sequence on each spoke of the wheel, working counterclockwise around the circle. For example, if you have Leo rising, then Virgo would be on the eight o'clock spoke, Libra on the seven o'clock spoke, Scorpio on the six o'clock spoke, Sagittarius on the five o'clock spoke, and so on around the wheel.

When you've completed your wheel, you'll have a rough approximation of the outline of your horoscope chart. It will not be exact, because there are many different systems of dividing the wheel, based on the precise moment of your birth. Each chart is a unique portrait of a moment in time, after all. However, this chart can be quite useful in helping you determine what Pluto is plotting in your life.

Each segment of the wheel, in astrology language, is called a "house" and represents an area of your life. The spokes are called "cusps" and the sign on the cusp is the one that influences happenings in that house. Each house is numbered, starting with the rising sign, which governs the first house, then working downward, counterclockwise around the wheel. Again, assuming Leo is the rising sign, the second house would have Virgo on the cusp, the third would be Libra, and so on. Sagittarius, our key house this year, would be on the 5th-house cusp. So our Leo-rising reader would have major emphasis on the 5th-house matters this year.

To make life even easier for you, here's a list of rising signs and their Sagittarius houses:

Aries rising—ninth house
Taurus rising—eighth house
Gemini rising—seventh house
Cancer rising—sixth house
Leo rising—fifth house
Virgo rising—fourth house
Libra rising—third house
Scorpio rising—second house
Sagittarius rising—first house
Capricorn rising—twelfth house
Aquarius rising—eleventh house
Pisces rising—tenth house

Pluto is a transformative planet; therefore, the events in your life that it activates are designed to bring up beliefs or circumstances that have been holding you back or limiting you in some way, and either resolve or eliminate these issues. You change with Pluto in such a way that there's no going back. However, the point is to help you evolve, to bring up those deep, hidden areas from Pluto's underworld "cave" for reexamination, and to eliminate or change them if necessary. Look upon this time of soul searching as a process that has been made necessary by the course of your life, not something that just happened out of the blue. It was precipitated by your previous attitudes and patterns. So rather than resist the elimination of old, outmoded patterns or cling to what has provided you with security, your best strategy is to examine why you are being asked to make this transformation. What deep, underlying concepts of reality are you required to change? What is getting in the way of becoming all you are meant to be?

As we've mentioned before, each house represents an area of your life. The following interpretations should help you determine where Pluto may transform your personal experience in the coming years. Keep in mind that Pluto works slowly, therefore the actual transformation may not be apparent for several years.

Another point to remember, since the houses in your chart usually occur later in the sign (rather than beginning at the actual first degree of the sign), is that Pluto is now traveling through the house *before* the one with the Sagittarius cusp. For instance, if Sagittarius is on your fifth-house cusp, it will be some time before Pluto actually travels over that cusp—at the moment, it is still in the fourth house. However, because the Sagittarius house will be transformed next, you should consider the changes that have happened over the past twelve years in the Scorpio area of your life, for a preview of what Pluto can do in the following house.

Pluto in the First House

This is a time when you make a break from the past. Whatever has been holding you back, whatever is outworn, outmoded, or outgrown, has to go. This powerful transit begins a new cycle in your evolution that involves a transformation in your outward identity, a challenge to add new dimensions to your personality. Often there is an actual physical transformation—you will look different to others. This could come from a conscious decision to change your appearance via plastic surgery or body building. Or you may suddenly look older, lose your hair, put on or lose weight. Some may go through a physical transition, such as menopause or pregnancy, or experience an illness that gives you a sense of your own mortality. Life-or-death questions about how you're going to survive in the future are possible.

In this house, Pluto will bring up the kind of situations that challenge your independence. For instance, you might break off relationships that are too confining, or become more assertive because of the new confidence gained from deep psychological or spiritual work.

Pluto in the Second House

Your sense of values and material resources now feel the transforming touch of Pluto. You'll ask yourself what is really important in life and why. There may be an increase or decrease in your material resources. You may decide to change the way you earn your living if your job is not truly meaningful to you. If your work is simply providing you with security, you may either be forced to change it or you may have a strong compulsion to do what you really want to do. If you are not using your own personal resources, you may find new ways to do so that will change your life in some way. Many of you will sell off property or possessions that have been weighing you down. Others will change how you handle finances or discover hidden sources of income.

Pluto in the Third House

Why do you think like you do? This process will transform the way you think, communicate, reach out to others. There could be a big difference in your perceptions of the world around you and the people in it. You may question and change some of the opinions and assumptions you've held for years. You may find yourself attacking others' ideas. Or, instead of agreeing with you, those who enter your life now could oppose your ideas. The challenge is to find out where you're coming from, bring in new information, and find out what has caused you to hold your strongest beliefs. Since your desire now is for deep knowledge, this is an excellent time for intensive study that will alter your perspective. Relatives and happenings on the local scene may have a very strong influence now.

Pluto in the Fourth House

This is your center, the place you call home, your deep sense of security and your ideas of family. Are you "at home" where you are? If you are too dependent, Pluto's transit can create some very uncomfortable times. However, through the experience of examining what makes you feel emotionally secure, and overcoming dependencies that have been holding you back, you'll emerge a much more productive individual. It is also a time to examine fears of abandonment and intimate family relationships, especially with your mother.

Pluto in the Fifth House

This is the time to ask if you're truly expressing yourself creatively. How are you giving of yourself to others? Here Pluto enforces the transformation of one's creative potential and self-expression. Many will do this through having a child or relating to a child in some way, or bringing out the creative "child within." If you already have children, your relationship with them could be transformed as deep feelings emerge.

Pluto can also transform the way you get recognition. Do others in your life give you the love and attention that encourages you to express yourself? If not, you may look for love elsewhere through an intense love affair, where you get swept away by romantic feelings, or you may have a series of affairs to provide you with all the attention you crave.

Pluto in the Sixth House

Does your life work? Or do you need to create new systems that support your ideas and can make them happen? If you're unfocused, with your energies scattered and your life cluttered, Pluto will make this clear to you. This transit brings much self-scrutiny and self-criticism. You may feel compelled to perfect your skills and techniques, to reorganize your life. Any areas that are out of control will be manifested. Health or diet issues become priorities, and any kind of self-indulgence or physical abuse over the years could surface as illness now. But this is an excellent opportunity to make changes that revitalize your body and create a healthier lifestyle for the future.

Pluto in the Seventh House

Is the one you love really holding you back? Now is when you'll find out. Here Pluto transforms close relationships, partnerships, and commitments you make to others. You'll feel the need to create a new way of being together with someone, a way that allows you both to grow. This is your chance to resolve issues that have been limiting the relationship, or if they can't be resolved, to break up. But, rather than taking sudden action, it is important to examine the deeper reasons why the relationship isn't working out, so both partners can understand that it has completed its mission in your lives and move on with no recriminations.

Pluto in the Eighth House

This is the power house, where you examine what you must give up to achieve a higher goal. Pluto here transforms how you exercise power over others. This is sure to be a very charismatic time, when you examine your own relationship to both internal and external power. It is a time when you empower yourself by facing your fears, risking insecurity, and moving forward. You may also feel powerless, at times, in the grip of forces you can't control. Since this is the house of strong sexual urges and mergers, you may find yourself in a relationship that's "bigger than both of us." On a material level, you'll transform the way you handle the powers that be: the IRS, banks, debts, credit cards.

Pluto in the Ninth House

Here is where you'll be confronting the limits in the systems you believe in. And, since this is the natural Sagittarius-ruled house, this should be a *very* powerful year, with both Pluto and Jupiter activating this area. You may feel compelled to free yourself from any obligations that keep you from expanding now. You'll be required to be on the move, stretching your limits and transforming your concept of reality through exposure to new ideas and interacting with people from many different cultures, with teachers or with religious leaders. As a result, you may change your direction in life or literally move to another location. The big question will be: What is truth for you? When you find out, you may become a teacher who shows others the way.

Pluto in the Tenth House

What does success mean to you? Is your choice career giving you the chance to express who you are and what you believe? Are you being true to yourself in the way you influence others? For those who are not happy with their position either on the job or in some other public capacity, Pluto here could transform your career or the way you take power in society. You might enter public life, become a boss, or restructure your career so that it is more relevant to your inner needs. If you've been a private "inside" person, you may surprise others by taking a more visible role in the outside world. Or you may quit a job or end a relationship that is keeping you from pursuing new goals you have set for yourself.

Pluto in the Eleventh House

Pluto here transforms how you deal with society at large. Who you identify with and why, or where you feel you belong are the deep issues that arise. You might transform your life by working with groups in some way. You may become more socially active or involved with clubs, teams, or professional organizations. You may question why you are so invested in a particular group, or in such an active social life, and you may change the groups you belong to. You may acquire a new political interest. Or you may sever long-standing associations with groups which are no longer relevant to your goals or beliefs.

Pluto in the Twelfth House

The last house of the zodiac is the place of spiritual consciousness, where you are inspired and where you have the most potential for divine illumination. It's also the place where you get "high" via natural or potentially abusive substances. In this house, you have no brakes or structures to keep you from enlightenment or chaos. (That's why it's often called "the house of self-undoing.") Institutions, which are ruled by this house, are places where you go when you are helpless and must be protected or isolated from the outside world, such as convents, hospitals, or prisons. However, when Pluto passes through this place of transformational insights, it's a wonderful time to do deep psychological or spiritual work. You may find that you need more time alone than usual and have more vivid dreams. Now you can tap the collective unconscious and effect a powerful transformation on others with the creative work you do. Some of our most transformative artists (Madonna and Michael Jackson, for instance) were born with this Pluto position.

CHAPTER 4

Introduction to Astrology— Questions and Answers

Even though astrology is a very precise art, the basic principles are not that difficult to learn. And once you know the basics, you can begin to penetrate beyond your sun sign into the realm of influence of the other planets. You'll find that the more you know, the more you'll want to explore further! Here are the questions most beginning astrology students ask.

- **What is a sign and how is it different from a constellation?**

A sign is actually a thirty-degree division of a circular belt of sky called the zodiac, which means "circle of animals" in Greek. The zodiac corresponds to the apparent path of the sun, moon, and planets around the earth. Of course, we know that the earth and other planets orbit around the sun, but astrology takes the planet where we are located as a reference point.

Originally, each division was marked by a constellation, most of which were named after animals (the lion, bull, goat, ram) or sea creatures (fishes, crab), but as the earth's axis changed over thousands of years, so did the stellar signposts. However the thirty-degree signs retained the names and symbolism of their original markers. In other words, a sign is always the same thirty-degree segment of the zodiac, but the original constellations have moved with time.

As the sun, moon, and planets appear to move (from our observation here on earth) around the zodiac, they pass through each sign. A person born while the sun is passing

31

through a sign is said to be a member of that sign. An Aries, for instance, was born while the sun was passing through the Aries portion of the zodiac.

- **I've heard that Pisces is a water sign, Aquarius is an air sign, and so on. What does that mean and how were these definitions determined?**

It's important to remember that the definitions of the signs were not determined by guesswork or chosen at random. They evolved systematically from several components that interrelate. These four different criteria are a sign's element, its quality, its polarity or sex, and its order on the zodiac belt. These all work together to tell us what the sign is like and how it behaves.

The system is magically mathematical: The number twelve—as in the twelve signs of the zodiac—is divisible by four, by three, and by two. Perhaps it is no coincidence that there are four elements, three qualities, and two polarities. These follow each other in sequence around the zodiac, starting with Aries.

The four elements (earth, air, fire, and water) are the building blocks of astrology. The use of an element to describe a sign probably dates from man's first attempts to categorize what and who he saw in the world. In ancient times, it was believed that all things were composed of combinations of earth, air, fire, and water. This included the human character, which was fiery/choleric, earthy/melancholy, airy/sanguine, or watery/phlegmatic. The elements also correspond to our emotional (water), physical (earth), mental (air), and spiritual (fire) natures. The energies of each of the elements were then observed to relate to the time of year when the sun was passing through a certain segment of the zodiac.

The fire signs—Aries, Leo, and Sagittarius—embody the characteristics of that element. Optimism, warmth, hot tempers, enthusiasm, and spirit are typical of these signs. Taurus, Virgo, and Capricorn are earthy—more grounded, physical, materialistic, organized, and deliberate than fire people. Air signs—Gemini, Libra, and Aquarius—are mentally oriented communicators. Water signs—Cancer, Scorpio, and Pisces—are emotional, creative, and caring.

Think of what each element does to the others: water puts out fire or evaporates with heat. Air fans the flames or blows them out. Earth smothers fire, drifts and erodes with too much wind, becomes mud or fertile soil with water. Those are often perfect analogies for the relationships between signs of these elements! This astro-chemistry was one of the first ways man described his relationships. Fortunately, no one is entirely air or fire. We all have a bit, or a lot, of each element in our horoscopes; this unique mix defines each astrological personality.

Within each element, there are three qualities, which describe how the sign behaves, how it works. Cardinal signs are the activists, the go-getters. These signs—Aries, Cancer, Libra, and Capricorn—begin each season. Fixed signs are the builders that happen in the middle of the season. You'll find that Taurus, Leo, Scorpio, and Aquarius are gifted with focused concentration, stubbornness, and stamina. Mutable signs—Gemini, Virgo, Sagittarius, and Pisces—are catalysts for change at the end of each season; these are flexible, adaptable, mobile signs.

The polarity of a sign is it's positive or negative "charge." It can be masculine, active, positive, or yang like the air and fire signs. Or it can be feminine, reactive, negative, or yin like the water and earth signs. The polarities of each sign alternate around the zodiac, like a giant battery.

Finally, we consider the sign's place in the order of the zodiac. This is vital to the balance of all the forces and the transmission of energy moving through the signs. Notice that each sign is quite different from its neighbors on either side. Yet each seems to grow out of its predecessor like links in a chain and transmits a synthesis of energy gathered along the chain to the following sign, beginning with the fire-powered active positive charge of Aries. Keep this in mind as you read through the descriptions.

ARIES: Fire element, cardinal quality, masculine polarity, first sign

Aries, the harbinger of spring, starts off the zodiac with a powerful charge. This is the youngest sign, the perennial baby, focused on the ego. Aries rushes forward, impatiently, always wanting to be first. This sign is active and assertive in everything it does.

TAURUS: Earth element, fixed quality, feminine polarity, second sign

Taurus is a growing period, a time to acclimate to the physical world and to explore the territory nearby. Taurus distinguishes between what's mine and what belongs to others. It is a sign that nurtures, that slows down and builds step by step after a fast start.

GEMINI: Air sign, mutable quality, masculine polarity, third sign

The third sign, Gemini, is ready to reach out actively to others, to communicate. This is an assertive, changeable, sociable sign that gathers information and breaks new ground.

CANCER: Water sign, cardinal quality, feminine polarity, fourth sign

After reaching out to others, comes an emotionally active sign with the feminine drive to nurture and bear fruit. Cancer, the first water sign, uses the emotions, and the first use of emotions is to nurture, protect, and mother others during the initial growing period of summer.

LEO: Fire sign, fixed quality, masculine polarity, fifth sign

After nurturing others, it is time to lead them into the world in the masculine sense. Leo is a sign to lean on, a bright and steady energy that asserts itself, builds strength and self-confidence.

VIRGO: Earth sign, mutable quality, feminine polarity, sixth sign

Time to stop, analyze. After the confident surge of Leo comes the practical down-to-earth Virgo, that makes sure everything is working well. It serves others by analyzing, teaching, criticizing, and improving what has been done.

LIBRA: Air sign, cardinal quality, masculine polarity, seventh sign

An active mental sign, Libra constantly weighs and balances objectively; sees both sides of the question; and asserts itself to maintain equilibrium and ideals of justice, balance, beauty.

SCORPIO: Water sign, fixed quality, feminine polarity, eighth sign

Coming after the mentally active Libra, we have the decisive, fixed sign of emotional extremes, of commitment. Scorpio is the proverbial still-waters-run-deep sign. It penetrates to the core, tends to be all or nothing. In this sign is the intense desire to procreate, the fascination with control and power.

SAGITTARIUS: Fire sign, mutable quality, masculine polarity, ninth sign

Here is a catalyst for growth, expansion, and change. This sign manifests fire's quest for spiritual development. This is a restless sign—a traveler always on the go who expands by relating to others and prepares the way for our relating to the world.

CAPRICORN: Earth sign, cardinal quality, feminine polarity, tenth sign

Now it is time to move into the world, to organize so we can function on a large scale, to organize. Capricorn is a dutiful sign that is conscious of the expectations of others, of one's status in the scheme of things.

AQUARIUS: Air sign, fixed quality, masculine polarity, eleventh sign

This mental sign is concerned with the correct social values, actively promoting the welfare of groups, discovering new inventions. It comes during the quiet time of winter, the right time for concentrated objective scientific thought, mass communication, planning for the future.

PISCES: Water sign, mutable quality, feminine polarity, twelfth sign

This sign's constantly changing emotions reflect the knowledge obtained in the trip through the other signs and prepare for the rebirth of spring in Aries. This sensitive sign must digest the impressions gathered; it's a creative time of dreams, and a time of contributing to others through service and caring.

• **Besides my "sun sign," how many other signs do I have?**

In compiling your astrological database, we consider eight planets, besides the moon and sun. Some astrologers also use asteroids, the moon's nodes, and certain sensitive points of the zodiac. The phrase "as above, so below" is often used to describe a chart as a microcosm of the universe. The three closest planets to the earth—Mercury, Mars, Venus, and the moon—affect your personal character. The next-farthest out—Jupiter and Saturn—affect influences from others, turning points and outside events, and significant cycles in your life. As we get farther out, the slower-moving planets—Uranus, Neptune, and Pluto—deal with mass trends that effect your whole generation. The zodiac, with its constellations of stars, represents the universal influences.

In the western systems of astrology, we confine our charts to the planets and stars within the zodiac. We would not consider the influence of the Big Dipper or Orion or black holes and supernovas.

The sign the planet is passing through at the time of your birth and that sign's location in the sky determine the way the planet will manifest itself in your life. For instance Mars in aggressive, impatient Aries will show a completely different energy than Mars in dreamy, creative Pisces.

The planets' influence in your horoscope is intensified if they are close together, or affecting another planet, which is called an "aspect." This term refers to a distance between two forces within the 360 degrees of the zodiac circle. Some aspects, such as the "trine" (120 degrees apart) and the "sextile" (60 degrees apart) are considered easy and harmonious. Others, such as the "square" (90 degrees) and the "opposition" (180 degrees) are tense, causing friction and conflict or, more positively, challenges.

Two or more planets traveling close together in the same sign (within ten degrees of each other) is called a "conjunction." Depending on the planets, the conjunction can be difficult or very beneficial. The sun works well with Mercury, Venus, and Jupiter. Mars, Uranus, and Saturn are best left alone. A conjunction will give much more importance to the sign it inhabits. When there are several planets crowding one sign, the activities of that area will dominate the horoscope.

• **What is a "ruling planet?"**
Each sign of the zodiac has a planet that corresponds to its energies. Mars rules the firey, assertive Aries. The sensual beauty and comfort-loving aspect of Venus rules Taurus, while the more idealistic side rules Libra. The quick-moving Mercury rules both Gemini and Virgo, showing its mental agility in Gemini and its critical, analytical side in Virgo. Emotional Cancer is ruled by the moon, while outgoing Leo is ruled by the sun. Scorpio was originally given Mars, but when Pluto was discovered in this century, its powerful magnetic energies were deemed more suitable to Scorpio. Disciplined Capricorn is ruled by Saturn. Expansive Sagittarius is ruled by Jupiter, unpredictable Aquarius by Uranus, and creative, impressionable Pisces by Neptune.

CHAPTER 5

Your Success Profile—
Astrological Self-Help to Tap
Your Potential

If you've ever wondered whether you're on the right track
with your life, if you're making the most of what you've
got, if you have undiscovered capabilities just waiting to
make your fortune, look no further. If you're thinking
about changing directions, trying on a new career for size,
here is a clear road map. Does this sound like a mailer for
one of the popular self-help courses? In a way, it does. The
fact is, that for centuries astrology has been used to help
people discover themselves and make important decisions.
And it's still one of the best ways to learn more about
yourself and what you can do best.

To know yourself astrologically, however, you must go
beyond your sun sign to examine a complete profile of your
personality, including all the planets in their positions at
the moment you were born. Besides the sun, there are nine
other planets (in astrology, by the way, the sun and moon
are usually referred to as planets) that work together to
create the unique astrological personality that is yours
alone. Each planet has a role to play in your total portrait
and each is a great source of information for getting to
know yourself. So if you've been just sticking with your sun
sign, come along with us in this chapter and find out how
much more there is to your astrological portrait.

For those of you who feel you're not typical of your sun
sign, this chapter may show you why. Having several planets in another sign can color your personality strongly with
that sign's characteristics. For instance, a Leo sun sign with

Venus, Mercury, and the moon in Virgo will come across as a much more conservative person than the Leo sun person who has Venus, Jupiter, and Mercury also placed in Leo.

And while you're studying the planets, you can use the charts in Chapter 7—"Look Up Your Planets," to get to know your friends, coworkers, loved ones, and that fascinating person who might be your soulmate.

The Sun: Your Confidence and Sense of Self

The sign of the sun when you were born is always given most importance. This is the sign that's center stage. It is the showoff sign that is the major indicator of your personality, your confidence, and your general sense of who you are. You can find out all about your sun sign in detail from the individual chapters at the end of the book. Astrologers focus on the sun sign in general books like these because the qualities of the sun are the most typical of people who were born when the sun was passing through a given sign. This is the common denominator. You may share other planets with someone, but it's your sun sign that will color your outward personality most strongly.

The Moon: What Do You Need?

Your moon sign reflects your subconscious needs and longings, as well as the kind of mothering and childhood conditioning you had. Your moon sign will tell you what you need to be emotionally happy (rather than what attracts you, which is Venus's territory).

Since accurate moon tables are too extensive to include in this book, we suggest you consult an astrologer or have a computer chart made to determine your correct moon sign.

MOON IN ARIES. Emotionally, you are independent and ardent. You are fulfilled by meeting challenges, overcoming obstacles, being "first." You have exceptional courage. You love the challenge of an emotional pursuit, and difficult situations in love only intensify your excitement. As the legendary film star Bette Davis, an archetypical Aries, once asked, "If it's too easy, where's the challenge?" But the catch-22 is that after you attain your goal to conquer whatever or whomever you're pursuing, your ardor is likely to cool down rapidly. To avoid continuous treat-'em-rough situations, work on developing patience and tolerance.

MOON IN TAURUS. Solid, secure, comfortable situations and relationships are fulfilling to you. You need plenty of open displays of affection, lots of hugs and touching. You'll also gravitate to those who provide you with material comforts as well as sensual pleasures. Your emotions are steady and nurturing in this strong moon sign, but could lean toward stubbornness when pushed. You could miss out on some of life's excitement by sticking to the safe, straight and narrow road.

MOON IN GEMINI. You need constant emotional stimulation and enjoy an outgoing, diversified lifestyle. You could have difficulty with commitment, and therefore may marry more than once or have a love life of changing partners. An outgoing, interesting, talented partner could merit your attention, however. You could spread yourself too thin to accomplish major goals, but watch a tendency to be emotionally fragmented. Find a creative way to express the range of your feelings, possibly through developing writing, speaking, or other communicative talents.

MOON IN CANCER. This is the most powerful moon position, one that can seem even stronger than the sun in the horoscope. You are the zodiac nurturer who needs to be needed. You have an excellent memory and an intuitive understanding of the needs of others. You are happiest at home and may work in a home office or turn your corner of the company into a home away from home. Work that supplies food and shelter, nurtures children, or involves occult studies and psychology could take advantage of this lunar position.

MOON IN LEO. You need to be treated like royalty! Strong support, loyalty, and loud applause win your heart. You rule over your territory and resent anyone who intrudes on your turf. Your attraction to the finer things in people and in your lifestyle could give you a snobbish outlook. But basically you have a warm, passionate, loyal, and emotional nature that gives generously to those you deem worthy. Children and leadership roles that express your creativity can bring you great satisfaction.

MOON IN VIRGO. This moon often draws you to situations where you play the role of healer, teacher, or critic. You may find it difficult to accept others as they are or enjoy what you have. Because you must analyze before you can give emotionally, the Virgo moon can seem hard on others and equally tough on yourself. Be aware that you may have impossible standards, and take it easier on others. A little tolerance goes a long way, and so does a bit of humor!

MOON IN LIBRA. Your emotional role is partnership oriented—you won't live or work alone for long! You may find it difficult to do things alone. You need the emotional balance of a strong "other." You thrive in an elegant, harmonious atmosphere, where you get attention and flattery. This moon needs to keep it light. Heavy emotions cause your Libran moon's scales to swing precariously. So does an overly possessive or demanding partner, so choose well. The right partner can make all the difference for the better in your life.

MOON IN SCORPIO. The moon is not totally comfortable in intense Scorpio, which is emotionally drawn to extremes and can be obsessive, suspicious, and jealous. You take disappointments very hard and are often drawn to issues of power and control. It's important to learn when to tone down those all-or-nothing feelings. Finding a healthy outlet in meaningful work could diffuse your intense needs. Medicine, occult work, police work, or psychology are good possibilities.

MOON IN SAGITTARIUS. This moon needs freedom—you can't stand to be possessed by anyone. You have emotional wanderlust and may need a constant dose of mental and spiritual stimulation. But you cope with the fluctuations of life with good humor and a spirit of adventure. You may find great satisfaction in exotic situations, foreign travels, philosophical and spiritual studies, rather than in intense one-on-one relationships.

MOON IN CAPRICORN. Here, the moon is cool and calculating—and very ambitious. You get a sense of security from achieving prestige and position in the outside world, rather than creating a cozy nest or cuddling romantically by the fire. Though you are dutiful toward those you love, your heart is in your climb to the top of the business or social ladder. Concrete achievement and improving your position in life bring you great satisfaction.

MOON IN AQUARIUS. This is a gregarious moon, happiest when surrounded by people. You're everybody's buddy, as long as no one gets too close. You'd rather stay pals. You make your own rules in emotional situations; you may have a radically different life-or love-style. Intimate relationships may feel too confining, for you need plenty of space.

MOON IN PISCES. This watery moon needs an emotional anchor to help you keep grounded in reality. Otherwise, you tend to escape to a fantasy world through intoxicating substances. Creative work could give you a far more productive way to express yourself and get away from it all. Working in a healing or helping profession is also good for you because you get satisfaction from helping the underdog. But, though you naturally attract people with sob stories, try to cultivate friends with a positive upbeat point of view.

Mercury: Your Mind Power

Mercury rules how your mind operates and how you communicate. Do you have a more disciplined, focused, one-track mind, or does your mind jump from idea to idea easily, perhaps a bit scattered? Or are you a visionary, poetic type? Do you communicate easily in speech or writing, or are you the type that spends a great deal of time thinking before you speak?

Since Mercury never moves more than a sign away from

the sun, check your sun sign and the signs preceding and following it to see which Mercury position most applies to you.

MERCURY IN ARIES never shies away from a confrontation. You say what you think; you are active and assertive. Your mind is sharp, alert, and impatient, but you may not be thorough.

MERCURY IN TAURUS is deliberate and thorough, with good concentration. You'll take the slow, methodical approach and leave no stone unturned. You'll see a problem through to the end, stick with a subject till you become an expert. You may talk very slowly, but in a melodious voice.

MERCURY IN GEMINI is a quick study. You can handle many subjects at once, jumping from one to the other easily. You may, however, spread yourself too thin. You express yourself easily both verbally and in writing. You are a "people person" who enjoys having others buzzing around and you are also skilled at communicating with a large audience.

MERCURY IN CANCER has great empathy for others—you can read their feelings. Your mind works intuitively rather than logically. And your thoughts are always colored by your emotions. You have an excellent memory and imagination.

MERCURY IN LEO has a flair for dramatic expression, and can hold the attention of others (and sometimes hog the limelight). This is also a placement of mental overconfidence. You think big and prefer to skip the details. However, this might make you an excellent salesperson or public speaker.

MERCURY IN VIRGO is a strong position. You're a natural critic, with an analytic, orderly mind. You pay attention to details and have a talent for thorough analysis and good organization, though you tend to focus on the practical side of things. Teaching and editing come naturally to you.

MERCURY IN LIBRA is a smooth talker, with a graceful gift of gab. Though gifted in diplomacy and debate, you may vacillate in making decisions, forever juggling the pros and cons. You speak in elegant, well-modulated tones.

MERCURY IN SCORPIO has a sharp mind that can be sarcastic and given to making cutting remarks. You have a penetrating insight and will stop at nothing to get to the heart of matters. You are an excellent and thorough investigator, researcher, or detective. You enjoy problems that challenge your skills in digging and probing.

MERCURY IN SAGITTARIUS has a great sense of humor but a tendency toward tactlessness. You enjoy telling others what you see as the truth "for their own good." This can either make you a great teacher or visionary, like poet Robert Bly, or it can make you dogmatic. When you feel you're in the right, you may expound endlessly on your own ideas. Watch a tendency to puff up ideas unrealistically (however, this talent could make you a super salesman).

MERCURY IN CAPRICORN has excellent mental discipline. You take a serious, orderly approach and play by the rules. You have a super-organized mind that grasps structures easily, though you may lack originality. You have a dry sense of humor.

MERCURY IN AQUARIUS is "exalted" and quite at home in this analytical sign. You have a highly original point of view, combined with good mental focus. An independent thinker, you'll break the rules, if this will help make your point. You are, however, fixed mentally, and reluctant to change your mind once it is made up. Therefore, you could sometimes come across as a "know it all."

MERCURY IN PISCES has a poetic mind that is receptive to psychic, intuitive influences. You may be vague, unclear in your expression and forgetful of details and find it difficult to work within a structure, but you are strong on creative communication and thinking. You'll express yourself in a very sympathetic, caring way. You should find work that uses your imaginative talents.

What Do You React To? What Attracts You? Look for Venus

Venus will show what turns a person on. It is the planet of romantic love, pleasure, and artistry. It shows your tastes and what you'll attract to you without trying. Venus will show you how to charm others in a way that's suited to you.

You can find your Venus placement on the chart in this book. Look for the year of your birth in the lefthand column, then follow the line across the page until you read the time of your birthday. The sign heading that column will be your Venus. If you were born on a day when Venus was changing signs, check the signs preceding or following that day. Here are the roles your Venus plays—and sings.

VENUS IN ARIES. Scarlett O'Hara probably had Venus here! You love a challenge that adds spice to life; you might even pick a fight now and then to "shake 'em up." Since a good chase revs up your romantic motor, you could abandon a romance if the going becomes too smooth. You're first on the block with the newest styles, and first out the door if you're bored or ordered around.

VENUS IN TAURUS. Venus is literally at home in Taurus. It's a terrific placement for a "material girl" or boy, an interior designer or a musician. You love to surround yourself with the very finest smells, tastes, sounds, visuals, textures. You'd run from an austere lifestyle or uncomfortable surroundings. Creature comforts turn you on. And so does a beautiful, secure nest—and nest egg. Not one to rush about, you take time to enjoy your pleasures and treasures.

VENUS IN GEMINI. You're a sparkler, like singer Cher, who loves the night life, with constant variety, and a frequent change of scenes and loves. You like lots of stimulation, a varied social life; you are better at light flirtations than at serious romances. You may be attracted to younger, playful lovers who have the pep and energy to keep up with you.

VENUS IN CANCER. You can be "daddy's girl" or "mama's boy," like the late Liberace. You love to be babied, coddled, and protected in a cozy, secure home. You are attracted to those who make you feel secure, well provided for. You could also have a secret love life or clandestine arrangement with a "sugar daddy." You love to "mother" others as well.

VENUS IN LEO. You're an "uptown" girl or boy who loves "Putting on the Ritz," where you can consort with elegant people, dress extravagantly, and be the center of attention. Think of Coco Chanel, who piled on the jewelry and decorated tweed suits with gold braid. You dress and act like a star, but you might often be more attracted to hangers-on and flatterers, rather than to those who can offer you a relationship with solid value.

VENUS IN VIRGO. This Venus is attracted to perfect order, but underneath your pristine white dress is some naughty black lace! You fall for those who you can make over or improve in some way. You may also fancy those in the medical profession. Here Venus may express itself best through some kind of service, by giving loving support. You may find it difficult to show your true feelings, to really let go in intimate moments. "I Can't Get No Satisfaction" could sometimes be your theme song.

VENUS IN LIBRA. "I Feel Pretty" sings this Venus. You love a beautiful, harmonious, luxurious atmosphere. Many artists and musicians thrive with this Venus, with its natural feeling for the balance of colors and sounds. In love, you make a very compatible partner in a supportive relationship where there are few confrontations. You can't stand arguments or argumentative people. The good looks of your partner may also be a deciding factor.

VENUS IN SCORPIO. "All or Nothing at All" could be your theme song. This Venus wants "Body and Soul." You're a natural detective who's attracted to a mystery. You know how to keep a secret, and have quite a few of your own. This is a very intense placement, where you can be preoccupied with sex and power. Living dangerously adds spice to your life, but don't get burned. All that's intense appeals to you: heady perfume, deep rich colors, dark woods, spicy foods.

VENUS IN SAGITTARIUS. "On the Road Again" sums up your Venus personality. Travel, athletics, New Age philosophies, and a casual, carefree lifestyle appeal to you. You are attracted to exciting, idealistic types who give you plenty of space. Large animals, especially horses, are part of your life. You probably have a four-wheel drive vehicle or a motorized skateboard—anything to keep moving.

VENUS IN CAPRICORN. "Diamonds Are a Girl's Best Friend" could characterize this ambitious Venus. You may seem cool and calculating, but underneath you're insecure and want a substantial relationship you can count on. It wouldn't hurt if your beloved could help you up the ladder professionally, either. This Venus is often attracted to objects and people of a different generation (like Clark Gable, you could marry someone much older—or younger)—antiques; traditional clothing (sometimes worn in a very "today" way, like Diane Keaton); and dignified, conservative behavior are trademarks.

VENUS IN AQUARIUS. "Just Friends, Lovers No More" is often what happens with Venus in Aquarius. You love to be surrounded by people, but are uncomfortable with intense emotions (steer clear of Venus in Scorpio!). You like a spontaneous lifestyle, full of surprises. You make your own rules in everything you do, including love. The avant-garde, high technology, and possibly unusual sexual experiences attract you.

VENUS IN PISCES. "Why not Take All of Me?" sings this exalted Venus, who loves to give. You may have a collection of stray animals, lost souls, the underprivileged, the lonely. (Try to assess their motives in a clear light.) You're a natural for theater, film, anything involving fantasy. Psychic or spiritual life also draws you, as does selfless service for a needy cause.

Your Drive and Motivation Come From Mars

Mars shows what you'll go for. This planet is your driving force, your active sexuality, what makes you run, your kind of energy. To find your Mars, refer to the Mars chart in this book. If the following description of your Mars sign doesn't ring true, you may have been born on a day when Mars was changing signs, so check the adjacent sign descriptions.

MARS IN ARIES runs in high gear, showing the full force of its energy. You have a fiery, explosive disposition, but are also very courageous, with enormous drive. You'll tackle problems head on and mow down anything that stands in your way. Though you're supercharged and can jump-start others, you are short on follow-through, especially when a situation requires diplomacy, patience, and tolerance.

MARS IN TAURUS could claim the motto, "Persistence alone is omnipotent." You're in it for the long haul, and you win the race with a slow, steady pace. Gifted with stamina and focus, this Mars may not be first out of the gate, but you're sure to finish. You tend to wear away or outlast your foes rather than bowl them over. Like Bruce Willis, this Mars is supersensual sexually—you take your time and enjoy yourself all the way. You'll probably accumulate many collections and material possessions.

MARS IN GEMINI holds the philosophy that "two loves are better than one," which could mean trouble. Your restless nature searches out stimulation and will switch rather than fight. Your life gets complicated, but that only makes it more interesting for you. You have a way with words and can "talk" with your hands. Since you tend to go all over the lot in your interests, you may have to work to develop focus and concentration.

MARS IN CANCER is given, in its fall, to moods and can be quite crabby. This may be due to a fragile sense of security. You are quite self-protective and secretive about your life, which might make you appear untrustworthy or manipulative to others. Try not to take things so much to heart—cultivate a sense of impersonality or detachment. Sexually, you are tender and sensitive, a very protective lover.

48

MARS IN LEO fills you with self-confidence and charisma. You'll use your considerable drive to get attention, coming on strong with show-biz flair, like Cher, who has this placement. In fact, you'll head right for the spotlight. Sexually, you're a giver—but you do demand the royal treatment in return. You enjoy giving orders and can create quite a scene if you're disobeyed. At some point, you may have to learn some lessons in humility.

MARS IN VIRGO is a worker bee, a "Felix Unger" character who notices every detail. This is a thorough, painstaking Mars that worries a great deal about making mistakes—this "worrier" tendency may lead to very tightly strung nerves under your controlled facade. Your energy can be expressed positively in a field like teaching or editing, but your tendency to fault-find could make you a hard-to-please lover. Learning to delegate and praise, rather than do everything perfectly yourself, could make you easier to live with. You enjoy good mental companionship, with less emphasis on sex and no emotional turmoil. If you do find the perfect lover, you'll tend to take care of that person.

MARS IN LIBRA is a passive-aggressor who avoids confrontations and charms people into doing what you want. You are best off in a position where you can exercise your great diplomatic skills. Mars is in its detriment in Libra, and expends much energy deciding which course of action to take. However, setting a solid goal in life—perhaps one that expresses your passion for beauty, justice, or art—could give you the vantage point you need to achieve success. In love, like Michael Douglas, you'll go for beauty in your partner and surroundings.

MARS IN SCORPIO has a powerful drive that could become an obsession. So learn to use this energy wisely and well, for Mars in Scorpio hates to compromise, loves with all-or-nothing fever (while it lasts), and can get jealous or manipulative if you don't get your way! But your powerful concentration and nonstop stamina is an asset in challenging fields like medicine or scientific research. You're the master planner, a super-strategist who, when well directed, can achieve important goals, like actors Larry Hagman and Bill Cosby, and scientist Jonas Salk.

MARS IN SAGITTARIUS is the conquering hero set off on a crusade. You're great at getting things off the ground. Your challenge is to consider the consequences of your actions. In love with freedom, you don't always make the best marriage partner. "Love 'em and leave 'em" could be your motto. You may also gravitate toward risk and adventure, and may have great athletic skill. You're best off in a situation where you can express your love of adventure, philosophy, and travel, or where you can use artistic talents to elevate the lives of others, like Johann Sebastian Bach.

MARS IN CAPRICORN is exalted, a "chief executive" placement that gives you a drive for success and the discipline to achieve it. You deliberately aim for status and a high position in life, and you'll keep climbing, despite the odds. This Mars will work for what you get. You are well organized and persistent—a winning combination. Sexually, you have a strong, earthy drive, but you may go for someone who can be useful to you, rather than someone flashy or fascinating.

MARS IN AQUARIUS Is a visionary and often a revolutionary who stands out from the crowd. You are innovative and highly original in your methods. Sexually, you could go for unusual relationships, like Hugh Hefner or Howard Hughes. You have a rebellious streak and like to shake people up a bit. Intimacy can be a problem—you may keep lots of people around you or isolate yourself to keep others from getting too close.

MARS IN PISCES likes to play different roles. Your ability to tune in and project others' emotions makes you a natural actor. There are many film and television personalities with this placement, such as Mary Tyler Moore, Jane Seymour, Cybill Shepherd, Burt Reynolds, and Jane Fonda. You understand how to use glamour and illusion for your own benefit. You can switch emotions on and off quickly, and you're especially good at getting sympathy. You'll go for romance, though real-life relationships never quite live up to your fantasies.

Your Enthusiasm and
Sales Ability Come from Jupiter

Are you enthusiastic, optimistic, willing to take a risk? Look for Jupiter. This planet is often viewed as the "Santa Claus" of the horoscope, a jolly, happy planet that brings good luck, gifts, success, and opportunities. Jupiter also embodies the functions of the higher mind, where you do complex, expansive thinking, and deal with the big overall picture rather than with the specifics (the province of Mercury).

Be sure to look up your Jupiter "lucky spot" in the tables in this book. But bear in mind that Jupiter gives growth without discrimination or discipline. A person with a strong Jupiter may be weak in common sense. This is also the place where you could have too much of a good thing, resulting in extravagance, excess pounds, laziness, or carelessness.

JUPITER IN ARIES. You have big ambitions and won't settle for second place. You are luckiest when you are pioneering an innovative project, when you are pushing to be "first." You can break new ground with this placement, but watch a tendency to be pushy and arrogant. You'll also need to learn patience and follow through in the house where Jupiter falls in your horoscope.

JUPITER IN TAURUS. You have expensive tastes and like to surround yourself with the luxuries money can buy. You acquire beauty and comfort in all its forms. You could tend to expand physically from overindulgence in good tastes! Dieting could be a major challenge. Land and real estate are especially lucky for you.

JUPITER IN GEMINI. You love to be in the center of a whirlwind of activity, talking a blue streak, with all phone lines busy. You have great facility in expressing yourself verbally or in writing. Work that involves communicating or manual dexterity is especially lucky for you. Watch a tendency to be too restless—slow down from time to time. Try not to spread yourself too thin.

JUPITER IN CANCER. This Jupiter has a big safe-deposit box, an attic piled to overflowing with boxes of treasures. You may still have your christening dress or your beloved high school sweater. This Jupiter loves to accumulate things, to save for a rainy day, or to gather collections. Negatively, you could be a hoarder with closets full of things you'll never use. Protective, nurturing Jupiter in Cancer often has many mouths to feed, human or animal. Naturally, this placement produces great restauranteurs and hotel keepers. The shipping business is also a good bet.

JUPITER IN LEO. Naturally warm, romantic, and playful, you can't have too much attention or applause. You bask in the limelight while others are still trying to find the stage. Politics or show business—anywhere you can perform for an audience—are lucky for you. You love the good life and are happy to share your wealth with others. Negatively, you could be extravagant and tend to hog center stage. Let others take a bow from time to time. Also, be careful not to overdo or overspend.

JUPITER IN VIRGO. You like to work! In fact, work can be more interesting than play for you. You have a sharp eye for details and pick out every flaw! Be careful not to get caught up in nitpicking. You expect nothing short of perfection from others. Finding practical solutions to problems and helping others make the most of themselves are better uses for this Jupiter. Consider a health field such as nutrition, medicine, or health education.

JUPITER IN LIBRA. You function best when you have a stimulating partner. You also need harmonious, beautiful surroundings. Chances are, you have closets full of fashionable clothes. The serious side of this Jupiter has an excellent sense of fair play, and can be a good diplomat or judge. Careers in law, the arts, or fashion are favored.

JUPITER IN SCORPIO. You love the power of handling other people's money—or lives. Others see you as having nerves of steel. You have luck in detective work, sex-related ventures, psychotherapy, research, the occult, or tax work—anything that involves a mystery. You're always going to extremes, as testing the limits gives you a thrill.

Your timing is excellent—you'll wait for the perfect moment to make your moves. Negatively, this Jupiter could use power to achieve selfish ends.

JUPITER IN SAGITTARIUS. In its strongest place, Jupiter compels you to expand your mind, travel far from home, collect college degrees. This is the placement of the philosopher, the gambler, the animal trainer, the publisher. You have an excellent sense of humor and a cheerful disposition. This placement often works with animals, especially horses, in some way.

JUPITER IN CAPRICORN. You are luckiest working in an established situation, within a traditional structure. In the sign of caution and restraint, Jupiter is thrifty rather than a big spender. You accumulate duties and responsibilities, which is fine for business leadership. You'll expand in any area where you can achieve respect, prestige, or social position. People with this position are especially concerned that nothing be wasted. You might have great luck in a recycling or renovation business.

JUPITER IN AQUARIUS. You are lucky when doing good in the world. You are extremely idealistic and think in the most expansive terms about improving society at large. This is an excellent position for a politician or labor leader. You're everybody's buddy who can relate to people of diverse backgrounds. You are luckiest when you can operate away from rigid rules and conservative organizations.

JUPITER IN PISCES. You work best in a creative field or in one where you are helping the downtrodden. You exude sympathy and gravitate toward the underdog. Watch a tendency to be too self-sacrificing, overly emotional. You should also be careful not to overindulge in alcohol or drugs. Some lucky work areas: oil, perfume, dance, footwear, alcohol, pharmaceuticals, and the arts, especially film.

Can You Get the Job Done?
Saturn Will Tell

Saturn is the planet of discipline, organization, and determination. It will show your ability to follow through and structure a project. It will also reveal your fears, and what you're afraid will be taken away from you.

Saturn has suffered from a bad reputation, always cast as the heavy in the horoscope. However, the flip side of Saturn is the teacher, the one whose class is the toughest in school, but, when you graduate, you never forget the lessons well learned. (They are the ones you came here on this planet to learn.) And the tests of Saturn, which come at regular seven-year exam periods, are the ones you need to pass to survive as a conscious, independent adult. Saturn gives us the grade we've earned—so, if we have studied and prepared for our tests, we needn't be afraid of the big bad wolf.

Your Saturn position can illuminate your fears, your hangups, your important lessons in life. Remember that Saturn is concerned with your maturity, what you need to know to survive in the world. Be sure to look it up in the Saturn chart in this book.

SATURN IN ARIES. "Don't push me around!" says this Saturn, which puts the brakes on Aries natural drive and enthusiasm. You'll have to learn to cooperate, tone down self-centeredness, and respect authorities, in order to get the job done. Bill Cosby, who has this placement, may have had the same lessons to learn.

SATURN IN TAURUS. "How am I going to pay the rent?" You'll have to stick out some lean periods and get control of your material life. Learn to use your talents to their fullest potential. In the same boat, Ben Franklin had the right idea: "A penny saved is a penny earned."

SATURN IN GEMINI. You're a deep thinker, with lofty ideals—a good position for scientific studies. You may be quite shy, speak slowly, or have fears about communicating, like Eleanor Roosevelt. Yet when you master these, you'll be able to sway the masses, just like she did. You'll tend to take shelter in abstract ideas, like Sigmund Freud, when dealing with emotional issues.

SATURN IN CANCER. Some very basic fears could center on your early home environment, overcoming a negative childhood influence to establish a sense of security.

You may fear being mothered or smothered and be tested in your female relationships. You may have to learn to be objective and distance yourself emotionally when threatened or when dealing with negative feelings such as jealousy or guilt. Bette Midler and Diane Keaton have this placement.

SATURN IN LEO. This placement can bring up ego problems. If you have not received the love you crave, you could be an overly strict, dictatorial parent. You may demand respect and a position of leadership at any cost. You may have to watch a tendency toward rigidity and withholding affection. You may have to learn to relax, have fun, lighten up!

SATURN IN VIRGO. You can be very hard on yourself, making yourself sick to your stomach by worrying about every little detail. You must learn to set priorities, discriminate, and laugh!

SATURN IN LIBRA. You may have your most successful marriage (or your first) later in life, because you must learn to stand on your own first. How to relate to others is one of your major lessons. Your great sense of fairness makes you a good judge or lawyer, or a prominent diplomat, like former Secretary of State Henry Kissenger.

SATURN IN SCORPIO. Your tests come when you handle situations involving control or power over others. You could fear depending on others financially or sexually, or there could be a blurring of the lines between sex and money. Sexual tests, periods of celibacy (resulting from fear of "merging" with another), or sex for money, are some ways this could manifest.

SATURN IN SAGITTARIUS. You accept nothing at face value. You are the opposite of the happy-go-lucky Sagittarius. With Saturn here, your beliefs must be fully examined and tested. Firsthand experience, without the guidance of dogma, gurus, or teachers, is your best education. This Saturn has little tolerance for another authority. You won't follow a dream unless you understand the idea behind it.

SATURN IN CAPRICORN. Saturn, which rules Capricorn, is sensitive to public opinion and achieving a high-status image. You are not a big risk taker because you do not want to compromise your position. In its most powerful place, Saturn is the teacher par excellence, giving structure and form to your life. Your persistence will assure you a continual climb to the top.

SATURN IN AQUARIUS. This is a Greta Garbo position, where you feel like an outsider, one who doesn't fit into the group. There may be a lack of trust in others, a kind of defensiveness that could engender defensiveness in return. Not a superficial social butterfly, your commitment to groups must have depth and humanitarian meaning.

SATURN IN PISCES. This position generates a feeling of helplessness, of being a victim of circumstances. You could underestimate yourself, lack a sense of self-power. However, this can give great wisdom if you can manage, like Edgar Cayce, to look inward, with contemplation and meditation, rather than outward, for solutions.

The Outer Planets: Uranus, Neptune, and Pluto

The three outer planets—Uranus, Neptune, and Pluto—are slow moving but powerful forces in our lives. Since they stay in a sign at least seven years, you'll share the sign placement with everyone you went to school with and probably your brothers and sisters. However, the specific place (house) in the horoscope where each one operates is yours alone, and depends on your moment in time—the exact time you were born. That's why it's important to have an exact birthchart. Look at the charts on pages 94–97 to find the signs of your outer planets.

Can You Work Independently? Are You a Rebel? An Original? Look at Uranus.

Uranus can be an excellent indicator of whether you stand out in a crowd. This is a brilliant, highly original, unpredictable planet who shakes us out of a rut and propels us forward.

URANUS IN ARIES. Yours was the generation that pioneered in electronics, developing the first computers and high-tech gadgets. Your powerful mixture of fire (Aries) and electricity (Uranus) propels you into exploring the unknown. Those of you born here, like Jacqueline Onassis, Andy Warhol, and Yoko Ono, probably have had sudden, violent changes in your lives and have a very headstrong, individualistic streak.

URANUS IN TAURUS. This generation became the "hippies" who rejected the establishment. The rise of communism and socialism happened during this period. You have bright ideas about making money and are a natural entrepreneur, but can have sudden financial shakeups.

URANUS IN GEMINI. The age of information begins. This generation was the first to be brought up on television. You stock up on cordless telephones, answering machines, faxes, modems, and car phones—any new way to communicate. You have an inquiring, curious, highly original mind. You're the talk-show person.

URANUS IN CANCER. You have unorthodox ideas about parenting, shelter, food, and child rearing. You are the "New Age" people, fascinated with the subconscious, memories, dreams, and psychic research. During this time period, the home was transformed with electronic gadgets. Many of you are sure to have home computers.

URANUS IN LEO. This period coincided with the rise of rock and roll and the heyday of Hollywood. Self-expression led to the exhibitionism of the Sixties. Electronic media was used skillfully for self-promotion and self-expression. This generation, now in your thirties, will have unusual love affairs and extraordinary children. You'll show the full force of your personality in a unique way.

URANUS IN VIRGO. This generation arrived at a time of student rebellions, the civil rights movement, and general acceptance of health foods. You'll be concerned with pollution and cleaning up the environment. You may revolution-ize the healing arts, making nontraditional methods acceptable. This generation also has campaigned against the use of dangerous pesticides and smoking in public spaces.

URANUS IN LIBRA. Born at a time when the divorce rate soared and the women's liberation movement gained ground, this generation will have some revolutionary ideas about marriage and partnerships. You may have an on-again, off-again relationship, prefer unusual partners, or prefer to stay uncommitted. This generation will pioneer concepts in justice and revolutionize the arts.

URANUS IN SCORPIO. Uranus here shook up our sexual ideas. And this generation, just beginning to enter adult-hood, will have unorthodox sex lives. You'll delve beneath the surface of life to explore life after death past lives and mediumship. This time period signaled the public aware-ness of the "New Age." Body and mind control will be an issue with the generation. You may make great break-throughs in scientific research and the medical field, espe-cially in surgery.

URANUS IN SAGITTARIUS. This generation rebels against orthodoxy and may invent some unusual modes of religion, education, or philosophy. In Sagittarius, Uranus will make breakthroughs in long-distance travel—these chil-dren may be the first to travel in outer space. When this placement happened earlier, the Wright Brothers began to fly and the aviator Charles Lindbergh was born.

URANUS IN CAPRICORN. For the past few years, Ura-nus is shaking up the established structures of society in Capricorn. Stock market ups and downs, the Berlin Wall crumbling, and new practical high-tech gadgets changed our lives. Long-established financial and technological struc-tures, like Pan Am airlines, are suddenly disappearing. Those born with this placement will take an innovative ap-proach to their careers. Capricorn likes tradition, while Ur-anus likes change. Therefore, this generation's task is to reconcile the two forces.

URANUS IN AQUARIUS. Uranus shines brightest in Aquarius, the sign it rules. During its previous transit, innovators such as Orson Welles and Leonard Bernstein were born, and breakthroughs in science and technology changed the way we view the world. Uranus will enter Aquarius again starting this year and lasting until 2002, when we can look forward to this planet performing at its most revolutionary, eccentric, and brilliant peak. Though this planet promises many surprises in store, we can be sure that the generation born during this time will be very concerned with global issues that are shared by all humanity, and with experimentation and innovation on every level.

URANUS IN PISCES. Many of the first television personalities were born with this placement, because this was the first generation to exploit the electronic media. This was the time of Prohibition (Pisces rules alcohol) and the development of the film industry (also Pisces-ruled). The next go-round, in the early 2000s, could bring on the Hollywood of the twenty-first century!

Are You Imaginative?
What Are Your Dreams, Fantasies, Ideals?
Neptune Will Tell

Neptune shows how well you and those of your generation create a world of illusion (very useful in creative work). Do you have an innate glamour you can tap? With Neptune, what you see is not what you get. Neptune is the planet of dissolution (it dissolves hard reality). It is not interested in the world at face value; it dons tinted glasses or blurs the facts with the haze of an intoxicating substance. Where Neptune is, you don't see things quite clearly. This planet's function is to express our visions, and it is most at home in Pisces, which it rules.

Neptune was in the following signs in this century:

NEPTUNE IN CANCER. Family ties were glamorized and extended to the nation. Motherhood and home cooking were cast in a rosy glow (Julia Child was born with this placement). People born then waved the flag, read Dr.

Spock, and watched Walt Disney. Many gave their lives for their homeland.

NEPTUNE IN LEO. Neptune in Leo brought the lavish spending and glamour of the 1920s, which blurred the harsh realities of the age. When Neptune left Leo and moved into Virgo in 1929, the stock market fell. This Neptune, which favored the entertainment industry, brought the golden age of Broadway and the rise of the star system. Those born with this placement have a flair for drama and may idealize fame without realizing there is a price to pay.

NEPTUNE IN VIRGO. Neptune in Virgo glamorizes health and fitness (Jane Fonda). This generation invented fitness videos, marathon running, and television sports. You may include psychotherapy as part of your mental-health regime. You glamorized the workplace and many became workaholics.

NEPTUNE IN LIBRA. Born at a time when "Ozzie and Harriet" was the marital ideal, this generation went on to glamorize "relating" in ways that idealized sexual equality and is still trying to find its balance in marriage. There have been many divorces as this generation tries to adapt traditional marriage to modern times and allow both sexes free expression.

NEPTUNE IN SCORPIO. This generation was born at a time which glamorized sex and drugs, and matured when the price was paid in AIDS and drug wars. The Berlin Wall was erected when they were born, torn down when they matured. Because of your intense powers of regeneration, part of your mission will be healing and transforming the earth after damage resulting from the delusions of the past is revealed.

NEPTUNE IN SAGITTARIUS. Spiritual and philosophical values were glamorized in the "New Age" period. Neptune brought out the truth-teller who revealed Watergate and unethical conduct in business. Space travel became a reality and children born with the placement could travel mentally or physically to other worlds.

NEPTUNE IN CAPRICORN. Now in Capricorn, Neptune brings illusions of material power, which were tested as Saturn passed by and were then shaken up by Uranus. It is a time when spiritual interests are commercialized and gain respectability. The business world, however, has been rocked with scandals and broken illusions, as management distances itself from the product and becomes engrossed in power plays. Those born during this period will embody these Neptune energies in some way and express them at maturity.

How Do You Handle Power?
Find Pluto in Your Chart!

Pluto is slow-moving, covering only seven signs in the past century. It tells lots about how your generation handles power, what makes it seem "cool" to others. This planet brings deep subconscious feelings to light, digging out our secrets though painful probing, to effect a total transformation. Nothing escapes—or is sacred—with Pluto.

PLUTO IN GEMINI. Some of our most transformative writers were born with Pluto in Gemini, such as Hemingway and F. Scott Fitzgerald. Sex taboos were broken by other writers such as Henry Miller, D. H. Lawrence and James Joyce. Muckraking journalism became an agent for transformation. Psychoanalysis (talk therapy) was developed.

PLUTO IN CANCER. Motherhood, security, and the breast became fetishes for this generation; it was also the generation that saw the rise of women's rights and of dictators who swayed the masses with emotional appeals and the rise of nationalism. This generation is deeply sentimental, placing great value on emotional security. This was also the time of the depression, the deprivation of food and security. This is the sign of mother power; intense, emotional sympathy; and an understanding of where others are emotionally dependent. Power issues center around using the understanding of where others need mothering to either "feed" them psychologically or literally, or to manipulate them.

PLUTO IN LEO. Self-expression becomes a power play for this generation, which invented rock and roll. The rise of television and the development of the entertainment business emphasize Leo's transformative power. This was the generation that "did its own thing" and demanded sexual freedom. These people will go to great lengths to get attention and recognition. This desire for personal recognition can lead to self-aggrandizement and extremes of self-promotion, such as baring innermost secrets on a talk show or to a tabloid. This generation also produced some of the most flamboyant entrepreneurs of the 80s—the big-spending billionaires who lived in the grand style. Pluto in Leo loves to see itself in everything. As this generation ages, it will remain extremely visible and demanding of attention.

PLUTO IN VIRGO. This generation returned to traditional values and became workaholics. Fitness, health, and career interests took over mass consciousness. To increase efficiency, this generation stocked up on high-tech gadgets such as faxes, computer dictionaries, time planners, and portable telephones. This generation uses power by discrimination. These became the "yuppies" who want the best of everything. A keen, judgmental mind, good organizational skills, and an extremely dutiful attitude characterize their exercise of power.

PLUTO IN LIBRA. This generation is just beginning to come into its own. At their birthtime, there was landmark legislation on life-or-death issues such as abortion and euthanasia. The ERA and gay rights movements were coming into mass attention. Marriage is being redefined as an equal partnership and parental roles are being shared. There may be a compulsive need to be in a relationship and to link with others. This generation will exercise power in a diplomatic way, working well in partnerships rather than independently. This is more of a "we" person than an independent operator.

PLUTO IN SCORPIO. Pluto has been in its ruling sign of Scorpio for the past seven years, and during this time has come as close to earth as its irregular orbit will allow. So it is no wonder that we have experienced the full force of this tiny planet. Somewhere in each of our lives, we have felt Pluto's transforming power, especially in 1989, when Pluto was at its perhelion.

For those of you who have felt "nuked" by Pluto (Scorpios and those with Scorpio rising, especially), it may be helpful to remember one of the key symbols for Scorpio— the phoenix rising from the ashes. Pluto clears the decks in order to create anew. In the Scorpio area of your life, you will go through changes in order to be "born again" and to make way for a period of optimism and expansion. Scorpion themes such as sexuality, birth, and death—and the transcendence of death—will be reflected in the way this generation exercises power.

PLUTO IN SAGITTARIUS (January 17, 1995—2008). This should signal a time of great optimism and spiritual development, bringing the century to an exciting close. The generation born now will be expansive on a mass level. In Sagittarius, the traveler, there's a good possibility that Pluto, the planet of extremes, will make space travel a reality for many of us. Look for new dimensions in publishing, emphasis on higher education, and a concern with animal rights issues. Religion will have a new emphasis in our lives and we'll certainly be developing far-reaching philosophies designed to elevate our lives with a new sense of purpose.

CHAPTER 6

How Your Rising Sign Can Change Your Outward Image

At the moment you were born, when you assumed a physical body and became an independent person, an astrological sign—that is, a specific thirty-degree portion of the zodiac—was passing over the eastern horizon. Called your "rising sign" or ascendant, this sign is very important in your horoscope because it sets your horoscope (or "astrological life") in motion. In effect, it says, "Here I am!" as it announces your arrival in the world.

Rising signs change every two hours with the Earth's rotation. If you were born early in the morning when the sun was on the horizon (which makes your sun sign also your rising sign), then you will come across to others like the prototype of your sun sign. That is also why we call those born with their sun sign on the horizon a "double Aquarius" or a "double Virgo." You have twice as much input from that sign.

If you were born with another sign on the horizon, you will advertise yourself more like that other sign. This other sign will mask slightly—or completely disguise—your basic sun-sign character. If people have difficulty guessing your sun sign, this is probably the reason, particularly if you have a very outgoing ascendant, such a Leo ascendant, and a rather shy sun sign, like Virgo.

On the other hand, a rather conservative Capricorn ascendant can tone down the intensity of a Scorpio or make a jovial Sagittarian seem far more serious than he really is. Your rising sign is your "cover" or mask. Often a person will project just one facet of a rising sign. For instance, one person with a Sagittarius rising would be a lover of horses and a world traveler; another with the same ascendant would project the more spiritual side of this sign.

In your horoscope chart, the other signs follow the rising sign in sequence, rotating counterclockwise over the houses of your chart and coloring each one with their personality. Therefore, the rising sign sets up the tone of your chart. It rules the first house, which is the physical body (your appearance) and also influences your style, tastes, health, and physical environment (where you are most comfortable working and living).

You'll find your rising sign on the chart on pages 69-70. Since rising signs move rapidly, you should know your birthtime as close to the minute as possible. If you are unsure about the exact time, but know within a few hours, check the following descriptions to see which is most like the personality you project.

ARIES RISING. You'll be the most aggressive version of your sun sign, coming across as a go-getter—headed for the fast track, dynamic, energetic, and assertive. Billy Graham and Bette Midler show the sparkle and fire of this ascendant. But since you can also be somewhat impatient and combative, try to either consider where the other person is coming from or head for an area where your feistiness will be appreciated. With this ascendant, you may prefer the color red—or wear it a lot—instinctively grabbing for the red sweater or tie. Many of you walk with your head thrust forward like the ram. You may also have prominent eyebrows or a very wide browline. At some point in your life, you may acquire a facial scar or a head injury.

TAURUS RISING. There is nothing lightweight about the impression you give. You have a strong, steady presence; you are not easily dismissed. You are more sensual, patient, and pleasure oriented than others of your sign. You love good food and may be an excellent cook. Green thumbs are also common with this nature-loving ascendant. You may have a very unusual and memorable voice and great concentration and stamina, like TV news anchor Dan Rather. Though your frame is often stocky, with a tendency to put on weight, some curvaceous beauty queens and sex goddesses are born with this placement.

GEMINI RISING. You're a great talker, in constant motion. You're a quick thinker and fast learner, like comedienne Phyllis Diller and rock star and songwriter Bruce Springsteen. On the minus side, you could come across as nervous, scattered, a jack-of-all-trades. Play up your analytical mind and your ability to communicate and to adapt to different people and environments. This ascendant could also give you writing talent or an affinity for work that uses your hands, such as massage or piano playing. Learning a keyboard is second nature to you. You gesture often and probably have light coloring and fine features.

CANCER RISING. You may come across as sensitive and caring, one who enjoys taking care of others. You may seem a bit moodier than others of your sign and more self-protective, like actor John Travolta. You have very quick responses to emotional situations. You are also very astute businesswise, with a sharp sense of what will sell, like H. Ross Perot, a double Cancer. You may choose work dealing with hotels or shelter business, decorating or working with children. Physically, you may be a lunar type, with a large chest area, a round face, and delicate sensitive skin. Or you may be a "crab" type, with wide-set eyes and prominent bone structure.

LEO RISING. You project a regal air of authority, which instills confidence in your abilities. You come across as someone who can take charge. You are very poised in the spotlight and you know how to present yourself to play up your special star quality, like Ava Gardner, ballerina Cynthia Gregory, or Marilyn Monroe. You attract attention and you tend to take center stage graciously. In business, you can be the epitome of executive style.

VIRGO RISING. Your style may be rather conservative, restrained, and classic, but your intelligence and your analytical ability shine brightly. You seem well organized, with a no-nonsense air of knowing what you're doing. Never one to slack off, you're a hard worker who gets on with it. Your manner may be a bit aloof, and you can be critical of others who don't share your sense of mastery of your craft, of doing it to perfection. But this critical quality serves you well as an editor, writer, or teacher. You may also be drawn

to the health or service fields. A high-profile example:
George Bush.

LIBRA RISING. You come across as charming, attractive, well dressed, and diplomatic. Like Nancy Reagan, the first impression you give is one of social ease and harmony. You enjoy working with others and it shows. You thrive in partnerships and relationships, rather than going it alone. You may have aesthetic concerns, such as fashion or design, or you could gravitate to the diplomatic or legal fields. Physically, you'll have delicate, harmonious features; graceful gestures; and a lovely, often dimpled, smile.

SCORPIO RISING. Even if you don't say a word, your presence carries a charge of excitement and an air of mystery. Margaret Thatcher and Jacqueline Kennedy Onassis are terrific examples. Intense and charismatic, you'll make your presence felt with a penetrating gaze. Be careful not to come on too overwhelmingly strong. You might consider toning down your intensity, tempering it with a touch of humor. Less open than others of your sign, you can be very manipulative when chasing your goals. You project an air of subtle sexuality, of a secret agenda that could fascinate others. Sexual expression will be an important issue for you. You may wear a great deal of the "no-color," black.

SAGITTARIUS RISING. This ascendant can push normally home-loving signs to exotic locales. Always on the go, you have energy to burn. You're a bouncy, athletic version of your sign, like Ted Turner, with an upbeat personality that exudes cheerful optimism. You adore competitive sports that require lots of leg power. You may also be drawn to horses or horse-related activities. You are frank and direct in manner and don't hesitate to say what you think, even if it means stepping on some tender toes. Travel excites you—the more exotic the destination, the better. You may be attracted to idealistic or philosophical activities, or to teaching, publishing, or religious careers. Your sense of humor wins fans, but some of you may have to work on developing tact and diplomacy. Another famous example: Raquel Welch.

CAPRICORN RISING. You are the serious, hard-working type with a very sharp business sense. (*Cosmopolitan* editor Helen Gurley Brown, who has this ascendant, has called herself a "mouseburger"). But you could also have the traditional flair of Fred Astaire. A great organizer, you function well in a structured or corporate environment. Not a frivolous type, you aim to be taken seriously, like Paul Newman. You'll easily adapt to present the classiest impression appropriate to your business. You understand how to delegate and to use the talents of others, which could land you a leadership position. You prefer a traditional atmosphere, antiques, and possessions of "quiet quality." Take special care of your knees, teeth and bone structure, which are vulnerable areas.

AQUARIUS RISING. Like daredevil Evil Knievel, you're charismatic and individualistic—you know how to get attention, sometimes in a startling way that shakes everyone up. You'll dress to please yourself—never mind the dress code. Be sure to find a business that appreciates your eccentric side, one with a cause or principles you believe in. Your job should give you plenty of space and allow you to work independently. You'll make your own rules and probably won't take well to authority or outside discipline—you know what's best for you, anyway. You may be attracted to a high-tech career or to one that probes the depths of the mind in some way.

PISCES RISING. You'll express the most artistic, romantic, and imaginative side of your sun sign. Like Phil Donohue, you'll come across as empathetic, a good listener who is able to cue in to where others are coming from—a valuable interview asset. You may be quite dramatic, and present yourself as a "character," like baseball's Yogi Berra or author Norman Mailer. You are very happy on the water, or in a home that overlooks water. You might gravitate to the theater, dance or film worlds, or to any creative environment. Or you could take another Pisces tack and show your more spiritual side, dedicating yourself to helping others. Beautiful eyes and talented dancing feet are frequent gifts of this ascendant. One of your most vulnerable points is your supersensitivity to drugs, chemicals, or alcohol. High-profile example: Richard Pryor.

RISING SIGNS—A.M. BIRTHS

	1 AM	2 AM	3 AM	4 AM	5 AM	6 AM	7 AM	8 AM	9 AM	10 AM	11 AM	12 NOON
Jan 1	Lib	Sc	Sc	Sc	Sag	Sag	Cap	Cap	Aq	Aq	Pis	Ar
Jan 9	Lib	Sc	Sc	Sag	Sag	Sag	Cap	Cap	Aq	Pis	Ar	Tau
Jan 17	Sc	Sc	Sc	Sag	Sag	Cap	Cap	Aq	Aq	Pis	Ar	Tau
Jan 25	Sc	Sc	Sag	Sag	Sag	Cap	Cap	Aq	Pis	Ar	Tau	Tau
Feb 2	Sc	Sc	Sag	Sag	Cap	Cap	Aq	Pis	Pis	Ar	Tau	Gem
Feb 10	Sc	Sag	Sag	Sag	Cap	Cap	Aq	Pis	Ar	Tau	Tau	Gem
Feb 18	Sc	Sag	Sag	Cap	Cap	Aq	Pis	Pis	Ar	Tau	Gem	Gem
Feb 26	Sag	Sag	Sag	Cap	Aq	Aq	Pis	Ar	Tau	Tau	Gem	Gem
Mar 6	Sag	Sag	Cap	Cap	Aq	Pis	Pis	Ar	Tau	Gem	Gem	Can
Mar 14	Sag	Cap	Cap	Aq	Aq	Pis	Ar	Tau	Tau	Gem	Gem	Can
Mar 22	Sag	Cap	Cap	Aq	Pis	Ar	Ar	Tau	Gem	Gem	Can	Can
Mar 30	Cap	Cap	Aq	Pis	Pis	Ar	Tau	Tau	Gem	Can	Can	Can
Apr 7	Cap	Cap	Aq	Pis	Ar	Ar	Tau	Gem	Gem	Can	Can	Leo
Apr 14	Cap	Aq	Aq	Pis	Ar	Tau	Tau	Gem	Gem	Can	Can	Leo
Apr 22	Cap	Aq	Pis	Ar	Ar	Tau	Gem	Gem	Can	Can	Leo	Leo
Apr 30	Aq	Aq	Pis	Ar	Tau	Tau	Gem	Can	Can	Can	Leo	Leo
May 8	Aq	Pis	Ar	Ar	Tau	Gem	Gem	Can	Can	Leo	Leo	Leo
May 16	Aq	Pis	Ar	Tau	Gem	Gem	Gem	Can	Can	Leo	Leo	Vir
May 24	Pis	Ar	Ar	Tau	Gem	Gem	Can	Can	Leo	Leo	Leo	Vir
June 1	Pis	Ar	Tau	Gem	Gem	Can	Can	Can	Leo	Leo	Vir	Vir
June 9	Ar	Ar	Tau	Gem	Gem	Can	Can	Leo	Leo	Leo	Vir	Vir
June 17	Ar	Tau	Gem	Gem	Can	Can	Can	Leo	Leo	Vir	Vir	Vir
June 25	Tau	Tau	Gem	Gem	Can	Can	Leo	Leo	Leo	Vir	Vir	Lib
July 3	Tau	Gem	Gem	Can	Can	Can	Leo	Leo	Vir	Vir	Vir	Lib
July 11	Tau	Gem	Gem	Can	Can	Leo	Leo	Leo	Vir	Vir	Lib	Lib
July 18	Gem	Gem	Can	Can	Can	Leo	Leo	Vir	Vir	Vir	Lib	Lib
July 26	Gem	Gem	Can	Can	Leo	Leo	Vir	Vir	Vir	Lib	Lib	Lib
Aug 3	Gem	Can	Can	Can	Leo	Leo	Vir	Vir	Vir	Lib	Lib	Sc
Aug 11	Gem	Can	Can	Can	Leo	Leo	Leo	Vir	Vir	Lib	Lib	Sc
Aug 18	Can	Can	Can	Leo	Leo	Vir	Vir	Vir	Lib	Lib	Sc	Sc
Aug 27	Can	Can	Leo	Leo	Leo	Vir	Vir	Lib	Lib	Lib	Sc	Sc
Sept 4	Can	Can	Leo	Leo	Leo	Vir	Vir	Vir	Lib	Lib	Sc	Sc
Sept 12	Can	Leo	Leo	Leo	Vir	Vir	Lib	Lib	Lib	Sc	Sc	Sag
Sept 20	Leo	Leo	Leo	Vir	Vir	Vir	Lib	Lib	Sc	Sc	Sc	Sag
Sept 28	Leo	Leo	Leo	Vir	Vir	Lib	Lib	Lib	Sc	Sc	Sag	Sag
Oct 6	Leo	Leo	Vir	Vir	Vir	Lib	Lib	Sc	Sc	Sc	Sag	Sag
Oct 14	Leo	Vir	Vir	Vir	Lib	Lib	Lib	Sc	Sc	Sag	Sag	Cap
Oct 22	Leo	Vir	Vir	Lib	Lib	Lib	Sc	Sc	Sc	Sag	Sag	Cap
Oct 30	Vir	Vir	Vir	Lib	Lib	Sc	Sc	Sc	Sag	Sag	Cap	Cap
Nov 7	Vir	Vir	Lib	Lib	Lib	Sc	Sc	Sc	Sag	Sag	Cap	Cap
Nov 15	Vir	Vir	Lib	Lib	Sc	Sc	Sc	Sag	Sag	Cap	Cap	Aq
Nov 23	Vir	Lib	Lib	Lib	Sc	Sc	Sag	Sag	Sag	Cap	Cap	Aq
Dec 1	Vir	Lib	Lib	Sc	Sc	Sc	Sag	Sag	Cap	Cap	Aq	Aq
Dec 9	Lib	Lib	Lib	Sc	Sc	Sag	Sag	Sag	Cap	Cap	Aq	Pis
Dec 18	Lib	Lib	Sc	Sc	Sc	Sag	Sag	Cap	Cap	Aq	Aq	Pis
Dec 28	Lib	Lib	Sc	Sc	Sag	Sag	Sag	Cap	Aq	Aq	Pis	Ar

RISING SIGNS—P.M. BIRTHS

	1 PM	2 PM	3 PM	4 PM	5 PM	6 PM	7 PM	8 PM	9 PM	10 PM	11 PM	12 MID-NIGHT
Jan 1	Tau	Gem	Gem	Can	Can	Can	Leo	Leo	Vir	Vir	Vir	Lib
Jan 9	Tau	Gem	Gem	Can	Can	Leo	Leo	Leo	Vir	Vir	Vir	Lib
Jan 17	Gem	Gem	Can	Can	Can	Leo	Leo	Vir	Vir	Vir	Lib	Lib
Jan 25	Gem	Gem	Can	Can	Leo	Leo	Leo	Vir	Vir	Lib	Lib	Lib
Feb 2	Gem	Can	Can	Can	Leo	Leo	Vir	Vir	Vir	Lib	Lib	Sc
Feb 10	Gem	Can	Can	Leo	Leo	Leo	Vir	Vir	Lib	Lib	Lib	Sc
Feb 18	Can	Can	Can	Leo	Leo	Vir	Vir	Vir	Lib	Lib	Sc	Sc
Feb 26	Can	Can	Leo	Leo	Leo	Vir	Vir	Lib	Lib	Lib	Sc	Sc
Mar 6	Can	Leo	Leo	Leo	Vir	Vir	Vir	Lib	Lib	Sc	Sc	Sc
Mar 14	Can	Leo	Leo	Vir	Vir	Vir	Lib	Lib	Lib	Sc	Sc	Sag
Mar 22	Leo	Leo	Leo	Vir	Vir	Lib	Lib	Lib	Sc	Sc	Sc	Sag
Mar 30	Leo	Leo	Vir	Vir	Vir	Lib	Lib	Sc	Sc	Sc	Sag	Sag
Apr 7	Leo	Leo	Vir	Vir	Lib	Lib	Lib	Sc	Sc	Sc	Sag	Sag
Apr 14	Leo	Vir	Vir	Vir	Lib	Lib	Sc	Sc	Sc	Sag	Sag	Cap
Apr 22	Leo	Vir	Vir	Lib	Lib	Lib	Sc	Sc	Sc	Sag	Sag	Cap
Apr 30	Vir	Vir	Vir	Lib	Lib	Sc	Sc	Sc	Sag	Sag	Cap	Cap
May 8	Vir	Vir	Lib	Lib	Lib	Sc	Sc	Sag	Sag	Sag	Cap	Cap
May 16	Vir	Vir	Lib	Lib	Sc	Sc	Sc	Sag	Sag	Cap	Cap	Aq
May 24	Vir	Lib	Lib	Lib	Sc	Sc	Sag	Sag	Sag	Cap	Cap	Aq
June 1	Vir	Lib	Lib	Sc	Sc	Sc	Sag	Sag	Cap	Cap	Aq	Aq
June 9	Lib	Lib	Lib	Sc	Sc	Sag	Sag	Sag	Cap	Cap	Aq	Pis
June 17	Lib	Lib	Sc	Sc	Sc	Sag	Sag	Cap	Cap	Aq	Aq	Pis
June 25	Lib	Lib	Sc	Sc	Sag	Sag	Sag	Cap	Cap	Aq	Pis	Ar
July 3	Lib	Sc	Sc	Sc	Sag	Sag	Cap	Cap	Aq	Aq	Pis	Ar
July 11	Lib	Sc	Sc	Sag	Sag	Sag	Cap	Cap	Aq	Pis	Ar	Tau
July 18	Sc	Sc	Sc	Sag	Sag	Cap	Cap	Aq	Aq	Pis	Ar	Tau
July 26	Sc	Sc	Sag	Sag	Sag	Cap	Cap	Aq	Pis	Ar	Tau	Tau
Aug 3	Sc	Sc	Sag	Sag	Cap	Cap	Aq	Aq	Pis	Ar	Tau	Gem
Aug 11	Sc	Sag	Sag	Sag	Cap	Cap	Aq	Pis	Ar	Tau	Tau	Gem
Aug 18	Sc	Sag	Sag	Cap	Cap	Aq	Pis	Pis	Ar	Tau	Gem	Gem
Aug 27	Sag	Sag	Sag	Cap	Cap	Aq	Pis	Ar	Tau	Tau	Gem	Gem
Sept 4	Sag	Sag	Cap	Cap	Aq	Pis	Pis	Ar	Tau	Gem	Gem	Can
Sept 12	Sag	Sag	Cap	Aq	Aq	Pis	Ar	Tau	Tau	Gem	Gem	Can
Sept 20	Sag	Cap	Cap	Aq	Pis	Pis	Ar	Tau	Gem	Gem	Can	Can
Sept 28	Cap	Cap	Aq	Aq	Pis	Ar	Tau	Tau	Gem	Gem	Can	Can
Oct 6	Cap	Cap	Aq	Pis	Ar	Ar	Tau	Gem	Gem	Can	Can	Leo
Oct 14	Cap	Aq	Aq	Pis	Ar	Tau	Tau	Gem	Gem	Can	Can	Leo
Oct 22	Cap	Aq	Pis	Ar	Ar	Tau	Gem	Gem	Can	Can	Leo	Leo
Oct 30	Aq	Aq	Pis	Ar	Tau	Tau	Gem	Gem	Can	Can	Leo	Leo
Nov 7	Aq	Aq	Pis	Ar	Tau	Tau	Gem	Can	Can	Can	Leo	Leo
Nov 15	Aq	Pis	Ar	Tau	Gem	Gem	Can	Can	Can	Leo	Leo	Vir
Nov 23	Pis	Ar	Ar	Tau	Gem	Gem	Can	Can	Leo	Leo	Leo	Vir
Dec 1	Pis	Ar	Tau	Gem	Gem	Can	Can	Can	Leo	Leo	Vir	Vir
Dec 9	Ar	Ar	Tau	Gem	Gem	Can	Can	Leo	Leo	Leo	Vir	Vir
Dec 18	Ar	Tau	Gem	Gem	Can	Can	Can	Leo	Leo	Vir	Vir	Vir
Dec 28	Tau	Tau	Gem	Gem	Can	Can	Leo	Leo	Vir	Vir	Vir	Lib

CHAPTER 7

Look Up Your Planets

The following tables are provided so that you can look up the signs of seven major planets—Venus, Mars, Saturn, Jupiter, Uranus, Neptune, and Pluto. We do not have room for tables for the moon and Mercury, which change signs often.

How to Use the Venus Table

Find the year of your birth in the vertical column on the left, then follow across the page until you find the correct date. The Venus sign is at the top of that column.

How to Use the Mars, Saturn, and Jupiter Tables

Find the year of your birth date on the left side of each column. The dates the planet entered each sign are listed on the right side of each column. (Signs are abbreviated to the first three letters.) Your birthday should fall on or between each date listed, and your planetary placement should correspond to the earlier sign of that period.

VENUS SIGNS 1901–2000

	Aries	Taurus	Gemini	Cancer	Leo	Virgo
1901	3/29-4/22	4/22-5/17	5/17-6/10	6/10-7/5	7/5-7/29	7/29-8/23
1902	5/7-6/3	6/3-6/30	6/30-7/25	7/25-8/19	8/19-9/13	9/13-10/7
1903	2/28-3/24	3/24-4/18	4/18-5/13	5/13-6/9	6/9-7/7	7/7-8/17 9/6-11/8
1904	3/13-5/7	5/7-6/1	6/1-6/25	6/25-7/19	7/19-8/13	8/13-9/6
1905	2/3-3/6 4/9-5/28	3/6-4/9 5/28-7/8	7/8-8/6	8/6-9/1	9/1-9/27	9/27-10/21
1906	3/1-4/7	4/7-5/2	5/2-5/26	5/26-6/20	6/20-7/16	7/16-8/11
1907	4/27-5/22	5/22-6/16	6/16-7/11	7/11-8/4	8/4-8/29	8/29-9/22
1908	2/14-3/10	3/10-4/5	4/5-5/5	5/5-9/8	9/8-10/8	10/8-11/3
1909	3/29-4/22	4/22-5/16	5/16-6/10	6/10-7/4	7/4-7/29	7/29-8/23
1910	5/7-6/3	6/4-6/29	6/30-7/24	7/25-8/18	8/19-9/12	9/13-10/6
1911	2/28-3/23	3/24-4/17	4/18-5/12	5/13-6/8	6/9-7/7	7/8-11/8
1912	4/13-5/6	5/7-5/31	6/1-6/24	6/24-7/18	7/19-8/12	8/13-9/5
1913	2/3-3/6 5/2-5/30	3/7-5/1 5/31-7/7	7/8-8/5	8/6-8/31	9/1-9/26	9/27-10/20
1914	3/14-4/6	4/7-5/1	5/2-5/25	5/26-6/19	6/20-7/15	7/16-8/10
1915	4/27-5/21	5/22-6/15	6/16-7/10	7/11-8/3	8/4-8/28	8/29-9/21
1916	2/14-3/9	3/10-4/5	4/6-5/5	5/6-9/8	9/9-10/7	10/8-11/2
1917	3/29-4/21	4/22-5/15	5/16-6/9	6/10-7/3	7/4-7/28	7/29-8/21
1918	5/7-6/2	6/3-6/28	6/29-7/24	7/25-8/18	8/19-9/11	9/12-10/5
1919	2/27-3/22	3/23-4/16	4/17-5/12	5/13-6/7	6/8-7/7	7/8-11/8
1920	4/12-5/6	5/7-5/30	5/31-6/23	6/24-7/18	7/19-8/11	8/12-9/4
1921	2/3-3/6 4/26-6/1	3/7-4/25 6/2-7/7	7/8-8/5	8/6-8/31	9/1-9/25	9/26-10/20
1922	3/13-4/6	4/7-4/30	5/1-5/25	5/26-6/19	6/20-7/14	7/15-8/9
1923	4/27-5/21	5/22-6/14	6/15-7/9	7/10-8/3	8/4-8/27	8/28-9/20
1924	2/13-3/8	3/9-4/4	4/5-5/5	5/6-9/8	9/9-10/7	10/8-11/12
1925	3/28-4/20	4/21-5/15	5/16-6/8	6/9-7/3	7/4-7/27	7/28-8/21

Libra	Scorpio	Sagittarius	Capricorn	Aquarius	Pisces
8/23-9/17	9/17-10/12	10/12-1/16	1/16-2/9	2/9	3/5-3/29
			11/7-12/5	12/5-1/11	
10/7-10/31	10/31-11/24	11/24-12/18	12/18-1/11	2/6-4/4	1/11-2/6
					4/4-5/7
8/17-9/6	12/9-1/5			1/11-2/4	2/4-2/28
11/8-12/9					
9/6-9/30	9/30-10/25	1/5-1/30	1/30-2/24	2/24-3/19	3/19-4/13
		10/25-11/18	11/18-12/13	12/13-1/7	
10/21-11/14	11/14-12/8	12/8-1/1/06			1/7-2/3
8/11-9/7	9/7-10/9	10/9-12/15	1/1-1/25	1/25-2/18	2/18-3/14
	12/15-12/25	12/25-2/6			
9/22-10/16	10/16-11/9	11/9-12/3	2/6-3/6	3/6-4/2	4/2-4/27
			12/3-12/27	12/27-1/20	
11/3-11/28	11/28-12/22	12/22-1/15			1/20-2/14
8/23-9/17	9/17-10/12	10/12-11/17	1/15-2/9	2/9-3/5	3/5-3/29
			11/17-12/5	12/5-1/15	
10/7-10/30	10/31-11/23	11/24-12/17	12/18-12/31	1/1-1/15	1/16-1/28
				1/29-4/4	4/5-5/6
11/19-12/8	12/9-12/31		1/1-1/10	1/11-2/2	2/3-2/27
9/6-9/30	1/1-1/4	1/5-1/29	1/30-2/23	2/24-3/18	3/19-4/12
	10/1-10/24	10/25-11/17	11/18-12/12	12/13-12/31	
10/21-11/13	11/14-12/7	12/8-12/31		1/1-1/6	1/7-2/2
8/11-9/6	9/7-10/9	10/10-12/5	1/1-1/24	1/25-2/17	2/18-3/13
	12-6/12-30	12/31			
9/22-10/15	10/16-11/8	1/1-2/6	2/7-3/6	3/7-4/1	4/2-4/26
		11/9-12/2	12/3-12/26	12/27-12/31	
11/3-11/27	11/28-12/21	12/22-12/31		1/1-1/19	1/20-2/13
8/22-9/16	9/17-10/11	1/1-1/14	1/15-2/7	2/8-3/4	3/5-3/28
		10/12-11/6	11/7-12/5	12/6-12/31	
10/6-10/29	10/30-11/22	11/23-12/16	12/17-12/31	1/1-4/5	4/6-5/6
11/9-12/8	12/9-12/31		1/1-1/9	1/10-2/2	2/3-2/26
9/5-9/30	1/1-1/3	1/4-1/29	1/29-2/22	2/23-3/18	3/19-4/11
	9/31-10/23	10/24-11/17	11/18-12/11	12/12-12/31	
10/21-11/13	11/14-12/7	12/8-12/31		1/1-1/6	1/7-2/2
8/10-9/6	9/7-10/10	10/11-11/28	1/1-1/24	1/25-2/16	2/17-3/12
	11/29-12/31				
9/21-10/14	1/1	1/2-2/6	2/7-3/5	3/6-3/31	4/1-4/26
	10/15-11/7	11/8-12/1	12/2-12/25	12/26-12/31	
11/3-11/26	11/27-12/21	12/22-12/31		1/1-1/19	1/20-2/12
8/22-9/15	9/16-10/11	1/1-1/14	1/15-2/7	2/8-3/3	3/4-3/27
		10-12/11-6	11/7-12/5	12/6-12/31	

VENUS SIGNS 1901–2000

	Aries	Taurus	Gemini	Cancer	Leo	Virgo
1926	5/7-6/2	6/3-6/28	6/29-7/23	7/24-8/17	8/18-9/11	9/12-10/5
1927	2/27-3/22	3/23-4/16	4/17-5/11	5/12-6/7	6/8-7/7	7/8-11/9
1928	4/12-5/5	5/6-5/29	5/30-6/23	6/24-7/17	7/18-8/11	8/12-9/4
1929	2/3-3/7 4/20-6/2	3/8-4/19 6/3-7/7	7/8-8/4	8/5-8/30	8/31-9/25	9/26-10/19
1930	3/13-4/5	4/6-4/30	5/1-5/24	5/25-6/18	6/19-7/14	7/15-8/9
1931	4/26-5/20	5/21-6/13	6/14-7/8	7/9-8/2	8/3-8/26	8/27-9/19
1932	2/12-3/8	3/9-4/3	4/4-5/5 7/13-7/27	5/6-7/12 7/28-9/8	9/9-10/6	10/7-11/1
1933	3/27-4/19	4/20-5/28	5/29-6/8	6/9-7/2	7/3-7/26	7/27-8/20
1934	5/6-6/1	6/2-6/27	6/28-7/22	7/23-8/16	8/17-9/10	9/11-10/4
1935	2/26-3/21	3/22-4/15	4/16-5/10	5/11-6/6	6/7-7/6	7/7-11/8
1936	4/11-5/4	5/5-5/28	5/29-6/22	6/23-7/16	7/17-8/10	8/11-9/4
1937	2/2-3/8 4/14-6/3	3/9-4/17 6/4-7/6	7/7-8/3	8/4-8/29	8/30-9/24	9/25-10/18
1938	3/12-4/4	4/5-4/28	4/29-5/23	5/24-6/18	6/19-7/13	7/14-8/8
1939	4-25/5/19	5/20-6/13	6/14-7/8	7/9-8/1	8/2-8/25	8/26-9/19
1940	2/12-3/7	3/8-4/3	4/4-5/5 7/5-7/31	5/6-7/4 8/1-9/8	9/9-10/5	10/6-10/31
1941	3/27-4/19	4/20-5/13	5/14-6/6	6/7-7/1	7/2-7/26	7/27-8/20
1942	5/6-6/1	6/2-6/26	6/27-7/22	7/23-8/16	8/17-9/9	9/10-10/3
1943	2/25-3/20	3/21-4/14	4/15-5/10	5/11-6/6	6/7-7/6	7/7-11/8
1944	4/10-5/3	5/4-5/28	5/29-6/21	6/22-7/16	7/17-8/9	8/10-9/2
1945	2/2-3/10 4/7-6/3	3/11-4/6 6/4-7/6	7/7-8/3	8/4-8/29	8/30-9/23	9/24-10/18
1946	3/11-4/4	4/5-4/28	4/29-5/23	5/24-6/17	6/18-7/12	7/13-8/8
1947	4/25-5/19	5/20-6/12	6/13-7/7	7/8-8/1	8/2-8/25	8/26-9/18
1948	2/11-3/7	3/8-4/3	4/4-5/6 6/29-8/2	5/7-6/28 8/3-9/7	9/8-10/5	10/6-10/31
1949	3/26-4/19	4/20-5/13	5/14-6/6	6/7-6/30	7/1-7/25	7/26-8/19
1950	5/5-5/31	6/1-6/26	6/27-7/21	7/22-8/15	8/16-9/9	9/10-10/3
1951	2/25-3/21	3/22-4/15	4/16-5/10	5/11-6/6	6/7-7/7	7/8-11/9

Libra	Scorpio	Sagittarius	Capricorn	Aquarius	Pisces
10/6-10/29	10/30-11/22	11/23-12/16	12/17-12/31	1/1-4/5	4/6-5/6
11/10-12/8	12/9-12/31	1/1-1/7	1/8	1/9-2/1	2/2-2/26
9/5-9/28	1/1-1/3	1/4-1/28	1/29-2/22	2/23-3/17	3/18-4/11
	9/29-10/23	10/24-11/16	11/17-12/11	12/12-12/31	
10/20-11/12	11/13-12/6	12/7-12/30	12/31	1/1-1/5	1/6-2/2
8/10-9/6	9/7-10/11	10/12-11/21	1/1-1/23	1/24-2/16	2/17-3/12
	11/22-12/31				
9/20-10/13	1/1-1/3	1/4-2/6	2/7-3/4	3/5-3/31	4/1-4/25
	10/14-11/6	11/7-11/30	12/1-12/24	12/25-12/31	
11/2-11/25	11/26-12/20	12/21-12/31		1/1-1/18	1/19-2/11
8/21-9/14	9/15-10/10	1/1-1/13	1/14-2/6	2/7-3/2	3/3-3/26
		10/11-11/5	11/6-12/4	12/5-12/31	
10/5-10/28	10/29-11/21	11/22-12/15	12/16-12/31	1/1-4/5	4/6-5/5
11/9-12/7	12/8-12/31		1/1-1/7	1/8-1/31	2/1-2/25
9/5-9/27	1/1-1/2	1/3-1/27	1/28-2/21	2/22-3/16	3/17-4/10
	9/28-10/22	10/23-11/15	11/16-12/10	12/11-12/31	
10/19-11/11	11/12-12/5	12/6-12/29	12/30-12/31	1/1-1/5	1/6-2/1
8/9-9/6	9/7-10/13	10/14-11/14	1/1-1/22	1/23-2/15	2/16-3/11
	11/15-12/31				
9/20-10/13	1/1-1/3	1/4-2/5	2/6-3/4	3/5-3/30	3/31-4/24
	10/14-11/6	11/7-11/30	12/1-12/24	12/25-12/31	
11/1-11/25	11/26-12/19	12/20-12/31		1/1-1/18	1/19-2/11
8/21-9/14	9/15-10/9	1/1-1/12	1/13-2/5	2/6-3/1	3/2-3/26
		10/10-11/5	11/6-12/4	12/5-12/31	
10/4-10/27	10/28-11/20	11/21-12/14	12/15-12/31	1/1-4/4	4/6-5/5
11/9-12/7	12/8-12/31		1/1-1/7	1/8-1/31	2/1-2/24
9/3-9/27	1/1-1/2	1/3-1/27	1/28-2/20	2/21-3/16	3/17-4/9
	9/26-10/21	10/22-11/15	11/16-12/10	12/11-12/31	
10/19-11/11	11/12-12/5	12/6-12/29	12/30-12/31	1/1-1/4	1/5-2/1
8/9-9/6	9/7-10/15	10/16-11/7	1/1-1/21	1/22-2/14	2/15-3/10
	11/8-12/31				
9/19-10/12	1/1-1/4	1/5-2/5	2/6-3/4	3/5-3/29	3/30-4/24
	10/13-11/5	11/6-11/29	11/30-12/23	12/24-12/31	
11/1-1/25	11/26-12/19	12/20-12/31		1/1-1/17	1/18-2/10
8/20-9/14	9/15-10/9	1/1-1/12	1/13-2/5	2/6-3/1	3/2-3/25
		10/10-11/5	11/6-12/5	12/6-12/31	
10/4-10/27	10/28-11/20	11/21-12/13	12/14-12/31	1/1-4/5	4/6-5/4
11/10-12/7	12/8-12/31		1/1-1/7	1/8-1/31	2/1-2/24

VENUS SIGNS 1901–2000

	Aries	Taurus	Gemini	Cancer	Leo	Virgo
1952	4/10-5/4	5/5-5/28	5/29-6/21	6/22-7/16	7/17-8/9	8/10-9/3
1953	2/2-3/13	3/4-3/31	7/8-8/3	8/4-8/29	8/30-9/24	9/25-10/18
	4/1-6/5	6/6-7/7				
1954	3/12-4/4	4/5-4/28	4/29-5/23	5/24-6/17	6/18-7/13	7/14-8/8
1955	4/25-5/19	5/20-6/13	6/14-7/7	7/8-8/1	8/2-8/25	8/26-9/18
1956	2/12-3/7	3/8-4/4	4/5-5/7	5/8-6/23	9/9-10/5	10/6-10/31
			6:24-8/4	8/5-9/8		
1957	3/26-4/19	4/20-5/13	5/14-6/6	6/7-7/1	7/2-7/26	7/7-8/19
1958	5/6-5/31	6/1-6/26	6/27-7/22	7/23-8/15	8/16-9/9	9/10-10/3
1959	2/25-3/20	3/21-4/14	4/15-5/10	5/11-6/6	6/7-7/8	7/9-9/20
					9/21-9/24	9/25-11/9
1960	4/10-5/3	5/4-5/28	5/29-6/21	6/22-7/15	7/16-8/9	8/10-9/2
1961	2/3-6/5	6/6-7/7	7/8-8/3	8/4-8/29	8/30-9/23	9/24-10/17
1962	3/11-4/3	4/4-4/28	4/29-5/22	5/23-6/17	6/18-7/12	7/13-8/8
1963	4/24-5/18	5/19-6/12	6/13-7/7	7/8-7/31	8/1-8/25	8/26-9/18
1964	2/11-3/7	3/8-4/4	4/5-5/9	5/10-6/17	9/9-10/5	10/6-10/31
			6/18-8/5	8/6-9/8		
1965	3/26-4/18	4/19-5/12	5/13-6/6	6/7-6/30	7/1-7/25	7/26-8/19
1966	5/6-6/31	6/1-6/26	6/27-7/21	7/22-8/15	8/16-9/8	9/9-10/2
1967	2/24-3/20	3/21-4/14	4/15-5/10	5/11-6/6	6/7-7/8	7/9-9/9
					9/10-10/1	10/2-11/9
1968	4/9-5/3	5/4-5/27	5/28-6/20	6/21-7/15	7/16-8/8	8/9-9/2
1969	2/3-6/6	6/7-7/6	7/7-8/3	8/4-8/28	8/29-9/22	9/23-10/17
1970	3/11-4/3	4/4-4/27	4/28-5/22	5/23-6/16	6/17-7/12	7/13-8/8
1971	4/24-5/18	5/19-6/12	6/13-7/6	7/7-7/31	8/1-8/24	8/25-9/17
1972	2/11-3/7	3/8-4/3	4/4-5/10	5/11-6/11		
			6/12-8/6	8/7-9/8	9/9-10/5	10/6-10/30
1973	3/25-4/18	4/18-5/12	5/13-6/5	6/6-6/29	7/1-7/25	7/26-8/19
1974						
	55-5/31	6/1-6/25	6/26-7/21	7/22-8/14	8/15-9/8	9/9-10/2
1975	2/24-3/20	3/21-4/13	4/14-5/9	5/10-6/6	6/7-7/9	7/10-9/2
					9/3-10/4	10/5-11/9

Libra	Scorpio	Sagittarius	Capricorn	Aquarius	Pisces
9/4-9/27	1/1-1/2	1/3-1/27	1/28-2/20	2/21-3/16	3/17-4/9
	9/28-10/21	10/22-11/15	11/16-12/10	12/11-12/31	
10/19-11/11	11/12-12/5	12/6-12/29	12/30-12/31	1/1-1/5	1/6-2/1
8/9-9/6	9/7-10/22	10/23-10/27	1/1-1/22	1/23-2/15	2/16-3/11
	10/28-12/31				
9/19-10/13	1/1-1/6	1/7-2/5	2/6-3/4	3/5-3/30	3/31-4/24
	10/14-11/5	11/6-11/30	12/1-12/24	12/25-12/31	
11/1-11/25	11/26-12/19	12/20-12/31		1/1-1/17	1/18-2/11
8/20-9/14	9/15-10/9	1/1-1/12	1/13-2/5	2/6-3/1	3/2-3/25
		10/10-11/5	11/6-12/16	12/7-12/31	
10/4-10/27	10/28-11/20	11/21-12/14	12/15-12/31	1/1-4/6	4/7-5/5
11/10-12/7	12/8-12/31		1/1-1/7	1/8-1/31	2/1-2/24
9/3-9/26	1/1-1/2	1/3-1/27	1/28-2/20	2/21-3/15	3/16-4/9
	9/27-10/21	10/22-11/15	11/16-12/10	12/11-12/31	
10/18-11/11	11/12-12/4	12/5-12/28	12/29-12/31	1/1-1/5	1/6-2/2
8/9-9/6	9/7-12/31		1/1-1/21	1/22-2/14	2/15-3/10
9/19-10/12	1/1-1/6	1/7-2/5	2/6-3/4	3/5-3/29	3/30-4/23
	10/13-11/5	11/6-11/29	11/30-12/23	12/24-12/31	
11/1-11/24	11/25-12/19	12/20-12/31		1/1-1/16	1/17-2/10
8/20-9/13	9/14-10/9	1/1-1/12	1/13-2/5	2/6-3/1	3/2-3/25
		10/10-11/5	11/6-12/7	12/8-12/31	
10/3-10/26	10/27-11/19	11/20-12/13	2/7-2/25	1/1-2/6	4/7-5/5
			12/14-12/31	2/26-4/6	
11/10-12/7	12/8-12/23		1/1-1/6	1/7-1/30	1/31-2/23
9/3-9/26	1/1	1/2-1/26	1/27-2/20	2/21-3/15	3/16-4/8
	9/27-10/21	10/22-11/14	11/15-12/9	12/10-12/31	
10/18-11/10	11/11-12/4	12/5-12/28	12/29-12/31	1/1-1/4	1/5-2/2
8/9-9/7	9/8-12/31		1/1-1/21	1/22-2/14	2/15-3/10
9/18-10/11	1/1-1/7	1/8-2/5	2/6-3/4	3/5-3/29	3/30-4/23
	10/12-11/5	11/6-11/29	11/30-12/23	12/24-12/31	
	11/25-12/18	12/19-12/31		1/1-1/16	1/17-2/10
10/31-11/24					
8/20-9/13		1/1-1/12	1/13-2/4	2/5-2/28	3/1-3/24
		10/9-11/5	11/6-12/7	12/8-12/31	
			1/30-2/28	1/1-1/29	
10/3-10/26	10/27-11/19	11/20-12/13	12/14-12/31	3/1-4/6	4/7-5/4
			1/1-1/6	1/7-1/30	1/31-2/23
11/10-12/7	12/8-12/31				

VENUS SIGNS 1901–2000

	Aries	Taurus	Gemini	Cancer	Leo	Virgo
1976	4/8-5/2	5/2-5/27	5/27-6/20	6/20-7/14	7/14-8/8	8/8-9/1
1977	2/2-6/6	6/6-7/6	7/6-8/2	8/2-8/28	8/28-9/22	9/22-10/17
1978	3/9-4/2	4/2-4/27	4/27-5/22	5/22-6/16	6/16-7/12	7/12-8/6
1979	4/23-5/18	5/18-6/11	6/11-7/6	7/6-7/30	7/30-8/24	8/24-9/17
1980	2/9-3/6	3/6-4/3	4/3-5/12	5/12-6/5	9/7-10/4	10/4-10/30
			6/5-8/6	8/6-9/7		
1981	3/24-4/17	4/17-5/11	5/11-6/5	6/5-6/29	6/29-7/24	7/24-8/18
1982	5/4-5/30	5/30-6/25	6/25-7/20	7/20-8/14	8/14-9/7	9/7-10/2
1983	2/22-3/19	3/19-4/13	4/13-5/9	5/9-6/6	6/6-7/10	7/10-8/27
					8/27-10/5	10/5-11/9
1984	4/7-5/2	5/2-5/26	5/26-6/20	6/20-7/14	7/14-8/7	8/7-9/1
1985	2/2-6/6	6/8-7/6	7/6-8/2	8/2-8/28	8/28-9/22	9/22-10/16
1986	3/9-4/2	4/2-4/26	4/26-5/21	5/21-6/15	6/15-7/11	7/11-8/7
1987	4/22-5/17	5/17-6/11	6/11-7/5	7/5-7/30	7/30-8/23	8/23-9/16
1988	2/9-3/6	3/6-4/3	4/3-5/17	5/17-5/27	9/7-10/4	10/4-10/29
			5/27-8/6	8/6-9/7		
1989	3/23-4/16	4/16-5/11	5/11-6/4	6/4-6/29	6/29-7/24	7/24-8/18
1990	5/4-5/30	5/30-6/25	6/25-7/20	7/20-8/13	8/13-9/7	9/7-10/1
1991	2/22-3/18	3/18-4/13	4/13-5/9	5/9-6/6	6/6-7/11	7/11-8/21
					8/21-10/6	10/6-11/9
1992	4/7-5/1	5/1-5/26	5/26-6/19	6/19-7/13	7/13-8/7	8/7-8/31
1993	2/2-6/6	6/6-7/6	7/6-8/1	8/1-8/27	8/27-9/21	9/21-10/16
1994	3/8-4/1	4/1-4/26	4/26-5/21	5/21-6/15	6/15-7/11	7/11-8/7
1995	4/22-5/16	5/16-6/10	6/10-7/5	7/5-7/29	7/29-8/23	8/23-9/16
1996	2/9-3/6	3/6-4/3	4/3-8/7	8/7-9/7	9/7-10/4	10/4-10/29
1997	3/23-4/16	4/16-5/10	5/10-6/4	6/4-6/28	6/28-7/23	7/23-8/17
1998	5/3-5/29	5/29-6/24	6/24-7/19	7/19-8/13	8/13-9/6	9/6-9/30
1999	2/21-3/18	3/18-4/12	4/12-5/8	5/8-6/5	6/5-7/12	7/12-8/15
					8/15-10/7	10/7-11/9
2000	4/6-5/1	5/1-5/25	5/25-6/13	6/13-7/13	7/13-8/6	8/6-8/31

Libra	Scorpio	Sagittarius	Capricorn	Aquarius	Pisces
9/1-9/26	9/26-10/20	1/1-1/26	1/26-2/19	2/19-3/15	3/15-4/8
		10/20-11/14	11/14-12/6	12/9-1/4	
10/17-11/10	11/10-12/4	12/4-12/27	12/27-1/20		1/4-2/2
8/6-9/7	9/7-1/7			1/20-2/13	2/13-3/9
9/17-10/11	10/11-11/4	1/7-2/5	2/5-3/3	3/3-3/29	3/29-4/23
		11/4-11/28	11/28-12/22	12/22-1/16	
10/30-11/24	11/24-12/18	12/18-1/11			1/16-2/9
8/18-9/12	9/12-10/9	10/9-11/5	1/11-2/4	2/4-2/28	2/28-3/24
			11/5-12/8	12/8-1/23	
10/2-10/26	10/26-11/18	11/18-12/12	1/23-3/2	3/2-4/6	4/6-5/4
			12/12-1/5		
11/9-12/6	12/6-1/1			1/5-1/29	1/29-2/22
9/1-9/25	9/25-10/20	1/1-1/25	1/25-2/19	2/19-3/14	3/14-4/7
		10/20-11/13	11/13-12/9		
10/16-11/9	11/9-12/3	12/3-12/27			1/4-2/2
8/7-9/7	9/7-1/7			1/20-3/13	2/13-3/9
9/16-10/10	10/10-11/3	1/7-2/5	2/5-3/3	3/3-3/28	3/28-4/22
		11/3-11/28	11/28-12/22	12/22-1/15	
10/29-11/23	11/23-12/17	12/17-1/10			1/15-2/9
8/18-9/12	9/12-10/8	10/8-11/5	1/10-2/3	2/3-2/27	2/27-3/23
			11/5-12/10	12/10-1/16	
10/1-10/25	10/25-11/18	11/18-12/12	1/16-3/3	3/3-4/6	4/6-5/4
			12/12-1/5		
8/21-12/6	12/6-12/31	12/21-1/25/92		1/5-1/29	1/29-2/22
8/31-9/25	9/25-10/19	10/19-11/13	1/25-2/18	2/18-3/13	3/13-4/7
			11/13-12/8	12/8-1/3	
10/16-11/9	11/9-12/2	12/2-12/26	12/26-1/19		1/3-2/2
8/7-9/7	9/7-1/7			1/19-2/12	2/12-3/8
9/16-10/10	10/10-11/13	1/7-2/4	2/4-3/2	3/2-3/28	3/28-4/22
		11/3-11/27	11/27-12/21	12/21-1/15	
10/29-11/23	11/23-12/17	12/17-1/10/97			1/15-2/9
8/17-9/12	9/12-10/8	10/8-11/5	1/10-2/3	2/3-2/27	2/27-3/23
			11/5-12/12	12/12-1/9	
9/30-10/24	10/24-11/17	11/17-12/11	1/9-3/4	3/4-4/6	4/6-5/3
11/9-12/5	12/5-12/31	12/31-1/24		1/4-1/28	1/28-2/21
8/31-9/24	9/24-10/19	10/19-11/13	1/24-2/18	2/18-3/12	3/13-4/6
			11/13-12/8	12/8	

1901	MAR	1	Leo		APR	28	Gem
	May	11	Vir		JUN	11	Can
	JUL	13	Lib		JUL	27	Leo
	AUG	31	Scp		SEP	12	Vir
	OCT	14	Sag		OCT	30	Lib
	NOV	24	Cap		DEC	17	Scp
1902	JAN	1	Aqu	1907	FEB	5	Sag
	FEB	8	Pic		APR	1	Cap
	MAR	19	Ari		OCT	13	Aqu
	APR	27	Tau		NOV	29	Pic
	JUN	7	Gem	1908	JAN	11	Ari
	JUL	20	Can		FEB	23	Tau
	SEP	4	Leo		APR	7	Gem
	OCT	23	Vir		MAY	22	Can
	DEC	20	Lib		JUL	8	Leo
1903	APR	19	Vir		AUG	24	Vir
	MAY	30	Lib		OCT	10	Lib
	AUG	6	Scp		NOV	25	Scp
	SEP	22	Sag	1909	JAN	10	Sag
	NOV	3	Cap		FEB	24	Cap
	DEC	12	Aqu		APR	9	Aqu
1904	JAN	19	Pic		MAY	25	Pic
	FEB	27	Ari		JUL	21	Ari
	APR	6	Tau		SEP	26	Pic
	MAY	18	Gem		NOV	20	Ari
	JUN	30	Can	1910	JAN	23	Tau
	AUG	15	Leo		MAR	14	Gem
	OCT	1	Vir		MAY	1	Can
	NOV	20	Lib		JUN	19	Leo
1905	JAN	13	Scp		AUG	6	Vir
	AUG	21	Sag		SEP	22	Lib
	OCT	8	Cap		NOV	6	Scp
	NOV	18	Aqu		DEC	20	Sag
	DEC	27	Pic	1911	JAN	31	Cap
1906	FEB	4	Ari		MAR	14	Aqu
	MAR	17	Tau		APR	23	Pic

	JUN	2	Ari		MAY	4	Tau
	JUL	15	Tau		JUN	14	Gem
	SEP	5	Gem		JUL	28	Can
	NOV	30	Tau		SEP	12	Leo
1912	JAN	30	Gem		NOV	2	Vir
	APR	5	Can	1918	JAN	11	Lib
	MAY	28	Leo		FEB	25	Vir
	JUL	17	Vir		JUN	23	Lib
	SEP	2	Lib		AUG	17	Scp
	OCT	18	Scp		OCT	1	Sag
	NOV	30	Sag		NOV	11	Cap
1913	JAN	10	Cap		DEC	20	Aqu
	FEB	19	Aqu	1919	JAN	27	Pic
	MAR	30	Pic		MAR	6	Ari
	MAY	8	Ari		APR	15	Tau
	JUN	17	Tau		MAY	26	Gem
	JUL	29	Gem		JUL	8	Can
	SEP	15	Can		AUG	23	Leo
1914	MAY	1	Leo		OCT	10	Vir
	JUN	26	Vir		NOV	30	Lib
	AUG	14	Lib	1920	JAN	31	Scp
	SEP	29	Scp		APR	23	Lib
	NOV	11	Sag		JUL	10	Scp
	DEC	22	Cap		SEP	4	Sag
1915	JAN	30	Aqu		OCT	18	Cap
	MAR	9	Pic		NOV	27	Aqu
	APR	16	Ari	1921	JAN	5	Pic
	MAY	26	Tau		FEB	13	Ari
	JUL	6	Gem		MAR	25	Tau
	AUG	19	Can		MAY	6	Gem
	OCT	7	Leo		JUN	18	Can
1916	MAY	28	Vir		AUG	3	Leo
	JUL	23	Lib		SEP	19	Vir
	SEP	8	Scp		NOV	6	Lib
	OCT	22	Sag		DEC	26	Scp
	DEC	1	Cap	1922	FEB	18	Sag
1917	JAN	9	Aqu		SEP	13	Cap
	FEB	16	Pic		OCT	30	Aqu
	MAR	26	Ari		DEC	11	Pic

1923	JAN	21	Ari		JUN	26	Tau
	MAR	4	Tau		AUG	9	Gem
	APR	16	Gem		OCT	3	Can
	MAY	30	Can		DEC	20	Gem
	JUL	16	Leo	1929	MAR	10	Can
	SEP	1	Vir		MAY	13	Leo
	OCT	18	Lib		JUL	4	Vir
	DEC	4	Scp		AUG	21	Lib
1924	JAN	19	Sag		OCT	6	Scp
	MAR	6	Cap		NOV	18	Sag
	APR	24	Aqu		DEC	29	Cap
	JUN	24	Pic	1930	FEB	6	Aqu
	AUG	24	Aqu		MAR	17	Pic
	OCT	19	Pic		APR	24	Ari
	DEC	19	Ari		JUN	3	Tau
1925	FEB	5	Tau		JUL	14	Gem
	MAR	24	Gem		AUG	28	Can
	MAY	9	Can		OCT	20	Leo
	JUN	26	Leo	1931	FEB	16	Can
	AUG	12	Vir		MAR	30	Leo
	SEP	28	Lib		JUN	10	Vir
	NOV	13	Scp		AUG	1	Lib
	DEC	28	Sag		SEP	17	Scp
1926	FEB	9	Cap		OCT	30	Sag
	MAR	23	Aqu		DEC	10	Cap
	MAY	3	Pic	1932	JAN	18	Aqu
	JUN	15	Ari		FEB	25	Pic
	AUG	1	Tau		APR	3	Ari
1927	FEB	22	Gem		MAY	12	Tau
	APR	17	Can		JUN	22	Gem
	JUN	6	Leo		AUG	4	Can
	JUL	25	Vir		SEP	20	Leo
	SEP	10	Lib		NOV	13	Vir
	OCT	26	Scp	1933	JUL	6	Lib
	DEC	8	Sag		AUG	26	Scp
1928	JAN	19	Cap		OCT	9	Sag
	FEB	28	Aqu		NOV	19	Cap
	APR	7	Pic		DEC	28	Aqu
	MAY	16	Ari	1934	FEB	4	Pic

	MAR	14	Ari		NOV	19	Pic
	APR	22	Tau	1940	JAN	4	Ari
	JUN	2	Gem		FEB	17	Tau
	JUL	15	Can		APR	1	Gem
	AUG	30	Leo		MAY	17	Can
	OCT	18	Vir		JUL	3	Leo
	DEC	11	Lib		AUG	19	Vir
1935	JUL	29	Scp		OCT	5	Lib
	SEP	16	Sag		NOV	20	Scp
	OCT	28	Cap	1941	JAN	4	Sag
	DEC	7	Aqu		FEB	17	Cap
1936	JAN	14	Pic		APR	2	Aqu
	FEB	22	Ari		MAY	16	Pic
	APR	1	Tau		JUL	2	Ari
	MAY	13	Gem	1942	JAN	11	Tau
	JUN	25	Can		MAR	7	Gem
	AUG	10	Leo		APR	26	Can
	SEP	26	Vir		JUN	14	Leo
	NOV	14	Lib		AUG	1	Vir
1937	JAN	5	Scp		SEP	17	Lib
	MAR	13	Sag		NOV	1	Scp
	MAY	14	Scp		DEC	15	Sag
	AUG	8	Sag	1943	JAN	26	Cap
	SEP	30	Cap		MAR	8	Aqu
	NOV	11	Aqu		APR	17	Pic
	DEC	21	Pic		MAY	27	Ari
1938	JAN	30	Ari		JUL	7	Tau
	MAR	12	Tau		AUG	23	Gem
	APR	23	Gem	1944	MAR	28	Can
	JUN	7	Can		MAY	22	Leo
	JUL	22	Leo		JUL	12	Vir
	SEP	7	Vir		AUG	29	Lib
	OCT	25	Lib		OCT	13	Scp
	DEC	11	Scp		NOV	25	Sag
1939	JAN	29	Sag	1945	JAN	5	Cap
	MAR	21	Cap		FEB	14	Aqu
	MAY	25	Aqu		MAR	25	Pic
	JUL	21	Cap		MAY	2	Ari
	SEP	24	Aqu		JUN	11	Tau

	JUL	23	Gem
	SEP	7	Can
	NOV	11	Leo
	DEC	26	Can
1946	APR	22	Leo
	JUN	20	Vir
	AUG	9	Lib
	SEP	24	Scp
	NOV	6	Sag
	DEC	17	Cap
1947	JAN	25	Aqu
	MAR	4	Pic
	APR	11	Ari
	MAY	21	Tau
	JUL	1	Gem
	AUG	13	Can
	OCT	1	Leo
	DEC	1	Vir
1948	FEB	12	Leo
	MAY	18	Vir
	JUL	17	Lib
	SEP	3	Scp
	OCT	17	Sag
	NOV	26	Cap
1949	JAN	4	Aqu
	FEB	11	Pic
	MAR	21	Ari
	APR	30	Tau
	JUN	10	Gem
	JUL	23	Can
	SEP	7	Leo
	OCT	27	Vir
	DEC	26	Lib
1950	MAR	28	Vir
	JUN	11	Lib
	AUG	10	Scp
	SEP	25	Sag
	NOV	6	Cap
	DEC	15	Aqu

1951	JAN	22	Pic
	MAR	1	Ari
	APR	10	Tau
	MAY	21	Gem
	JUL	3	Can
	AUG	18	Leo
	OCT	5	Vir
	NOV	24	Lib
1952	JAN	20	Scp
	AUG	27	Sag
	OCT	12	Cap
	NOV	21	Aqu
	DEC	30	Pic
1953	FEB	8	Ari
	MAR	20	Tau
	MAY	1	Gem
	JUN	14	Can
	JUL	29	Leo
	SEP	14	Vir
	NOV	1	Lib
	DEC	20	Scp
1954	FEB	9	Sag
	APR	12	Cap
	JUL	3	Sag
	AUG	24	Cap
	OCT	21	Aqu
	DEC	4	Pic
1955	JAN	15	Ari
	FEB	26	Tau
	APR	10	Gem
	MAY	26	Can
	JUL	11	Leo
	AUG	27	Vir
	OCT	13	Lib
	NOV	29	Scp
1956	JAN	14	Sag
	FEB	28	Cap
	APR	14	Aqu
	JUN	3	Pic

	DEC	6	Ari
1957	JAN	28	Tau
	MAR	17	Gem
	MAY	4	Can
	JUN	21	Leo
	AUG	8	Vir
	SEP	24	Lib
	NOV	8	Scp
	DEC	23	Sag
1958	FEB	3	Cap
	MAR	17	Aqu
	APR	27	Pic
	JUN	7	Ari
	JUL	21	Tau
	SEP	21	Gem
	OCT	29	Tau
1959	FEB	10	Gem
	APR	10	Can
	JUN	1	Leo
	JUL	20	Vir
	SEP	5	Lib
	OCT	21	Scp
	DEC	3	Sag
1960	JAN	14	Cap
	FEB	23	Aqu
	APR	2	Pic
	MAY	11	Ari
	JUN	20	Tau
	AUG	2	Gem
	SEP	21	Can
1961	FEB	5	Gem
	FEB	7	Can
	MAY	6	Leo
	JUN	28	Vir
	AUG	17	Lib
	OCT	1	Scp
	NOV	13	Sag
	DEC	24	Cap
1962	FEB	1	Aqu

	MAR	12	Pic
	APR	19	Ari
	MAY	28	Tau
	JUL	9	Gem
	AUG	22	Can
	OCT	11	Leo
1963	JUN	3	Vir
	JUL	27	Lib
	SEP	12	Scp
	OCT	25	Sag
	DEC	5	Cap
1964	JAN	13	Aqu
	FEB	20	Pic
	MAR	29	Ari
	MAY	7	Tau
	JUN	17	Gem
	JUL	30	Can
	SEP	15	Leo
	NOV	6	Vir
1965	JUN	29	Lib
	AUG	20	Scp
	OCT	4	Sag
	NOV	14	Cap
	DEC	23	Aqu
1966	JAN	30	Pic
	MAR	9	Ari
	APR	17	Tau
	MAY	28	Gem
	JUL	11	Can
	AUG	25	Leo
	OCT	12	Vir
	DEC	4	Lib
1967	FEB	12	Scp
	MAR	31	Lib
	JUL	19	Scp
	SEP	10	Sag
	OCT	23	Cap
	DEC	1	Aqu
1968	JAN	9	Pic

	FEB	17	Ari		DEC	24	Tau
	MAR	27	Tau	1974	FEB	27	Gem
	MAY	8	Gem		APR	20	Can
	JUN	21	Can		JUN	9	Leo
	AUG	5	Leo		JUL	27	Vir
	SEP	21	Vir		SEP	12	Lib
	NOV	9	Lib		OCT	28	Scp
	DEC	29	Scp		DEC	10	Sag
1969	FEB	25	Sag	1975	JAN	21	Cap
	SEP	21	Cap		MAR	3	Aqu
	NOV	4	Aqu		APR	11	Pic
	DEC	15	Pic		MAY	21	Ari
1970	JAN	24	Ari		JUL	1	Tau
	MAR	7	Tau		AUG	14	Gem
	APR	18	Gem		OCT	17	Can
	JUN	2	Can		NOV	25	Gem
	JUL	18	Leo	1976	MAR	18	Can
	SEP	3	Vir		MAY	16	Leo
	OCT	20	Lib		JUL	6	Vir
	DEC	6	Scp		AUG	24	Lib
1971	JAN	23	Sag		OCT	8	Scp
	MAR	12	Cap		NOV	20	Sag
	MAY	3	Aqu	1977	JAN	1	Cap
	NOV	6	Pic		FEB	9	Aqu
	DEC	26	Ari		MAR	20	Pic
1972	FEB	10	Tau		APR	27	Ari
	MAR	27	Gem		JUN	6	Tau
	MAY	12	Can		JUL	17	Gem
	JUN	28	Leo		SEP	1	Can
	AUG	15	Vir		OCT	26	Leo
	SEP	30	Lib	1978	JAN	26	Can
	NOV	15	Scp		APR	10	Leo
	DEC	30	Sag		JUN	14	Vir
1973	FEB	12	Cap		AUG	4	Lib
	MAR	26	Aqu		SEP	19	Scp
	MAY	8	Pic		NOV	2	Sag
	JUN	20	Ari		DEC	12	Cap
	AUG	12	Tau	1979	JAN	20	Aqu
	OCT	29	Ari		FEB	27	Pic

	APR	7	Ari		MAR	15	Tau
	MAY	16	Tau		APR	26	Gem
	JUN	26	Gem		JUN	9	Can
	AUG	8	Can		JUL	25	Leo
	SEP	24	Leo		SEP	10	Vir
	NOV	19	Vir		OCT	27	Lib
1980	MAR	11	Leo		DEC	14	Scp
	MAY	4	Vir	1986	FEB	2	Sag
	JUL	10	Lib		MAR	28	Cap
	AUG	29	Scp		OCT	9	Aqu
	OCT	12	Sag		NOV	26	Pic
	NOV	22	Cap	1987	JAN	8	Ari
	DEC	30	Aqu		FEB	20	Tau
1981	FEB	6	Pic		APR	5	Gem
	MAR	17	Ari		MAY	21	Can
	APR	25	Tau		JUL	6	Leo
	JUN	5	Gem		AUG	22	Vir
	JUL	18	Can		OCT	8	Lib
	SEP	2	Leo		NOV	24	Scp
	OCT	21	Vir	1988	JAN	8	Sag
	DEC	16	Lib		FEB	22	Cap
1982	AUG	3	Scp		APR	6	Aqu
	SEP	20	Sag		MAY	22	Pic
	OCT	31	Cap		JUL	13	Ari
	DEC	10	Aqu		OCT	23	Pic
1983	JAN	17	Pic		NOV	1	Ari
	FEB	25	Ari	1989	JAN	19	Tau
	APR	5	Tau		MAR	11	Gem
	MAY	16	Gem		APR	29	Can
	JUN	29	Can		JUN	16	Leo
	AUG	13	Leo		AUG	3	Vir
	SEP	30	Vir		SEP	19	Lib
	NOV	18	Lib		NOV	4	Scp
1984	JAN	11	Scp		DEC	18	Sag
	AUG	17	Sag	1990	JAN	29	Cap
	OCT	5	Cap		MAR	11	Aqu
	NOV	15	Aqu		APR	20	Pic
	DEC	25	Pic		MAY	31	Ari
1985	FEB	2	Ari		JUL	12	Tau

	AUG	31	Gem		
	DEC	14	Tau		
1991	JAN	21	Gem		
	APR	3	Can		
	MAY	26	Leo		
	JUL	15	Vir		
	SEP	1	Lib		
	OCT	16	Scp		
	NOV	29	Sag		
1992	JAN	9	Cap		
	FEB	18	Aqu		
	MAR	28	Pic		
	MAY	5	Ari		
	JUN	14	Tau		
	JUL	26	Gem		
	SEP	12	Can		
1993	APR	27	Leo		
	JUN	23	Vir		
	AUG	12	Lib		
	SEP	27	Scp		
	NOV	9	Sag		
	DEC	20	Cap		
1994	JAN	28	Aqu		
	MAR	7	Pic		
	APR	14	Ari		
	MAY	23	Tau		
	JUL	3	Gem		
	AUG	16	Can		
	OCT	4	Leo		
	DEC	12	Vir		
1995	JAN	22	Leo		
	MAY	25	Vir		
	JUL	21	Lib		
	SEP	7	Scp		
	OCT	20	Sag		
	NOV	30	Cap		
1996	JAN	8	Aqu		

	FEB	15	Pic
	MAR	24	Ari
	MAY	2	Tau
	JUN	12	Gem
	JUL	25	Can
	SEP	9	Leo
	OCT	30	Vir
1997	JAN	3	Lib
	MAR	8	Vir
	JUN	19	Lib
	AUG	14	Scp
	SEP	28	Sag
	NOV	9	Cap
	DEC	18	Aqu
1998	JAN	25	Pic
	MAR	4	Ari
	APR	13	Tau
	MAY	24	Gem
	JUL	6	Can
	AUG	20	Leo
	OCT	7	Vir
	NOV	27	Lib
1999	JAN	26	Scp
	MAY	5	Lib
	JUL	5	Scp
	SEP	2	Sag
	OCT	17	Cap
	NOV	26	Aqu
2000	JAN	4	Pic
	FEB	12	Ari
	MAR	23	Tau
	MAY	3	Gem
	JUN	16	Can
	AUG	1	Leo
	SEP	17	Vir
	NOV	4	Lib
	DEC	23	Scp

JUPITER SIGN 1901—2000

1901	JAN	19	Cap
1902	FEB	6	Aqu
1903	FEB	20	Pic
1904	MAR	1	Ari
	AUG	8	Tau
	AUG	31	Ari
1905	MAR	7	Tau
	JUL	21	Gem
	DEC	4	Tau
1906	MAR	9	Gem
	JUL	30	Can
1907	AUG	18	Leo
1908	SEP	12	Vir
1909	OCT	11	Lib
1910	NOV	11	Scp
1911	DEC	10	Sag
1913	JAN	2	Cap
1914	JAN	21	Aqu
1915	FEB	4	Pic
1916	FEB	12	Ari
	JUN	26	Tau
	OCT	26	Ari
1917	FEB	12	Tau
	JUN	29	Gem
1918	JUL	13	Can
1919	AUG	2	Leo
1920	AUG	27	Vir
1921	SEP	25	Lib
1922	OCT	26	Scp
1923	NOV	24	Sag
1924	DEC	18	Cap
1926	JAN	6	Aqu
1927	JAN	18	Pic
	JUN	6	Ari
	SEP	11	Pic
1928	JAN	23	Ari
	JUN	4	Tau
1929	JUN	12	Gem

1930	JUN	26	Can
1931	JUL	17	Leo
1932	AUG	11	Vir
1933	SEP	10	Lib
1934	OCT	11	Scp
1935	NOV	9	Sag
1936	DEC	2	Cap
1937	DEC	20	Aqu
1938	MAY	14	Pic
	JUL	30	Aqu
	DEC	29	Pic
1939	MAY	11	Ari
	OCT	30	Pic
	DEC	20	Ari
1940	MAY	16	Tau
1941	MAY	26	Gem
1942	JUN	10	Can
1943	JUN	30	Leo
1944	JUL	26	Vir
1945	AUG	25	Lib
1946	SEP	25	Scp
1947	OCT	24	Sag
1948	NOV	15	Cap
1949	APR	12	Aqu
	JUN	27	Cap
	NOV	30	Aqu
1950	APR	15	Pic
	SEP	15	Aqu
	DEC	1	Pic
1951	APR	21	Ari
1952	APR	28	Tau
1953	MAY	9	Gem
1954	MAY	24	Can
1955	JUN	13	Leo
	NOV	17	Vir
1956	JAN	18	Leo
	JUL	7	Vir
	DEC	13	Lib

1957	FEB	19	Vir		1973	FEB	23	Aqu
	AUG	7	Lib		1974	MAR	8	Pic
1958	JAN	13	Scp		1975	MAR	18	Ari
	MAR	20	Lib		1976	MAR	26	Tau
	SEP	7	Scp			AUG	23	Gem
1959	FEB	10	Sag			OCT	16	Tau
	APR	24	Scp		1977	APR	3	Gem
	OCT	5	Sag			AUG	20	Can
1960	MAR	1	Cap			DEC	30	Gem
	JUN	10	Sag		1978	APR	12	Can
	OCT	26	Cap			SEP	5	Leo
1961	MAR	15	Aqu		1979	FEB	28	Can
	AUG	12	Cap			APR	20	Leo
	NOV	4	Aqu			SEP	29	Vir
1962	MAR	25	Pic		1980	OCT	27	Lib
1963	APR	4	Ari		1981	Nov	27	Scp
1964	APR	12	Tau		1982	DEC	26	Sag
1965	APR	22	Gem		1984	JAN	19	Cap
	SEP	21	Can		1985	FEB	6	Aqu
	NOV	17	Gem		1986	FEB	20	Pic
1966	MAY	5	Can		1987	MAR	2	Ari
	SEP	27	Leo		1988	MAR	8	Tau
1967	JAN	16	Can			JUL	22	Gem
	MAY	23	Leo			NOV	30	Tau
	OCT	19	Vir		1989	MAR	11	Gem
1968	FEB	27	Leo			JUL	30	Can
	JUN	15	Vir		1990	AUG	18	Leo
	NOV	15	Lib		1991	SEP	12	Vir
1969	MAR	30	Vir		1992	OCT	10	Lib
	JUL	15	Lib		1993	NOV	10	Scp
	DEC	16	Scp		1994	DEC	9	Sag
1970	APR	30	Lib		1996	JAN	3	Cap
	AUG	15	Scp		1997	JAN	21	Aqu
1971	JAN	14	Sag		1998	FEB	4	Pic
	JUN	5	Scp		1999	FEB	13	Ari
	SEP	11	Sag			JUN	28	Tau
1972	FEB	6	Cap			OCT	23	Ari
	JUL	24	Sag		2000	FEB	14	Tau
	SEP	25	Cap			JUN	30	Gem

SATURN SIGN 1903–2000

1903 JAN	19	Aqu
1905 APR	13	Pic
AUG	17	Aqu
1906 JAN	8	Pic
1908 MAR	19	Ari
1910 MAY	17	Tau
DEC	14	Ari
1911 JAN	20	Tau
1912 JUL	7	Gem
NOV	30	Tau
1913 MAR	26	Gem
1914 AUG	24	Can
DEC	7	Gem
1915 MAY	11	Can
1916 OCT	17	Leo
DEC	7	Can
1917 JUN	24	Leo
1919 AUG	12	Vir
1921 OCT	7	Lib
1923 DEC	20	Scp
1924 APR	6	Lib
SEP	13	Scp
1926 DEC	2	Sag
1929 MAR	15	Cap
MAY	5	Sag
NOV	30	Cap
1932 FEB	24	Aqu
AUG	13	Cap
NOV	20	Aqu
1935 FEB	14	Pic
1937 APR	25	Ari
OCT	18	Pic
1938 JAN	14	Ari
1939 JUL	6	Tau
SEP	22	Ari
1940 MAR	20	Tau
1942 MAY	8	Gem
1944 JUN	20	Can
1946 AUG	2	Leo
1948 SEP	19	Vir
1949 APR	3	Leo
MAY	29	Vir
1950 NOV	20	Lib
1951 MAR	7	Vir
AUG	13	Lib
1953 OCT	22	Scp
1956 JAN	12	Sag
MAY	14	Scp
OCT	10	Sag
1959 JAN	5	Cap
1962 JAN	3	Aqu
1964 MAR	24	Pic
SEP	16	Aqu
DEC	16	Pic
1967 MAR	3	Ari
1969 APR	29	Tau
1971 JUN	18	Gem
1972 JAN	10	Tau
FEB	21	Gem
1973 AUG	1	Can
1974 JAN	7	Gem
APR	18	Can
1975 SEP	17	Leo
1976 JAN	14	Can
JUN	5	Leo
1977 NOV	17	Vir
1978 JAN	5	Leo
JUL	26	Vir
1980 SEP	21	Lib
1982 NOV	29	Scp
1983 MAY	6	Lib
AUG	24	Scp

1985	NOV	17	Sag		1994	JAN	28	Pic
1988	FEB	13	Cap		1996	APR	7	Ari
	JUN	10	Sag		1998	JUN	9	Tau
	NOV	12	Cap			OCT	25	Ari
1991	FEB	6	Aqu		1999	MAR	1	Tau
1993	MAY	21	Pic		2000	AUG	10	Gem
	JUN	30	Aqu			OCT	16	Tau

How to Use the Uranus, Neptune, and Pluto Tables

Find your birthday in the list following each sign.

Look up your Uranus placement by finding your birthday on the following lists.

URANUS IN ARIES BIRTH DATES

March 31–November 4, 1927
January 13, 1928–June 6, 1934
October 10, 1934–March 28, 1935

URANUS IN TAURUS BIRTH DATES

June 6, 1934–October 10, 1935
March 28, 1935–August 7, 1941
October 5, 1941–May 15, 1942

URANUS IN GEMINI BIRTH DATES

August 7–October 5, 1941
May 15, 1949–August 30, 1948
November 12, 1948–June 10, 1949

URANUS IN CANCER BIRTH DATES

August 30–November 12, 1948
June 10, 1942–August 24, 1955
January 28–June 10, 1956

URANUS IN LEO BIRTH DATES

August 24, 1955–January 28, 1956
June 10, 1956–November 1, 1961
January 10–August 10, 1962

URANUS IN VIRGO BIRTH DATES

November 1, 1961–January 10, 1962
August 10, 1962–September 28, 1968
May 20, 1969–June 24, 1969

URANUS IN LIBRA BIRTH DATES

September 28, 1968–May 20, 1969
June 24, 1969–November 21, 1974
May 1–September 8, 1975

URANUS IN SCORPIO BIRTH DATES

November 21, 1974–May 1, 1975
September 8, 1975–February 17, 1981
March 20–November 16, 1981

URANUS IN SAGITTARIUS BIRTH DATES

February 17–March 20, 1981
November 16, 1981–February 15, 1988
May 27, 1988–December 2, 1988

URANUS IN CAPRICORN BIRTH DATES

December 20, 1904–January 30, 1912
September 4–November 12, 1912
February 15–May 27, 1988
December 2, 1988–April 1, 1995
June 9, 1995–January 12, 1996

URANUS IN AQUARIUS BIRTH DATES

January 30–September 4, 1912
November 12, 1912–April 1, 1919
August 16, 1919–January 22, 1920

URANUS IN PISCES BIRTH DATES

April 1–August 16, 1919
January 22, 1920–March 31, 1927
November 4, 1927–January 13, 1928

Look up your Neptune placement by finding your birthday on the following lists.

NEPTUNE IN CANCER BIRTH DATES

July 19–December 25, 1901
May 21, 1902–September 23, 1914
December 14, 1914–July 19, 1915
March 19–May 2, 1916

NEPTUNE IN LEO BIRTH DATES

September 23–December 14, 1914
July 19, 1915–March 19, 1916
May 2, 1916–September 21, 1928
February 19, 1929–July 24, 1929

NEPTUNE IN VIRGO BIRTH DATES

September 21, 1928–February 19, 1929
July 24, 1929–October 3, 1942
April 17–August 2, 1943

NEPTUNE IN LIBRA BIRTH DATES

October 3, 1942–April 17, 1943
August 2, 1943–December 24, 1955
March 12–October 9, 1956
June 15–August 6, 1957

NEPTUNE IN SCORPIO BIRTH DATES

December 24, 1955–March 12, 1956
October 9, 1956–June 15, 1957
August 6, 1957–January 4, 1970
May 3–November 6, 1970

NEPTUNE IN SAGITTARIUS BIRTH DATES

January 4–May 3, 1970
November 6, 1970–January 19, 1984
June 23–November 21, 1984

NEPTUNE IN CAPRICORN BIRTH DATES

January 19, 1984–June 23, 1984
November 21, 1984–January 29, 1998

Find your Pluto placement in the following list:

Pluto in Gemini—Late 1800s until May 28, 1914
Pluto in Cancer—May 26, 1914–June 14, 1939
Pluto in Leo—June 14, 1939–August 19, 1957
Pluto in Virgo—August 19, 1957–October 5, 1971
              April 17, 1972–July 30, 1972
Pluto in Libra—October 5, 1971–April 17, 1972
              July 30, 1972–August 28, 1984
Pluto in Scorpio—August 28, 1984–January 17, 1995
Pluto in Sagittarius—starting January 17, 1995

CHAPTER 8

Astrology's Glyphs and the Myths Behind Them

Your horoscope chart is written in a special language known to astrologers all over the world. An astrologer in South America could read it as easily as an astrologer in Moscow could. However, if you don't know the meaning of the symbols covering your chart, the language of "astrologese" might look like a difficult code to crack.

If you have ordered one of the popular computer astrology programs, or if you have ordered your chart from one of the many computer services, you'll want to learn the meaning of the symbols. You probably know a few already, like the one for your sun sign, and the moon. It's easy to learn the meaning of the symbols, or "glyphs," for the other signs and planets.

Those little characters, twelve symbols for the astrological signs and 10 for planets, each contain information about their identity—and the hidden meaning of what they represent—within their design. Some are so obvious they give themselves away, like the symbol for the moon. Others take a bit of detective work, like a game of hide-and-seek. But the meaning is expressed right there in that combination of circles, wavy lines, and crosses. In fact, those readers who have already memorized the glyphs may not have realized how much of their meaning is revealed.

Let's start with the symbols for the planets. Look for them inside the "houses" (wedge-shaped segments) of your chart.

Glyphs for the Planets

Almost all the glyphs of the planets are derived from a combination of three basic forms—the circle, the half-circle or arc, and the cross (though this may not be immediately apparent because several symbols have become highly stylized over the years). Each element has a special meaning in relation to the others, which adds to the significance of the completed glyph.

The circle, with no beginning or end, is one of the oldest symbols of spirit or spiritual forces. All of the early diagrams of the heavens—spiritual territory—are shown in circular form. The arc or semicircle is the receptive symbol of the soul. The soul is finite, yet there is spiritual potential. The vertical line symbolizes movement from heaven to earth. The horizontal line describes temporal movement, in time and in space. Superimposed together, they become the cross, symbolizing manifestation in the material world.

THE SUN GLYPH ☉

The sun is always shown by this powerful solar symbol, a circle with a point in the center. It is you, your spiritual center, your infinite personality incarnating into the finite cycles of birth and death.

This symbol was brought into common use in the 16th century, after a German occultist and scholar, Cornelius Agrippa (1486–1535) wrote a book called *De Occulta Philosophia,* which became accepted as the standard work in its field. Agrippa collected many medieval astrological and magical symbols in this book, which were used by astrologers thereafter, copied from those found in Agrippa's book. In the light of what we have written about Pluto in Sagittarius in other chapters in this book, it's especially interesting that Agrippa's influential philosophical treatise was written during a previous time when Pluto was in Sagittarius (the sign that rules philosophy).

THE MOON GLYPH ☽

The easiest symbol to spot on a chart, the moon glyph is a left-facing arc stylized into the crescent moon, which perfectly captures the reactive, receptive, emotional nature of the moon.

As part of a circle, the arc symbolizes the potential fulfillment of the entire circle. It is the life force that is still incomplete. Unlike the circle, it is in a receptive state.

THE MERCURY GLYPH ☿

With a stretch of the imagination, can't you see the winged cap of Mercury the messenger? You might also think of the upturned crescent as little antennae that tune in and transmit messages from the sun, signifying that Mercury is the way you communicate, the way your mind works. The upturned arc is receiving energy into the spirit or solar disk, which will later be translated into action on the material plane, symbolized by the cross. All the elements are equally sized—because Mercury is neutral and doesn't play favorites—this planet symbolizes objective, detached, dispassionate thinking.

THE VENUS GLYPH ♀

Here the relationship is between two elements, the circle of spirit above the cross of matter. Spirit is elevated over matter, pulling it upward. Venus asks, "What is beautiful? What do you like best, what do you love to have done to you?" Venus determines both your ideal of beauty and what feels good sensually. It governs your own allure and power to attract, as well as what attracts and pleases you.

THE MARS GLYPH ♂

In this glyph, the cross of matter is stylized into an arrowhead pointed up and outward, propelled by the circle of spirit. You can deduce that Mars embodies your spiritual energy projected into the outer world. It's your assertiveness, your initiative, your aggressive drive, what you like to do to others, your temper. Your task is to use your outgoing Mars energy wisely and well.

THE JUPITER GLYPH ♃

Jupiter is the basic cross of matter, with a large stylized crescent perched on the left side of the horizontal, temporal plane. You might think of the crescent as an open hand—one meaning of Jupiter is "luck," what's handed to you. You don't work for what you get from Jupiter—it comes to you if you're open to it.

The Jupiter glyph might also remind you of a jumbo jet plane with a huge tail fin, about to take off. This is the planet of travel, mental and spiritual, of expanding your horizons via new ideas, new spiritual dimensions, and new places. Jupiter embodies the optimism and enthusiasm of the traveler about the embark on an exciting adventure.

THE SATURN GLYPH ♄

Flip Jupiter upside down and you've got Saturn. (This might not be immediately apparent, because Saturn is usually stylized into an "h" form like the one shown here.) But the principle it expresses is the opposite of Jupiter's expansive tendencies. Saturn pulls you back to earth—the receptive arc is pushed down underneath the cross of matter. Before there is any expansion, the duties and obligations of the material world must be considered. Saturn says, "Stop, wait, finish your chores before you take off!"

Saturn's glyph also resembles the sickle of old "Father Time." Saturn was first known as Chronos, the Greek god of time, for time brings all matter to an end. When it was the most distant planet (before the discovery of Uranus), it was thought to be the place where time stopped. After the soul, having departed from earth, journeyed back to the outer reaches of the universe, it finally stopped at Saturn, at the end of time.

THE URANUS GLYPH ⛢

The glyph for Uranus is often stylized to form a capital "H" after Sir William Herschel, the name of the planet's discoverer. But the more esoteric version curves the two pillars of the H into crescent antennae, like satellite discs receiving signals from space, perched on the material plane of the cross of matter and pushed from below by the circle of the spirit (a bit like an orbiting satellite). Uranus channels the highest energy of all, the white electrical light of the universal spiritual sun. This pure electrical energy picks up impulses from the deepest reaches of the universe. Because it doesn't follow the ordinary drumbeat, it can't be controlled or predicted (which is also true of those who are strongly influenced by this eccentric planet). This light of spirit is manifested through the balance of polarities (the two arms of the glyph).

THE NEPTUNE GLYPH ♆

Neptune's glyph is usually stylized to look like a trident, the weapon of the Roman god Neptune. However, on a more esoteric level, it shows the large upturned crescent of the soul pierced through by the cross of matter. Neptune nails down, or materializes, soul energy, bringing impulses from the soul level into manifestation. That is why Neptune is associated with imagination, making an image of the soul. Neptune works through feeling, sensitivity and mystical capacity to bring the divine into the earthly realm.

THE PLUTO GLYPH ♇ or ♇

Pluto is written two ways. One is a composite of the letters PL, the first two letters of the word Pluto and coincidentally the initials of Percival Lowell, one of the planet's discoverers. The other, more esoteric symbol is a small circle above a large open crescent surmounting the cross of matter. This depicts Pluto's power to regenerate—you might imagine from this glyph a new little spirit emerging from the sheltering cup of the soul. Pluto rules the forces of life and death—after a Pluto experience, you are transformed, reborn in some way.

Sci-fi fans might visualize this glyph as a small satellite

being launched. It was shortly after Pluto's discovery that we learned how to harness the nuclear forces that made space exploration possible. Pluto rules the transformative power of atomic energy, which totally changed our lives and from which there was no turning back.

The Glyphs for the Signs

On your chart, the glyphs for the sign will appear after the planet. You'll see something like (moon) 23 (Taurus) 44. That means that the moon is located at 23 degrees of Taurus, 44 minutes. At the dividing points (or cusps) between the houses on your chart, you'll also see a symbol for the sign that rules each house.

Glyphs for the signs are much harder to define visually than those of the planets. Many have been passed down from ancient Egyptian and Chaldean civilizations with few modifications. Others have been adapted over the centuries. In deciphering many of the glyphs, you'll often find the dual nature of a sign revealed that is not always obvious from sun-sign descriptions. The Gemini glyph is much like a Roman numeral for two, and reveals the sign's longing for the twin soul. The Cancer glyph may be interpreted as either nurturing, like the breast, or self-protective, like the crab. Libra's glyph embodies the duality of the spirit balanced with material reality. The Sagittarius glyph shows that the aspirant must also carry along the earthy animal nature. The Capricorn sea goat climbs high, yet is pulled back by the deep waters of the unconscious. Aquarius embodies the double waves of detachment and friendliness. And finally the two fishes of Pisces, forever tied together, show the duality of the soul and spirit that must be reconciled.

THE ARIES GLYPH ♈

Since the symbol for Aries is the ram, this glyph's most obvious association is with a ram's horns, which characterizes one aspect of the Aries personality—an aggressive, me-first, leaping-head-first attitude. But the symbol may have other meanings for you, too. Some astrologers liken it to a fountain of energy, which Aries people also embody. The

102

first sign of the zodiac bursts on the scene eagerly, ready to go. Another analogy is to the eyebrows and nose of the human head, which Aries rules, and the thinking power that is initiated in the brain.

One theory of the origin of this symbol links it to the Egyptian god Amun, represented by a ram. As Amon-Ra, this god was believed to embody the creator of the universe, the leader of all the other gods. This relates easily to the position of Aries as the leader (or first sign) of the zodiac, which begins at the spring equinox, a time of the year when nature is renewed.

THE TAURUS GLYPH ♉

This is another easy glyph to draw and identify. It takes little imagination to decipher the bull's head with long curving horns. Like the bull, the archetypal Taurus is slow to anger but ferocious when provoked, as well as stubborn, steady, and sensual. Another association is the larynx (and thyroid) of the throat area (ruled by Taurus) and the eustachian tubes running up to the ears, which coincides with the relationship of Taurus to the voice, song, and music. Many famous singer, musicians, and composers have prominent Taurus influences.

Many ancient religions involve a bull as a central figure in certain rites of fertility or initiation, usually symbolizing the victory of man over his animal nature. Another possible origin is in the sacred bull of Egypt, who embodied the incarnate form of Osiris, god of death and resurrection. In early Christian imagery, the Taurean bull represented St. Luke.

THE GEMINI GLYPH ♊

The standard glyph immediately calls to mind the Roman numeral for two and the symbol for Gemini, the "twins." In almost all images for this sign, the relationship between two persons is emphasized. This is the sign of communication, human contact brings with it the desire to share. Many of the figurative images for Gemini show twins with their arms around each other, emphasizing that they are sharing the same ideas and the same ground. In the glyph, the top line indicates mental communication, while the bottom line indicates shared physical space.

The most prevalent Gemini legend is that of the twin sons, Castor and Pollux, one of whom had a mortal father, while the other was the son of Zeus, king of the gods. When it came time for the mortal twin to die, his grief-stricken brother pleaded with Zeus, who agreed to let them spend half the year on earth, in mortal form, and half in immortal life with the gods on Mt. Olympus. This reflects the basic nature of humankind, which possesses an immortal soul, yet is also subject to the limits of mortality.

THE CANCER GLYPH ♋

Two convenient images relate to the Cancer glyph. The easiest to picture is the curving claws of the Cancer symbol, the crab. Like the crab, Cancer's element is water. This sensitive sign also has a hard protective shell to protect its tender interior. It is wily to escape predators, scampering sideways and hiding shyly under rocks. The crab also responds to the cycles of the moon, as do all shellfish. The other image is that of two female breasts, which Cancer rules, showing that this is a sign that nurtures and protects others as well as itself.

In ancient Egypt, Cancer was also represented by the scarab beetle, a symbol of regeneration and eternal life.

THE LEO GLYPH ♌

Lions have belonged to the sign of Leo since earliest times, and it is not difficult to imagine the king of beasts with his sweeping mane and curling tail from this glyph. The upward sweep of the glyph easily describes the positive energy of Leos; the flourishing tail, their flamboyant qualities. Another analogy, which is a stretch, is that of a heart leaping up with joy and enthusiasm—also very typical of Leo. Notice that the Leo glyph seems to be an extension of Cancer's glyph; however, in the Cancer glyph, the figures are folding inward, protectively, while the Leo glyph expresses energy outward and there is no duality in the symbol (or in Leo). In early Christian imagery, the winged Leo lion represented St. Mark.

THE VIRGO GLYPH ♍

You can read much into this mysterious glyph. The initials of "Mary Virgin," female genitalia, and a young woman holding a staff of wheat are common interpretations. The "M" shape might also remind you that Virgo is ruled by Mercury. The cross beneath the symbol could indicate the grounded, practical nature of this earth sign.

The earliest zodiacs link Virgo with the Egyptian goddess Isis, who gave birth to the god Horus after her husband Osiris had been killed, in the archetype of a miraculous conception. There are many statues of Isis nursing her baby son, which are reminiscent of medieval Virgin and Child motifs. This sign has also been associated with the image of the Holy Grail, when the Virgo symbol was substituted with a chalice.

THE LIBRA GLYPH ♎

It is not difficult to read the standard image for Libra, the scales, into this glyph. There is another meaning, however, that is equally relevant: the setting sun as it descends over the horizon. Libra's natural position on the zodiac wheel is the descendant or sunset position (as Aries' natural position is the ascendant, or rising sign). Both images relate to Libra's personality. Libra is always weighing pros and cons for a balanced decision. In the sunset image, the sun (male) hovers over the horizontal Earth (female) before setting. Libra is the space between these lines, harmonizing yin and yang, spiritual and material, ideal and real worlds. The glyph has also been linked to the kidneys, which are ruled by Libra.

THE SCORPIO GLYPH ♏

With its barbed tail, this glyph is easy to identify with the sign of the Scorpion. It also represents the male sexual parts, over which the sign rules. However, some earlier symbols for Scorpio, such as the Egyptian, represent it as an erect serpent. You can also draw the conclusion that Mars is its ruler by the arrowhead.

Another image for Scorpio, which is not identifiable in this glyph, is the eagle. Scorpios can go to extremes, soaring like the eagle or self-destructing like the Scorpion. In early Christian imagery, which often used zodiacal symbols, the Scorpio eagle was chosen to symbolize the intense apostle St. John the Evangelist.

THE SAGITTARIUS GLYPH ♐

This glyph is one of the easiest to spot and draw—an upward pointing arrow lifting up a cross. The arrow is pointing skyward, while the cross represents the four elements of the material world, which the arrow must convey. Elevating materiality into spirituality is an important Sagittarius quality, which explains why this sign is associated with higher learning, religion, philosophy, travel—the aspiring professions. Sagittarians can also send barbed arrows of frankness in their pursuit of truth. (This is also the sign of the super-salesman.)

Sagittarius is symbolically represented by the centaur, a mythological creature who is half-man, half-horse, aiming his arrow toward the skies. Though Sagittarius is motivated by spiritual aspiration, it also must balance the powerful appetites of the animal nature. The centaur Chiron, a figure in Greek mythology, became a wise teacher, after many adventures and world travels.

THE CAPRICORN GLYPH ♑

One of the most difficult symbols to draw, this glyph may take some practice. It is a representation of the seagoat: a mythical animal that is a goat with a curving fish's tail. The goat part of Capricorn wants to leave the waters of the emotions and climb to the elevated areas of life. But the fish part is the unconscious, the deep chaotic psychic level that draws the goat back. Capricorn is often trying to escape the deep, feeling part of life by submerging himself in work, steadily climbing to the top. To some people, the glyph represents a seated figure with a bent knee, since Capricorn governs the knee area of the body.

An interesting aspect of this figure is how the sharp

pointed horns of this figure, which represent the penetrating, shrewd, conscious side of Capricorn, contrast with the swishing tail, which represents its serpentine, unconscious, emotional force. One Capricorn legend dates from Roman times. The earthy fertility god, Pan, tried to save himself from uncontrollable life forces by jumping into the Nile. His upper body then turned into a goat, while the lower part became a fish. Then Jupiter gave him a save have in the skies, as a constellation.

THE AQUARIUS GLYPH ≈

This ancient water symbol can be traced back to an Egyptian hieroglyph representing streams of life force. Symbolized by the water bearer, Aquarius is distributor of the waters of life—the magic liquid of regeneration. The two waves can also be linked to the positive and negative charges of the electrical energy that Aquarius rules, a sort of universal wavelength. Aquarius is tuned in intuitively to higher forces via this electrical force. The duality of the glyph could also refer to the dual nature of Aquarius, a sign that runs hot and cold, is friendly but also detached in the mental world of air signs.

In Greek legends, Aquarius was represented by Ganymedes, who was carried to heaven by an eagle in order to become the cup bearer of Zeus, and to supervise the annual flooding of the Nile. The sign became associated with aviation and notions of flight.

THE PISCES GLYPH){

Here is an abstraction of the familiar image of Pisces, two fishes swimming in opposite directions, bound together by a cord. The fishes represent spirit, which yearns for the freedom of heaven, while the soul remains attached to the desires of the temporal world. During life on earth, the spirit and the soul are bound together, and when they complement each other, instead of pulling in opposite directions, this facilitates the creative expression for which Pisceans are known. The ancient version of this glyph, taken from the Egyptians, had no connecting line, which was added in the fourteenth century.

Another interpretation is that the left fish indicates the

direction of involution or the beginning of a cycle; the right-hand fish, the direction of evolution, the way to completion of a cycle. It's an appropriate meaning for Pisces, the last sign of the zodiac.

CHAPTER 9

Ten Sure-fire Ways to Thrive in '95!

Wouldn't you like to use the power of the planets to help you achieve your goals? By flowing with the major planetary movements of 1995, you can master your own particular universe. Scheduling activities to coincide with the most favorable cosmic trends is a technique that rulers, presidents, and financiers have been using for centuries. Now you have the same kind of information that was once a highly guarded secret available right in this chapter.

Some very predictable movements of the planet Mercury, for instance, could cause your big plans to stall or go into reverse motion. Perhaps someone might not get an urgent message on time. Or a plane trip might be unaccountably delayed. Knowing what Mercury's up to in advance, you'll double check reservations, and give yourself plenty of options and a double dose of patience. Other planetary movements could bring a situation you've been barely tolerating to a dramatic head, causing tempers to flare. That's when your Dr. Jekyll turns into Mr. Hyde and comes out of hiding. However, these topsy-turvy times might also serve a useful purpose, by forcing you to slow down, reevaluate your life, or blast yourself out of a rut.

Several kinds of events can throw your daily life off track. One possible cause is a retrograding planet. Periodically, most planets seem to tread backward (retrograde) from our point of view on Earth. (Planets don't actually move backward; it just looks that way from here.) If you have a new project planned for those times, you'll know enough to provide for possible delays and tie-ups. On the other hand, you'll have much more success with the kinds of activities that require reaction rather than direct action. If you learn not to push against the tide, but to flow with it, you'll have a big advantage!

Here's our ten-point plan for getting the most out of '95:

1. Promote Yourself When You'll Be Most Attractive to Others

When Venus is in your sign, you can be sure that your charm will be appreciated. Since Venus spends about a month in each sign, time your big sales pitches for the month when it passes through your sun Sign. That's when to flirt up a storm with someone who hasn't been giving you the time of day. Socialize and network with potential clients and contacts. Wear the colors of your sun Sign and play up all your natural sun-sign charms. You'll be the flavor of the month! For example, from January 7 to February 4, Venus is passing through Sagittarius, so Sagittarians will be most appealing. But signs of the same fire-sign family as Sagittarius (Leo and Aries) will also benefit from Venus in Sagittarius. It's also good for air signs (Libra, Aquarius, and Gemini).

So it pays to look for the times when Venus is in your sign, putting a rosy glow on the signs most compatible with yours. For a brief review, fire and air signs generally click. Water and earth signs are generally compatible. The glow will "rub off" on you!

Your Venus Timetable for 1995

As the year begins: Venus is in Scorpio

January 7:	Venus moves to Sagittarius
February 4:	Venus to Capricorn
March 2:	Venus enters Aquarius
March 28:	Venus enters Pisces
April 22:	Venus to Aries
May 16:	Venus to Taurus
June 10:	Venus to Gemini
July 5:	Venus to Cancer
July 29:	Venus to Leo

August 23:	Venus to Virgo
September 16:	Venus to Libra
October 10:	Venus to Scorpio
November 3:	Venus to Sagittarius
November 27:	Venus to Capricorn
December 21:	Venus to Aquarius

2. Make Your Big Push When You'll Have Energy to Burn

Mars is often called the great motivator—it shows how to get where you want to go. It's your personal battery charger, so knowing where this planet is traveling at any given time can help you take the initiative and schedule your major moves for days when you can get ahead fast. At other times, you may be much better off kicking back and reacting to what's happening around you.

Your best times to forge ahead are during the weeks when Mars is traveling through your sun sign or your Mars sign (you can look your Mars Sign up in the chapter on how to find your planets). Also consider times when Mars is in a compatible sign (fire with air signs, or earth with water signs). You'll be sure to have plenty of fuel to get where you're going.

Hold your fire, however, from January 2 until March 24 this year, when Mars retrogrades back from Virgo to Leo, especially if your sun or Mars is in either of those signs. This is the time to exercise diplomacy, let someone else run with the ball, or fight city hall. You may feel that you are not accomplishing as much as you'd like. The key here for everybody when Mars retrogrades is patience. Slow down and work off any frustrations with constructive physical activity (get on that Stairmaster; start pumping iron). It's also best to postpone buying mechanical devices (Mars-ruled) and take extra care when handling sharp objects.

Your Mars Timetable for 1995

January 2:	* Mars turns retrograde in Virgo
January 22:	* Mars retrogrades back to Leo
March 24:	Mars turns direct in Leo

May 25:	Mars reenters Virgo
July 21:	Mars to Libra
September 7:	Mars to Scorpio
October 20:	Mars to Sagittarius
November 30:	Mars to Capricorn

3. Play Your Cards on Your Best Days Every Month and Your High Times Each Year

Your birthday is literally a new birth, when you begin a new solar cycle. This is truly the high time of the year, when the qualities of your sun sign predominate in the overall atmosphere. Take advantage of this time to get new projects under way, especially at the time of the new moon in your sign. This is a powerful time to try new things, to take off in a different direction.

For about two days every month, as the moon passes through your sun sign, the emotional energies are in tune with you. This is also an excellent time to make your moves. Use the moon listings, which accompany your daily forecasts in this book, to schedule key activities.

4. Take It Easy During Your Personal "Low" Times

There are two times during the year when you may feel you are out of sync with what's happening around you. One time is right before your birthday, when the sun is passing through the sign preceding yours. This is a slowdown time, before the annual rebirth on your birthday. You may be feeling a bit vulnerable and reflective, more like keeping to yourself than socializing. (That's good—it's what you're supposed to do at this time!) This is a time to toss away ideas that have outlived their usefulness and unproductive ways of using your time. If you reflect on where you're going and why, then this can be one of your most profitable times of the year. It's also the ideal time to meditate and spend time in more spiritual pursuits.

The other time of year when you may feel at odds with the world is when the sun is passing through the sign opposite yours. If you are a Pisces, for instance, you may feel a sense of unease when the sun is in down-to-earth Virgo, which favors efficient, routine work, rather than creative, imaginative activity. On the other hand, this may be the perfect time to get your life in order. When the full moon is in Pisces, which occurs during this period, you Pisceans may feel especially emotional, as if you're pulled in different directions.

During each month, when the moon passes through your opposite sign, play it cool, doing a few things you've been avoiding. Pisces could clean up clutter when the moon is in Virgo; Aries might be more diplomatic when the moon is in Libra. The idea is to look at the other side of the coin and act accordingly.

5. Gear Up for Saturn's Testing Times

You'll discover strengths you didn't know you had when Saturn comes calling! With a Saturn transit, obstacles appear and our dreams often get doused with a cold splash of reality. However, if these dreams have a chance of really happening, Saturn will provide the structure that will make them materialize. So don't knock Saturn! If you pass this planet's tests, you'll be a much stronger, more grown-up, and more capable person.

Important Saturn times are those when Saturn returns to the position it occupied when you were born, every twenty-eight years or so. At these times, if you don't think about duties and obligations, settling down, and taking on responsibilities, events may force you to do so. Other significant times are when Saturn crosses your rising sign and when it passes your natal sun.

Since Saturn will be traveling through the second half of Pisces all year long, those with Pisces placements will find that they're having some of Saturn's learning experiences. You might find that you are restricted or constrained in some area of your life. (If you're astrology aware, look up the house Saturn is passing through to discover what kind of experiences to expect.) If you ask yourself what the lessons are in these experiences, you might discover that they

113

involve adjusting your dreams to reality and dealing with the responsibilities of being an adult. You'll grow up fast during a Saturn transit.

When Saturn retrogrades, from July 6 to November 21, all signs may feel a lack of discipline. It may be difficult to get things done when you'd rather indulge yourself. You're more likely to give in to daydreaming or overspending when Saturn's restraints are lifted. (Don't worry—you'll put your nose to the grindstone later!)

The best times of this year's Saturn transit could be when Saturn sextiles Neptune (the ruler of Pisces). This happens twice this year, on June 27 and August 17). During this favorable aspect, your dreams have a good chance of becoming realities. On the other hand, it's "chin-up" time in November, when first Jupiter (November 11) and then Mars (November 15) in Sagittarius form an unfriendly angle to Saturn. Things should get back on track after November 21, when Saturn swings into forward motion.

If Saturn is putting on the brakes in your life, remember that Father Time (Saturn) is a fair teacher. You'll get the grades you earn. This planet can be very kind to those who have progressed in maturity and learned their lessons well. It is those who need to learn discipline and responsibility (not the strong points of Sagittarius and Gemini) who will face the most difficult tests.

6. Outwit Mercury Mischief!

If there's one planet that is guaranteed to cause mischief with your scheduling, it's Mercury. This little planet, which rules communications, turns retrograde three times each year for three weeks at a time, when it wreaks havoc with computers, telephones, and traffic of all kinds. People don't get your message or they misunderstand you. Your answering machine breaks down. Computer terminals at your travel agency will somehow put you on the wrong flight. Then your baggage gets lost.

Your best ammunition against the woes of Mercury retrograde is a sense of humor. This diabolical little planet seems to be saying "Don't take it all so seriously!" If traveling, carry a good book or some work to do during delays. Put on your favorite tape when stuck in traffic. Keep your options open and double-check all reservations. Try not to sign contracts or make major purchases during this period. If you're traveling for pleasure, revisit favorite places, leaving exploring the unknown for another time.

This is also a time when people or things from the past could turn up again. You might reignite a former passion or plan a reunion with school buddies. While you're cleaning out your files, you might find an important document you'd lost. Look in the back of your closet—you could uncover a forgotten dress or jacket that could be recycled now. Revisit favorite places. Spend a weekend with your first love in a small hotel filled with memories. You might run into an old friend. At work, go for repeat business. Call up customers you haven't heard from in a while, look up old business contacts, renew subscriptions to professional journals.

This year, Mercury turns retrograde in air signs (Aquarius, Gemini, and Libra), so mark the dates on your calendar. Those born in air signs could feel especially confused or unfocused. Give yourself plenty of options; double-check all communication; and try not to make commitments, sign leases, or make contracts. Instead, use this time to reevaluate your plans and strategies. And remember, in just three weeks, it will be over!

Mercury Retrogrades for 1995

January 26:	Mercury turns retrograde in Aquarius
February 16:	Mercury direct in Aquarius
May 24:	Mercury turns retrograde in Gemini
June 17:	Mercury direct in Gemini
September 22:	Mercury turns retrograde in Libra
October 14:	Mercury direct in Libra

7. Could You Get Lucky This Year? Put Your Money on Sagittarius!

Jupiter represents the principle of expansion—think of hot-air balloons, Santa Claus, and "Luck Be a Lady Tonight." The flipside of Jupiter is that there are no limits—you can expand right off the planet, which is why Jupiter is also called the gateway to heaven. Many people pass on with a Jupiter transit or overextend themselves in some way. Jupiter promotes optimism and enthusiasm, as well as overconfidence, so you'll need a good set of brakes when this planet steps on the gas.

This year, Jupiter is especially strong as it passes through the sign it rules, Sagittarius. This makes for a blast of optimism, enthusiasm, and risk taking in Sagittarian-ruled things. Since Pluto is also powering up the beginning of Sagittarius, it's fair to bet on horses, publishing ventures, higher education, gambling, the travel business, and religious-themed products.

Doing foreign business? Consider Chile, Czechoslovakia, Saudi Arabia, Spain, Toronto, Provence (France), Singapore, Stuttgart (Germany), or Madagascar—all Sagittarius-influenced.

However, be careful of overoptimism during the April 1–August 2 period, when Jupiter will be retrograding, which can deflate enthusiasm and cause powers of persuasion to fall flat. There may be delays and foul-ups in Jupiter-ruled areas, so postpone your risk-taking adventures until after Jupiter turns direct!

Another period to note is the time around November 11, when Jupiter forms a tense aspect with Saturn, which will apply the brakes to any overinflated ventures. However, if your schemes pass Saturn's test, you can be sure they're winners!

Movements of Jupiter in 1995

April 1:	Jupiter turns retrograde in Sagittarius
August 2:	Jupiter direct in Sagittarius
November 11:	Jupiter in Sagittarius squares Saturn in Pisces

8. Oh, Those Ominous Eclipses!

Eclipses have had an ominous reputation since man first panicked at the blackout of one of the celestial lights. If you've ever witnessed a total solar eclipse, you'll agree it's an awesome spectacle. Even today, people in many parts of the world cling to their superstitions about the negative effects of eclipses. During the total solar eclipse of July 1991, villagers in Mexico painted fruit trees red and wore red ribbons and underwear to deflect "evil rays." Then everyone retreated inside to track the eclipse on TV.

Could you be eclipsed by an eclipse? Not if you know how to turn one of nature's most fascinating events to your advantage. Lunar eclipses happen at the time of a full moon, when emotions would normally come to a head and be released—this is the monthly climax of events. Then, after the full moon comes a winding-down period before the next new moon starts the cycle rolling again. At a lunar eclipse, however, the release, which is usually triggered by the tension of the sun opposing the moon, is intercepted by the Earth, which passes exactly between the two bodies and cuts off the exchange of energy, like a football player intercepting a long pass. The effect can be either confusion or clarity, as subconscious energies are let loose, bringing insights and events that can change the pattern of our lives. Whether this creates disorientation or divine insight depends on each individual's reaction. However, change is the key word.

When a solar eclipse occurs, the moon is the interfering body, blocking the sun's energy from the Earth. Since this always happens at the new moon, which begins the monthly cycle, the alignment of sun and moon energies becomes super-intense, with the moon's emotional nature taking over. It's not a time for objective clarity! Emotions can get out of hand as the ego (sun) goes into hiding. But what a time for spiritual or psychic experiences!

Because the exact alignments of eclipses create such a concentration of energy, everything from birds, animals, fish—even oysters—become disoriented. But if we look behind eclipse-related crises, we often find that there is some deep, positive force activated—a change that needed to happen.

How should you handle an eclipse? Mark your calendar the week before the eclipse, a few days after the previous quarter moon, when energies start to build up. Clearly this would not be a good time to make a serious commitment, an important decision, or a major purchase that requires measured, rational thinking. Generally, stick to low-stress activities, since your energy and immune system may be lower than usual. If at all possible, avoid surgery, risky sports, handling sharp or dangerous objects. And be especially careful with any form of drug or alcohol use.

However, if you'd like to catch someone off guard, this would be the time to do it! Let the competition make a move, while you sit patiently and wait until at least three days after the eclipse before you act.

New Moons, Full Moons, and Eclipses in 1995

January 1:	New moon in Capricorn
January 16:	Full moon in Cancer
January 30:	New moon in Aquarius
February 15:	Full moon in Leo
March 1:	New moon in Pisces
March 17:	Full moon in Virgo
March 31:	New moon in Aries
**April 15:	Full moon/lunar eclipse in Libra
**April 29:	New moon/solar eclipse in Taurus
May 14:	Full moon in Scorpio
May 29:	New moon in Gemini
June 13:	Full moon in Sagittarius
June 27:	New moon in Cancer
July 12:	Full moon in Capricorn
July 27:	New moon in Leo
August 10:	Full moon in Aquarius
August 26:	New moon in Virgo
September 9:	Full moon at Pisces
September 24:	New moon in Libra
**October 8:	Full moon/lunar eclipse in Aries
**October 24:	New moon/solar eclipse in Scorpio
November 7:	Full moon in Taurus
November 22:	New moon in Scorpio again
December 7:	Full moon in Gemini
December 21:	New moon in Sagittarius

9. Process What You Learned over the Last Two Years

The outer planets, Uranus and Neptune, have been making the news since 1993, when they lined up in Capricorn for a monumental happening that takes place only once every

171 years. Many of us experienced the fallout from natural shakeups—floods, wars, personal confusion—which served to break down traditional structures in all areas of our lives, redefine our priorities, and put us on new ground for the next century. Now, as both planets prepare to leave Capricorn, you should be making significant progress based on what you've learned over the past two years.

Pay attention when both these planets turn retrograde this year. At these times, watch for delays and setbacks in areas where there have been revolutionary changes in the last two years. This is a pause to gather energy for a great shift in the atmosphere next year. During late November and December, when Venus, Mars, and Mercury pass by Uranus and Neptune, their energies will be strongly activated once again. Expect the unexpected!

In June and August, Neptune's sextile to Saturn, which is passing through Neptune-ruled Pisces, could have a very constructive effect in our lives by providing an understanding of the lessons we learned over the past two years.

Uranus, often called the awakener, has certainly done its work over the past two years. This year, it begins to move into Aquarius, the sign it rules, where its influence is strongest. More than ever, it seems to say, "Make way for the new!" This is a transition time between the breaking up of old structures and the beginning of a more expansive and more advanced era. Uranus will confirm this as it nods to Pluto on April 10 and August 7, signaling a shift in energy that should bring hope to everyone.

Movements of Uranus in 1995

April 1:	Uranus enters Aquarius, its planetary ruler
April 10:	Uranus sextiles Pluto in Sagittarius
May 5:	Uranus turns retrograde in Aquarius
June 8:	Uranus retrogrades back to Capricorn
August 7:	Uranus in Capricorn Sextiles Pluto in Scorpio again
October 6:	Uranus turns direct in Capricorn

Movements of Neptune in 1995

April 27:	Neptune turns retrograde in Capricorn
June 27:	Saturn (Pisces) sextiles Neptune (Capricorn)

August 17: Saturn (retrograding in Pisces) sextiles Nep-
          tune (Capricorn) for the second time.
October 5: Neptune turns direct in Capricorn

10. Watch Pluto Switch on a New Kind of Power!

Pluto shows where the power is on a mass level. And if you have strong Sagittarius placements, you're sure to feel the intense transformative power of Pluto in the next few years. Everyone else could also benefit by some Pluto awareness. Though this tiny planet moves very slowly through the zodiac, it's an amazingly accurate barometer of what's really happening on a deep, subconscious level. Since we've covered the main event this year (Pluto's move into Sagittarius) in a separate chapter, this should serve as an extra reminder to tune in to Pluto and mark its movements on your calendar.

After moving into Sagittarius on January 17, giving us a taste of things to come, Pluto turns retrograde on March 3, moving back to Scorpio and, after turning direct on August 8, it finally enters Sagittarius on November 10. You may be able to feel the energy as it shifts from the intensity of Scorpio to the light, jovial optimism of Sagittarius. We'll all be transformed in our attitudes toward the very serious life-and-death issues that Scorpio rules. Now we can look forward to a spiritual shift with the potential to uplift our lives!

Movements of Pluto

**January 17:	Pluto enters Sagittarius, a major event
March 3:	Pluto turns retrograde in Sagittarius
April 10:	Uranus sextiles Pluto in Sagittarius
April 21:	Pluto retrogrades back to Scorpio
August 8:	Pluto turns direct in Scorpio
November 10:	Pluto enters Sagittarius

CHAPTER 10

Find Your Love in the Sun-Sign Personals

For some lucky people, the love of their lives is waiting in their favorite newspaper or magazine. There, in the back pages, could be a "successful entrepreneur looking for a curvaceous cutie." Further down the column is a "sensuous, brilliant blonde." Or how about the sports fan who's looking for someone who likes tennis and kayaking.

Since "personals" columns are taking up more and more classified ad space, many people must be getting together via the printed media. And some love seekers include either their own astrological sign, or the sign they'd most like to meet, in their qualifications.

Astrology-savvy sleuths might be able to detect a certain sign's style from the wording of the ad. Who but a Leo would be so confident in print? And doesn't that long list of qualifications sound like a Virgo's ad? But first, you have to know what a given sun sign's line might be. One easy way to do this is to guess which sign wrote the following ads. Then ask yourself who you'd be most likely to respond to it.

The ad writer's astrological identity will be revealed at the end of the chapter.

Women Seeking Men

1. RESCUE ME! I've been looking for love in all the wrong places. I need a special someone who is successful, sincere, and ready for a permanent commitment. I'm a magical dreamer who could invent some fantasies you'd love to fulfill. If you like affectionate, adorable, offbeat ladies, who are interested in music, art, and romantic candlelit dinners, I'll be happy to start over again with you.

2. LOOKING FOR THE REAL THING. Are you a steadfast, caring go-getter, who not only appreciates the best things in life but wants to have them! Are you the ritzy romantic who'll break down my reserve, the man of substance who can also make me laugh? I'm a hard-working, ambitious professional who'll make romance a high priority with an equally accomplished soulmate. I'll give you good value if you'll cater to my needs.

3. FIRE UP YOUR ENGINE! I'm looking for my knight riding a red Miata, Jeep or dirt bike. Let's hit the road and talk. I'm a feminine feminist, financially independent and frisky. I love the simple joy of wind in my hair, would rather have a mountaintop picnic than a posh night out. My guy is in good shape, has high energy, and is brave enough to have an equal relationship. Adventure and wild passion are ahead for us both.

4. PRESCRIPTION FOR PASSION. I'm waiting for a doting doctor with a logical mind and a poetic soul. You need tender loving care from a sweet-tempered nurse who is intelligent, informed, and a good conversationalist. I need a responsible, rational Romeo who's fit physically and financially. You should be a nonsmoker, brainy, funny, and confident, but also shy, gentle, and gallant. Since casual encounters are not my style, please be serious about having a meaningful relationship.

5. WOMAN OF DEPTH, looking for a man of substance. If you're smart, sexy, and do what you do with passion, we should meet. Why settle for less? This passionate, attractive, super-sensual seductress is looking for her match. I have some wild ideas, but old-fashioned values. I'm ready to be your one-and-only, so say good-bye to all your exes, and let's get back to basics together.

6. LET'S BE FRIENDS FIRST, LOVERS LATER. I'm a loving visionary who cares about making the world a better place. I'm looking for a Renaissance man who's unconventional, bright, and strong, who dances to his own tune, a like-minded lover who will hold me lightly. If you'd like to be the wind beneath my wings, let's get together and reach for the stars.

7. BIG SPENDER WANTS MILLIONAIRE IN TRAINING.
Let's conquer the world together. I'm a warm, ultra-feminine head-turner who's as gorgeous in jeans as in a ball gown. If you deserve the best, look no further. My best man has George Hamilton's wardrobe, Bill Clinton's power, and Schwartzenegger's muscles. But if you've just got a heart of gold, you might still be The One for me.

8. I'M THRILLED BY CREATURE COMFORTS.
Breakfast in bed, fresh flowers, gourmet dinners, velvet gowns. I'm looking for someone to share earthly pleasures and earthy passion. Let's indulge each other! I could make beautiful music with someone who's generous, sensual, and single. You'll be rewarded with all the cuddling and laughter you can handle!

9. ARE THERE ANY GUYS LEFT who like nice old-fashioned girls like me?
I'm pretty, full figured, and want a solid relationship with a man of morals, manners, and means, who can take time to be loving and tender. Please be a family man who'll bring me home to mother, introduce me to your kids, wolf down the wonderful meals I'll cook for you, and hold hands under the full moon.

10. SPORTS FAN.
Blond personal trainer, 5'10", looking for someone who likes football as much as I do. Interested in meeting upbeat, honest, athletic male for tennis or biking, as well as Monday-night TV games. If you love travel to exotic places, have a sharp mind in a fit body, I'll take a gamble on you. Let's go jogging or walk our dogs together. Who knows where we'll end up?

11. DESIGNING WOMAN SEEKS A LEADING MAN.
If you appreciate the finer things in life (and can afford them), let me surround you with romance. I'm a beautiful balance of cool logic and vulnerability; I love togetherness, but also need my own well-decorated space. Please be an unencumbered potential mate with good looks, good man-

ners, and a great lifestyle. If you believe success is better when shared, then I'm the elegant lady who can take you from here to eternity.

12. GOT A TWINKLE IN YOUR EYE? Then I'll be no trivial pursuit. If we can talk a good game, then we might be lifetime playmates. You've got a lot to say and a witty way to say it; you're a playful party-goer, a sharp dresser who can make me laugh. Would a sophisticated, brainy beauty, who'll never give you a dull moment, make you happy? Then let's talk!

Men Seeking Women

1. TRY A LITTLE TENDERNESS. I'm romantic; I love moonlight and old-fashioned girls. I'm looking for someone to share long walks by the sea, old movies, and cozy candlelit dinners we'll cook together. You should be gentle and feminine, soft spoken and affectionate, with family values. We'll go antiquing, make love in a canopy bed, share our secrets. I love children, good wine, good company. Intimacy is my specialty. Let me provide a warm, supportive nest for you.

2. YOUR BEST INVESTMENT. Established professional, very financially secure, seeks an attractive, classy, charming lady to get serious about. Am interested in raising a family. You should also be marriage minded, intelligent, and well educated. I offer you a life of art, music, and mental stimulation. Please be slim, between 25–35, and physically fit. You may be a career woman by day, but be a homebody by night.

3. READ MY LIPS. Young-looking, young-at-heart, divorced male with eclectic tastes. I'm looking for a stunning, spirited companion with a zest for life. Great sense of humor a must. I'm whimsical, unencumbered, fun-loving, and communicative. Be ready for laughter and loving combined. If you like a varied menu of activities with lots of spice and sweet words, can we talk?

4. DOES KAYAKING IN ALASKA LEAVE YOU COLD? If so, you're not the spirited, adventurous, outdoor gal I'm looking for. Be in good shape or willing to get there fast. You should also like camping, animals, and weekends away from it all. If you're an optimist who cares about making the world a better place; if you're a brainy, insightful lady with great legs, then let's try out that kayak! Keep your bags packed and your passport updated.

5. LIVE OUT YOUR FANTASIES. I'm the man you meet in your dreams, the one who knows your thoughts before you speak, who treats you like the special person you are. I'll listen to your innermost confidences, give you my shoulder to cry on. Please be sweet but strong willed. Let me be the dreamer, while you be the doer. If you've been overworking, I'll de-stress you with caresses, give you the romance you've been missing.

6. LET ME BE YOUR TEDDYBEAR. I'm looking for a curvaceous cutie to huddle and cuddle with. Be my favorite pet and we'll satisfy our appetites in the kitchen and bedroom. You won't have to diet for me! I like you full figured and fabulous, wearing silk blouses, fluffy sweaters, and French perfumes. If you're a peaceful, home-loving lady with feet on the ground, let's get together. If you're a great cook, even better.

7. BE MY PRETTY WOMAN. I'll show you how beautiful life can be. Let's be Nick and Nora, Fred and Ginger, Bill and Hillary. I'm slim and handsome, and I have a passion for the arts and fine dining. I love entertaining and am as comfortable in a tux as I am in a jogging suit. I'd like a committed relationship with my female counterpart, who's up on the latest fashions and exudes elegance. Come share my social whirl!

8. WHERE'S MY QUEEN OF HEARTS? I'm a handsome, high-powered executive looking for a princess to share my castle. I'd love to hear from a beautiful, intelligent, passionate woman who feels good about herself and would like to share life's pleasures with a very generous man. If you're a warm, sunny head-turner with a radiant smile, I'll give you the royal treatment.

9. ALL OR NOTHING AT ALL. A woman of depth and sensuality who'll be my body and soulmate. If you're a one-man woman who's ready to be cherished forever, I'd like to meet you. I could get serious about someone who is intensely feminine, proud and passionate, erotically inventive. Let's rendezvous in a haunted mansion, read each other's tarot cards and snack on caviar. Wear slinky black—or nothing at all—under your trenchcoat.

10. LOOKING FOR BEAUTY AND BRAINS. Successful M.D. seeks lady to share the best things in life. I'm looking for a foxy lady who exudes style, class, and great taste in all she does. Dazzle me with your brilliant mind and fascinate me with witty conversation. You should also be in great shape, slim, and health conscious. Be conservative in public, and an uninhibited vixen in private. For Ms. Perfect, I'll cure your insecurities and be your significant other.

11. I'M OPEN-MINDED AND WILLING TO TRY ANYTHING ONCE. Surprise me! I'm slightly eccentric—a Renaissance man with Tom Selleck's looks, Einstein's mind, and Yeltsin's guts. You're your own person, strong in spirit and body. Be adventurous, unconventional, open minded, and future oriented. Material girls need not apply. Be my best friend as well as my lover, and I'll be yours for keeps.

12. LIGHT MY FIRE! I'm a strong, confident macho man who's looking for a kindred spirit to share life's challenges. You should be athletic, energetic, and ready for lots of action. If you spark my interest, I'll give you plenty of fireworks—get ready to be swept off your feet, wooed, and pursued like you've never been before. My white charger's waiting for the right fair damsel.

Who Placed the Personal Ads?

Women Seeking Men

1. Pisces
2. Capricorn
3. Aries
4. Virgo
5. Scorpio
6. Aquarius
7. Leo
8. Taurus
9. Cancer
10. Sagittarius
11. Libra
12. Gemini

Men Seeking Women:

1. Cancer
2. Capricorn
3. Gemini
4. Sagittarius
5. Pisces
6. Taurus
7. Libra
8. Leo
9. Scorpio
10. Virgo
11. Aquarius
12. Aries

CHAPTER 11

Let the Stars Guide You to Your True-Love Type

Ladies, does the sensitivity of Tom Cruise and the smooth style of Harrison Ford appeal to you most? Or do you prefer the dash of Dennis Quaid and Alec Baldwin? Guys, do you dream of Kim Basinger? Or are Julia Roberts and Demi Moore more your type?

It's amazing how many celebrities embody the qualities of their sun sign. And it's amazing, too, what your favorite celebrity's sign can reveal about your potential soulmate. To prove (or disprove) this point, circle the celebrities that appeal to you on the following lists. Some are all-time classic film personalities; others might be the talk-show host you watch most often, or the celebrity you'd like most to have dinner with. You may be surprised to find out how many of your choices fall under one or two signs. Then look up the sun sign type at the end of the lists and learn more about who really turns you on (it could be quite a different sign than the one you expect)!

Type A: Dashing and Daring

MALES

Alec Baldwin
Al Gore
Gregory Peck
Spencer Tracy
Matthew Broderick
Timothy Dalton

FEMALES

Ellen Barkin
Diana Ross
Emma Thompson
Leeza Gibbons
Paulina Porizkova
Mariah Carey

Dennis Quaid
Warren Beatty
David Letterman
Eddie Murphy

Reba McEntire
Shannon Doherty
Marilu Henner
Ali MacGraw

Type B: Earthy Sensualists

MALES

FEMALES

Daniel Day Lewis
Jack Nicholson
Jay Leno
Randy Travis
Al Pacino
Pierce Brosnan
Tony Danza
David Byrne
Billy Joel
Emilio Estevez

Michelle Pfeiffer
Janet Jackson
Candice Bergen
Andie MacDowell
Debra Winger
Shirley Maclaine
Sheena Easton
Cher
Bea Arthur
Jessica Lange

Type C: Charm to Spare

MALES

FEMALES

Tom Berenger
Clint Eastwood
Parker Stevenson
Donald Trump
Tony Geary
Tristan Rogers
Prince
Johnny Depp
Paul McCartney
John Goodman

Elle MacPherson
Brooke Shields
Isabella Rossellini
Nicole Kidman
Joan Rivers
Kathleen Turner
Lisa Hartman
Phylicia Rashad
Joan Collins
Connie Selleca

Type D: Tender and Caring

FEMALES

Princess Diana
Linda Ronstadt
Kim Alexis
Meryl Streep
Diahann Carroll
Phoebe Cates
Isabelle Adjani
Jerry Hall
Angelica Huston
Brigitte Neilson

MALES

Tom Cruise
Harrison Ford
Geraldo Rivera
Bill Cosby
Jimmy Smits
Robin Williams
George Michael
John Tesh
Alex Trebek
Sylvester Stallone

Type E: Big-time Romantics

MALES

Mick Jagger
Arnold Schwartzenegger
President Bill Clinton
Steve Martin
Kenny Rogers
Peter Jennings
Magic Johnson
Robert de Niro
Robert Redford
Patrick Swayze

FEMALES

Madonna
Jackee
Whitney Houston
Lynda Carter
Delta Burke
Connie Chung
Kathie Lee Gifford
Deborah Norville
Iman
Loni Anderson

Type F: They Love Taking Care of You

FEMALES

Shelley Long
Joan Lunden
Raquel Welch
Sophia Loren
Jacqueline Bisset
Faith Ford

MALES

Richard Gere
Jeremy Irons
Harry Connick, Jr.
Billy Ray Cyrus
David Soul
Corbin Bernson

Rebecca DeMornay
Ann Archer
Amy Irving
Linda Gray

John Ritter
Sean Connery
Michael Keaton
Mark Harmon

Type G: The Beauty Lover

MALES

FEMALES

Michael Douglas
Armand Assante
Julio Iglesias
Marcello Mastroianni
Luciano Pavarotti
John Lithgow
Sting
Jesse Jackson
Bryant Gumbel
Charleton Heston

Susan Sarandon
Sigourney Weaver
Suzanne Somers
Cheryl Tiegs
Catherine Deneuve
Heather Locklear
Brigitte Bardot
Angela Lansbury
Julie Andrews
Deborah Kerr

Type H: Intense and Passionate

FEMALES

MALES

Jodie Foster
Goldie Hawn
Roseanne Arnold
Demi Moore
Julia Roberts
Whoopi Goldberg
Meg Ryan
Mary Elizabeth
   Mastrantonio
Mary Hart
Maria Shriver

Sam Sheppard
Dan Rather
Larry King
Kevin Kline
Harry Hamlin
Burt Lancaster
Richard Burton
Danny DeVito
Pat Sajak
Ted Turner

Type I: Call Me Lucky

MALES	**FEMALES**
Don Johnson	Kim Basinger
Billy Idol	Darryl Hannah
Frank Sinatra	Jane Fonda
Jeff Bridges	Sinead O'Connor
John F. Kennedy, Jr.	Bette Midler
Kirk Douglas	Robin Givens
Michael Nouri	Susan Dey
Richard Pryor	Tina Turner
Phil Donohue	Teri Garr
Woody Allen	Liv Ullman

Type J: Home Is Where the Heart Is

FEMALES	**MALES**
Katie Courec	David Bowie
Diane Sawyer	Elvis Presley
Diane Keaton	Rod Stewart
Kirstie Alley	Denzel Washington
Victoria Principal	Ted Danson
Faye Dunaway	Nicholas Cage
Susan Lucci	Mel Gibson
Dolly Parton	Kevin Costner
Marlene Dietrich	Cary Grant
Ava Gardner	Anthony Hopkins

Type K: Mr. or Ms. Charisma

MALES	**FEMALES**
Clark Gable	Geena Davis
Michael Jordan	Ann Jillian
Axl Rose	Farrah Fawcett
Burt Reynolds	Morgan Fairchild
Tom Selleck	Meg Tilly
Garth Brooks	Lana Turner

Lorenzo Lamas	Cybill Shepherd
Paul Newman	Jane Seymour
Richard Dean Anderson	Vanna White
John Travolta	Oprah Winfrey

Type L: The Fantasy Lover

FEMALES	**MALES**
Cindy Crawford	Michael Bolton
Drew Barrymore	Edward James Olmos
Bernadette Peters	William Hurt
Glenn Close	Raul Julia
Rue McClanahan	Chuck Norris
Sharon Stone	Billy Crystal
Paula Zahn	Erik Estrada
Faith Daniels	James Taylor
Sally Jessy Raphael	Harry Belafonte
Elizabeth Taylor	Willard Scott

• **IF MOST OF YOUR CHOICES ARE TYPE A, YOUR FANTASY SOULMATE IS ARIES.** These are the macho men and liberated women of the zodiac. You are probably also fascinated by such classic stars as Bette Davis, Marlon Brando, and Joan Crawford. Aries men are the type who sweep you off your feet, with plenty of enthusiasm. They may, however, cool down just as fast as they heated up. This sign has produced some noted playboys, including the founder of *Playboy* magazine, Hugh Hefner, as well as Warren Beatty and Marlon Brando. The women are some of the most exciting in the zodiac. These are assertive take-charge women who usually have dynamic careers. Obstacles only make life more challenging for lady Aries, who needs someone who'll let her take the lead—or have her own turf.

• **IF MOST ARE TYPE B, YOUR FANTASY SOUL-MATE IS TAURUS.** This sign experiences the world through the five senses—whatever or whoever feels good, tastes good, smells good, sounds good, looks good, is the one they love. This is the sign that stops to smell the roses, and probably planted them in the first place. This sign likes control, and stars of this sign, like Barbra Streisand and

Shirley Maclaine, usually call their own shots. Men of this sign, like Jack Nicholson and Daniel Day Lewis, have an earthy kind of sensuality. They're the type that responds to good food, comfort, and physical beauty in a woman. The gorgeous Taurus stars like Candice Bergen, Michelle Pfeiffer, and Andie McDowell have a flowerlike femininity that is down to earth and a bit maternal—someone you'd love to come home to.

• **IF MOST ARE TYPE C, YOUR FANTASY SOUL-MATE IS GEMINI.** Gemini celebrities are known for their great lines. When we say, "Can we talk?" or "Make my day," or when we mention "the art of the deal," we conjure up images of Joan Rivers, Clint Eastwood, or Donald Trump. Joan Collins's TV character on "Dynasty" was as famous for her quick wit as her beauty. Never bored or boring, Gemini values mental stimulation more than the physical pleasures or material rewards. One example is Gemini beauty Brooke Shields, who cut her career short to finish college. Rather than be typecast, Kathleen Turner and Isabella Rossellini experiment with many kinds of roles. Rare is the Gemini who has only one career or one marriage. George Bush was the exception—but he was married to Barbara, another Gemini. Variety is the key to Gemini's appeal, and it's also the secret to their ability to communicate with so many different kinds of people.

• **IF MOST ARE TYPE D, YOUR FANTASY SOUL-MATE IS CANCER.** Women born under this sign are among the most classically feminine and nurturing in the zodiac. However, that same caring nature can make them powerful mother figures, like Princess Diana, Nancy Reagan, and Imelda Marcos. If you're attracted to this type, you love their strong femininity and depth of feelings. Actresses like Meryl Streep and Angelica Huston have an intuitive understanding of character that helps them turn in award-winning performances. The Cancer male, like Robin Williams or Tom Cruise, also accesses that uncanny intuition. Here is a man who is more comfortable with women than any other sign. This man is a born romantic, whose understanding of a woman's emotions and insecurities makes him one of the zodiac's most tender and sympathetic lovers.

• **IF MOST ARE TYPE E, YOUR FANTASY SOUL-MATE IS LEO.** This sign does everything in a big way. They crave lots of attention, and you'd better be ready to provide it if you fall in love with this sign. President Bill Clinton and Arnold Schwartzenegger are prototypes of the larger-than-life Leo male. Though not on the list, Stormin' Norman Schwartzkopf is another. Even Leos who are less than impressive physically make their presence felt—Dustin Hoffman and Mick Jagger are two examples. The women of this sign are regal romantics who need a lover who knows how to pay court. Many Leo stars were beauty queens or involved with the pageants, like Delta Burke, Lynda Carter, and Kathie Lee Gifford. Many Leo stars are powerful enough to be known by only one name, like Madonna, Iman, Jackee, or Jackie O. If she can learn to share the spotlight sometimes, this sign makes a warm, loving mate who radiates positive energy.

• **IF MOST ARE TYPE F, YOUR FANTASY SOUL-MATE IS VIRGO.** It may come as a surprise that the sign of the virgin contains some of the sexiest celebrities, like Sophia Loren, Sean Connery, Raquel Welch, and Jaqueline Bisset. Yet these are not types who bestow affection lightly. There is always an idealism, a search for the perfect lover, behind their quest. The Virgo male type, like Jeremy Irons and Corbin Bernsen, appreciates brains as well as beauty—and that's a big part of his appeal. And this is one man that can sing about an "Achey Breakey Heart" (Billy Ray Cyrus) and have women lining up to cure it. Virgo women, sensuous though they may be, always have an air of discipline and discrimination. Like Raquel, they watch what they eat and exercise every day. But it's this blend of sensuality and practicality that makes this sign so appealing. If they take such good care of themselves, imagine how well they'll take care of you!

• **IF MOST ARE TYPE G, YOUR FANTASY SOUL-MATE IS LIBRA.** Libra is an aesthetic sign that is able to project an ideal kind of beauty, like Catherine Deneuve, Deborah Kerr, or Brigitte Bardot. When this sign's scales are balanced, Libra combines charm, style, and ideals of fairness. The men of this sign are often style setters, like Bryant Gumbel, Marcello Mastroianni, or Ralph Lauren, yet they always retain an air of detachment as they examine everyone and everything from many perspectives. The women are ultra-feminine but fight fiercely for justice, as shown by the Libran celebrities' roles. Sigourney Weaver in *Aliens* and Susan Sarandon in *Thelma and Louise* are two examples. And in real life, there are forceful Libra heroines like Eleanor Roosevelt and Margaret Thatcher.

• **IF MOST ARE TYPE H, YOUR FANTASY SOUL-MATE IS SCORPIO.** This category shows an attraction to intense characters. Both male and female Scorpios love to exercise power and control over others. You'll find many female Scorpio stars firmly holding the reins, involved in all aspects of their shows. Jodie Foster, Roseanne Arnold, and Goldie Hawn are all active players in the Hollywood power scene. Hillary Rodham Clinton wields Scorpio female political power. Scorpio men, like Kevin Kline, have strong sexual magnetism, even when playing comedy roles. Often they come across as low key, like Sam Sheppard or anchorman Dan Rather—but never underestimate their underlying drive. To intrigue a Scorpio, keep your air of mystery. Don't tell all. Scorpio loves to delve into your deep secrets.

• **IF MOST ARE TYPE I, YOUR FANTASY SOUL-MATE IS SAGITTARIUS.** When Frank Sinatra sings "I Did It My Way," he's singing the Sagittarius theme song. This sign hates to take orders and needs to keep some independence in any relationship. The male Sagittarius is a romantic wanderer, but so much fun that he's easier to forgive than other zodiac Don Juans. This sign is also compelled to voice its opinions, controversial as they may be. You may be attracted by the outspoken, sometimes outrageous qualities of Sagittarius stars like Sinead O'Connor, Bette Midler, and Phil Donohue. This sign is very sports minded, whether as a participant or spectator, and adores being on the road. Sagittarius women, like Jane Fonda and Liv Ullman, usually have interests that reach beyond their profession. Sagittarians are big risk takers, whether it be a new business venture or a night at the casino. Fortunately, luck usually smiles on this sign, perhaps because these folks are among the most optimistic positive thinkers of the zodiac.

• **IF MOST ARE TYPE J, YOUR FANTASY SOUL-MATE IS CAPRICORN.** It may come as a surprise that a sign that contains David Bowie, Rod Stewart, and Elvis Presley, could be called home loving and traditional. But male Capricorns like the little woman to stay in the background, helping them rise to the top, and they usually do not tolerate a two-career marriage for long. Women of this sign also combine ambition with traditional values. Dolly Parton has lovingly restored the backwoods cabin where she grew up. Throughout her long career, Marlene Dietrich returned to her husband's chicken farm and stayed married to the same man in spite of her legendary love life. This combination of the devoted girl or boy next door with worldly success is one thing that keeps Capricorn stars like Cary Grant, Ava Gardner, and Loretta Young on our mind.

• **IF MOST ARE TYPE K, YOUR FANTASY SOUL-MATE IS AQUARIUS.** Charisma is the word for the electric appeal of Aquarius, which grows ever stronger over high-tech media like television and video. This sign understands the secret of universal appeal. They're everyone's friend and can reach out to groups of people easily, like Oprah Winfrey or Paul Newman. The men of this sign easily embody an archetypal masculinity, like Clark Gable or Burt Reynolds. However, on a personal level they tend to be remote. There's always a fascinating elusive quality that can't quite be pinned down. To have a lasting relationship with this sign, you've got to be a friend as well a lover. It also helps if you share plenty of outside activities and interests—this is not a sign who'll focus on you alone.

• **IF MOST ARE TYPE L, YOUR FANTASY SOUL-MATE IS PISCES.** Pisces celebrities wrap their talent in an air of illusion. They rarely come on strong. Instead, they have an undefinable ease and glamour that lures admirers. Like the actors Michael Caine, Glen Close, or Raul Julia, Pisces artists seem to do what they do effortlessly, as if they're hardly trying. No one can guess the hard work behind their talented facade. They love to help the needy (and often attract people with problems). Pisces, like Elizabeth Taylor, will champion the most controversial causes. The Pisces female, like Cindy Crawford, epitomizes feminine glamour, but there is always a caring, emotional quality as well. The Pisces male is home loving and sensual. He's the dreamy kind of romantic, who will make you feel as if you're the center of his universe and that he understands everything you're going through. If he's in a field where he can use his creative talents, he's sure to be a success.

CHAPTER 12

The Astrology Bulletin—How to Make Your Own Astrology Connections

If you've caught the "astrology bug," you'll want to go even further than the scope of this book. Perhaps you'll begin by having your chart done, then deepen your knowledge by taking courses or attending conferences, subscribing to astrology-oriented magazines, or trying your hand at doing charts yourself on your personal computer. If you are buying a computer with astrology use in mind, you'll want to know where to find the right program for your needs and expertise.

To help you in your quest, here is what you can expect from a typical astrological reading, some tips on the newest computer programs, plus a resource list of reputable companies and organizations at the end of the chapter.

Whether you're new to astrology or already hooked, you'll find the more you get involved, the more you'll be fascinated by its accuracy and relevance to your life. And the more there is to challenge you!

When to Have a Reading

If you've been wondering about whether an astrological reading could give you the competitive edge in business, help you break through a personal dilemma, decide on the best day for a key event in your life, or help you make a career change, this may be the time to have a personal consultation. An astrologer might give you reassurance and validation at a turning point or crisis time in your life, or simply help you get where you want to go. Though you can learn much about astrology from books such as this one, or you can choose from a varied menu of computer readings (there are some quite sophisticated readings done by world-famous astrologers), nothing compares to a personal consultation with a professional astrologer who has analyzed thousands of charts and who can pinpoint the winning potential within yours. With your astrologer, you can address specific problems in your life that may be holding you back. For instance, if you are not getting along with your mate or coworker, you could leave the reading with some new insights and some constructive ways to handle the situation. There's no question that a good astrologer can help you create a more fulfilling future by understanding your own tendencies as well as your place in the cosmic scheme.

YOU'LL NEED TO GIVE THE ASTROLOGER THIS INFORMATION BEFOREHAND. Before your reading, a reputable astrologer will ask you for the date, time (as accurately as possible), and place of birth of the subject of the reading. A horoscope can be cast about anything that has a specific time and place. Most astrologers will enter this information into a computer, which will then calculate your chart in seconds. From the resulting chart, the astrologer will do an interpretation.

WHAT TO DO IF YOU ARE NOT SURE OF YOUR EXACT BIRTH TIME. If you don't know your exact birth time, you can usually find it filed at the Bureau of Vital Statistics at the city hall or county seat of the state where you were born. If you have no success in getting your time of birth, some astrologers specialize in rectification, using past events of your life to estimate an approximate birth time.

How to Find a Good Astrologer

Your first priority should be to choose a qualified astrologer. Rather than relying on hearsay or grandiose advertising claims, do this with the same care you would choose any trusted adviser such as a doctor, lawyer, or banker.

Unfortunately, anyone can claim to be an astrologer—to date, there is no licensing of astrologers or established professional criteria. However, there are nationwide organizations of serious, committed astrologers that can help you in your search.

Good places to start your investigation are organizations such as the American Federation of Astrologers or the National Council for Geocosmic Research (NCGR), which offers a program of study and certification. If you live near a major city, there is sure to be an active NCGR chapter or astrology club in your area—many are listed in astrology magazines available at your local newsstand. In response to many requests for referrals, the NCGR has compiled a directory of professional astrologers, which includes a glossary of terms and an explanation of specialties within the astrological field. Contact the NCGR headquarters (see the resource list at the end of this chapter) to order a copy.

As a potentially lucrative freelance business, astrology has always attracted self-styled experts who may not have the technique or the counseling experience to give an accurate, helpful reading. These astrologers can range from the well-meaning amateur to the charlatan or street-corner gypsy who has for many years given astrology a bad name. Be very wary of astrologers who claim to have occult powers or who make pretentious claims of celebrated clients or miraculous achievements. You can often tell from the initial phone conversation if the astrologer is legitimate. He or she should ask for your birthday time and place and conduct the conversation in a professional way. Any astrologer who gives a reading based only on your sun sign is highly suspect.

When you arrive at the reading, the astrologer should be prepared. The consultation should be conducted in a private, quiet place. The astrologer should be interested in your problems of the moment. A good reading involves feedback on your part, so if the reading is not relating to your concerns, you should let the astrologer know. You should feel free to ask questions and get clarification of technical terms. The reading should be an interaction between two people rather than a solo performance. The more you actively participate, rather than expecting the astrologer to carry the reading or come forth with oraclar predictions, the more meaningful your experience will be.

An astrologer should help you validate your current experience and be frank about possible negative happenings, but be helpful about pointing your life in the most positive direction.

In their approach to a reading, some astrologers may be more literal, some more intuitive. Those who have had counseling training may take a more psychological approach. Though some astrologers may seem to have an almost psychic ability, extrasensory perception or any other parapsychological talent is not necessary to be a good astrologer. A very accurate picture can be drawn from factual data.

An astrologer may do several charts for each client—one for the time of birth, one for the current date, and a "progressed" chart showing the evolution from the birth time to the present. According to your individual needs, there are many other possibilities, such as a chart for a different location, if you are contemplating a change of place. Relationships between any two people, things, or events can be interpreted with a "synastry" chart, which compares the chart of one birth date with the chart of another date. Another type of relationship chart is the composite chart, which uses the midpoints between planets in two individual charts to describe the relationship.

An astrologer will be particularly interested in transits—planets passing over the planets or sensitive points in your chart during the upcoming year, which signal important times for you.

Another option is a taped reading—the astrologer will mail you a previously taped reading based on your birth chart. This type of reading if more personal than a computer printout and can give you valuable insights, but it is not equivalent to a live reading, when you have a dialogue with the astrologer and can cover your specific interests.

Astrology on Your Home Computer

Your PC is an excellent tool for learning about astrology. There are basic programs especially for students, which cost under $100, such as "Chartwheels" from Astrolabe. No longer do you have to spend hours on tedious calculations or rely on guesswork when you set up a chart. The computer does this for you in seconds and runs off a great-looking chart.

Software is now available for every computer and for all levels of astrological expertise. Some will provide pages of interpretations. Others simply run off a chart with technical information. Others give you mind-boggling menus enabling you to choose from many different zodiacs, house systems, and types of charts. If, like most of our readers, you will only be using the program occasionally for fun, then you really don't need an expensive and complicated program. If you are motivated to study astrology in depth, however, you may want to investigate the more challenging programs.

There are several companies on the resource list at the end of this chapter that produce or distribute astrological software. Most are happy to offer support and advice. If you give them the make and model of your computer and your level of astrological knowledge, they will recommend a program and even help you get started. Some offer chart services to print up charts and interpretations for those who do not have a computer or do not want to invest in a program.

BUYING A COMPUTER TO DO ASTROLOGY. There are programs available for all operating systems, although most are created for IBM compatibles. At this writing, one of the top astrology software companies, Astrolabe, is offering thirty programs for IBM PC compatibles, thirteen for Macintoshes, and one for the Commodore Amiga. It also continues to stock some older programs for Apple II, earlier Commodores, and CPM-compatible machines, so don't despair if you are still working on a "dinosaur."

If you're buying a new computer and want to run state-of-the-art programs, most software vendors recommend an 80386 to 80486 processor chip, at least 640K RAM (though most current software runs on 512 K RAM), a speed of 16 megaHertz or faster, and DOS 3.3 or higher. A hard disk with 40 or more megabytes and at least one floppy are recommended. As for monitors, color displays are not necessary; however, there are some gorgeous graphic astrology charts coming out that will require an auto VGA. Otherwise, a high-resolution one-color monitor with a Hercules monographics card is fine.

If you are buying a new printer, graphics look sharpest on a laser printer, but many astrologers are very content with a 9- or 24-pin printer. Those of you who use Windows will find that several of the companies listed at the end of the chapter are now doing programs for this environment, with pull-down menus and graphics. "Solar Fire" from Astrolabe is one such program.

Where to Connect with Other Astrologers

Check your local metaphysical bookstore for flyers or a bulletin board posting astrological events in your area. Many New Age centers offer courses with astrologers visiting your area, when you can meet kindred souls.

You can contact other astrologers or learn about astrological happenings in your area and nationwide through computer networks which have astrological SIG's (Special Interest Groups). These are often reviewed or listed in astrology magazines, so, if you have a modem, why not tune in? If you already belong to a network or to Compuserve, check to see if there are astrology fans online.

Another way of finding an astrology class is to contact one of the regional astrology groups across the country that have regular meetings. Ask at your local metaphysical or New Age bookstore or look for listings in an astrology magazine such as *American Astrology* or *Dell's Horoscope*. Astrological organizations like the National Council for Geocosmic Research may give classes in your area. Several times a year, these organizations sponsor regional astrology conferences where you can meet some of the best teachers, as well as broaden your knowledge and socialize with other astrology fans.

Several astrologers are running mating-and-dating services, using astrological savvy to bring cosmically connected couples together. It is possible that one of your local astrologers is running a comparable service. This could be a "personals" column with astrological information about the participants that you then follow up on your own, or the astrologer may do a more personalized search for you, involving individual chart comparisons, personal interviews, and video interviews.

Some Other Ways to Study Astrology

First, consider attending one of the several yearly regional conferences sponsored by the major astrological organizations. Most offer programs at several levels of expertise. You could also connect with a teacher who would help you further your studies.

If you cannot go to conferences, you can still hear many of the lectures and workshops on tape cassetes in your home or car. See the resource list to order catalogues of regional and national conferences. Taped instruction is also advertised in the more specialized astrology magazines such as *Planet Earth* or *Mountain Astrologer.*

Another option, which might interest those who live in out-of-the-way places or who are unable to fit classes into their schedule, are study-by-mail courses that are offered by several astrological computing services and astrology magazines. Some courses will send you a series of tapes; others use workbooks or computer printouts.

An Astrology Resource List

Nationwide Astrology Organizations

(Conferences, Workshops, Local Meetings, Conference

Tapes, Referrals)

National Council for Geocosmic Research
(For Directory of Professional Astrologers, classes, tape catalogue, and conference schedule.)
105 Snyder Avenue
Ramsey, NJ 07446
201-818-2871

American Federation of Astrologers (A.F.A.)
P.O. Box 22040
Tempe, AZ 85382

A.F.A.N.
(Networking, Legal Issues.)
8306 Wilshire Blvd.
Berkeley Hills, CA 90211

ARC Directory
(Listing of astrologers worldwide)
2920 E. Monte Vista
Tucson, AZ 85716
602-321-1114

Computer Programs

Matrix Software
(Programs for IBM Compatibles, at the student and professional level.)
315 Marion Avenue
Big Rapids, MI 49307
(1-800-PLANETS)

Astro Communications Services
(Programs for IBM compatibles and MAC, variety of computer charts, Telephone Consultations.)
Dept. AF693, PO Box 34487
San Diego, CA 92163-4487
(1-800-888-9983)

Astrolabe
(Variety of programs for all computers, beginner to professional level, wide selection of computer readings.)
Box 1750—R
Brewster, MA 02631
1-800-843-6682

A.R.T. Software
(Programs for the Mac.)
P.O. Box 191
Cumberland Center, ME 04021

Microcycles
PO Box 78219
Los Angeles, CA 90016-0219
(1-800-CYCLES)

Air Software
115 Caya Avenue
West Hartford, CT 06110
(1-800-659-1AIR)

Time Cycles Research
(Programs for the Macintosh.)
27 Dimmock Road
Waterford, CT 06385

Astro-Cartography
(Charts for location changes.)
Astro-Numeric Service
Box 336-AD
Ashland, OR 97520
1-800-MAPPING

Conference and Workshop Tapes

Pegasus Tapes
P.O. Box 419
Santa Ysabel, CA 92070

National Council for Geocosmic Research
(Conference tapes.)
NCGR Headquarters
105 Snyder Avenue
Ramsey, NJ 07446
201-818-2871

International Society for Astrological Research (ISAR)
(Lectures, workshops, seminars.)
P.O. Box 38613
Los Angeles, CA 90038

ISIS Institute
P.O. Box 21222
El Sobrante, CA 94820-1222

Astro Analytics Productions
P.O. Box 16927
Encino, CA 914116-6927
818-997-8684

Astrology Schools

New York School of Astrology
(Intensive curriculum, seminars, bookstore, conferences, public events.)
545 Eighth Avenue-10th Floor
New York, NY 10018-4307
212-947-3609

Astrology Magazines

American Astrology
475 Park Avenue South
New York, NY 10016

Dell Horoscope
P.O. Box 53352
Boulder, CO 80321-3342

Aspects
Aquarius Workshops
P.O. Box 260556
Encino, CA 91426

Planet Earth
The Great Bear
P.O. Box 5164
Eugene, OR 97405

The Mountain Astrologer
P.O. Box 11292
Berkeley, CA 94701

CHAPTER 13

Your Year-Round Calendar for Creating a Healthier Lifestyle

Of the big changes in the past few years, those involving our health care may have the greatest effect on our future well-being. At this writing, as Pluto, the planet of transformation, is winding up its trip through Scorpio, the sign that rules insurance and life-or-death matters, we are scheduled for sweeping health-care reforms. It should be no surprise that the one who designed and launched the transformation in American health care should be an intense and dedicated Scorpio, Hillary Rodham Clinton.

At the same time, Saturn is moving through Pisces, which rules hospitals. This planet calls attention to what isn't working, and while in Pisces, it calls for devotion to helping others. Over this year, many health-care institutions are sure to be reexamined and restructured. With monumental changes shaking up our health-care system, we'll be asked to take on more responsibility for our own health, beginning with adopting a healthier lifestyle.

Astrology can help you sort out your health priorities and put your life on a healthier course by getting in step with these times of reform. Since astrology began, different parts of the body, and their potential illnesses, have been associated with specific signs of the zodiac. Today's astrologers still work with these ancient associations, using them not only to locate potential health problems, but also to help clients harmonize their activities with those favored by each sign.

Using the stars as a guide, you can create your own master plan for a healthier lifestyle by focusing on the part of your body that is ruled by each sign, during that sun-sign period. For example, during Pisces, the sign that rules the feet, you might evaluate your shoes for fit and comfort or start a walking program. You could step up to an aerobics class or regular tennis games during Mars-ruled Aries, a high-energy sign. During nature-oriented Taurus, you should switch to more outdoor exercise, like hiking. This approach varies your workout routine to harmonize with the astrological atmosphere. And you'll be more likely to sustain your fitness program if there is enough variety to keep you from getting bored. If you follow this sign by sign pathway, by the end of the year you'll have improved your health from head to toe.

The following guide should help you select activities which harmonize with each sun-sign period.

Capricorn—a great time to get started!
(December 22–January 19)

You couldn't pick a better time to start off on a new health and fitness regime than discipline-oriented Capricorn. Maybe that's why this is the busiest time of the year for gyms and health spas. Why not give yourself a Christmas present of a membership in a local gym or YMCA? Under Capricorn, which favors structure and organization of all kinds, you'll be motivated to start off the new year by getting into an exercise routine. However, it's important to find a plan you can stick with, so consider first consulting with a coach or a personal trainer who'll design a routine that's best for you.

Capricorn rules the skeletal structure, which makes this a great time to look at the state of your posture, your bones and joints. It's never too early to counteract osteoporosis by adding weight-bearing exercise to your routine. If your knees or joints are showing early signs of arthritis, you may need to add calcium supplements to your diet. Check your posture, which affects your looks and your health. Remember to protect your knees when you work, perhaps adding exercises to strengthen this area.

Capricorn, the sign of Father Time, brings up the subject of aging. If sags and wrinkles are keeping you from looking as young as you feel, you may want to investigate plastic surgery. Many foods have antiaging qualities and might be worth adding to your diet. Teeth are also ruled by this sign—a reminder to have regular cleanings and dental checkups.

Capricorn is also the sign of the workaholic, so be sure not to overdo in your quest for health. Keep a steady, even pace for lasting results. Remember to include pleasurable activities in your self-care program. Grim determination can be counterproductive if you're also trying to relieve tension. Take up a sport for pure enjoyment, not necessarily to become a champion.

Your Capricorn-time stress-busters: Check your office environment for hidden health saboteurs, like air quality, lighting, and comfort. Get a back-support cushion if your chair is uncomfortable. If you work at a computer, check your keyboard and the height of the computer screen for ergonomic comfort.

Aquarius—individualize! (January 20–February 18th)

Aquarius, the sign of high-tech gadgets and new ideas, should inspire you with new ways to get fit and healthy. You don't have to follow the crowd to keep fit. There are many ways to adapt your exercise routine to your personal needs. If your schedule makes it difficult to get to the gym or take regular exercise classes, look over the vast selection of exercise videos available and take class anytime you want. Or set up a gym at home with portable home exercise equipment.

New Age health treatments are favored by Aquarius, which makes this an ideal month to consider alternative approaches to health and fitness. Since Aquarius rules the circulatory system, you might benefit from a therapeutic massage, a relaxing whirlpool, or one of the new electronic massage machines.

Calves and ankles are also Aquarius territory and should be emphasized in your exercise program. Be sure your ankles are well supported, and be careful of sprains.

This is also a good time to consider the air quality around you. Aquarians are often vulnerable to airborn allergies and are highly sensitive to air pollution. Do some air quality control on your environment with an air purifier, ionizer, or humidifier. Since this is flu season, read up on ways to strengthen your immune system.

Aquarius is a sign of reaching out to others, a cue to

make your health regime more social—doing your exercises with friends could make staying fit more fun.

Pisces—feet first! (February 19–March 20)

Perhaps it's no accident that we often do spring cleaning during Pisces. The last sign of the zodiac, which rules the lymphatic system, is super-sensitive to toxins. This is the ideal time to detox your system with a liquid diet or supervised fast. This may also help you get rid of water retention, a common Pisces problem.

Feet are Pisces territory. Consider how often you take your feet for granted and how miserable life can be when your feet hurt. Since our feet reflect and affect the health of the entire body, devote some time this month to pampering them. Check your walking shoes or buy some shoes tailored for your kind of exercise. Investigate orthotics, especially if you walk or run a lot. These custom-molded inserts could make a big difference in your comfort and performance.

The soles of our feet connect with all other parts of our body, just as the sign of Pisces embodies all the previous signs. This is the theory behind reflexology, a therapeutic foot massage which treats all areas of the body via the nerve endings on the soles of the feet. For the sake of your feet, as well as your entire body, consider treating yourself to a session with a local practitioner of this technique.

Pisces is the ideal time to start walking outdoors again, enjoying the first signs of spring. Try doing local errands on foot, as much as possible.

Aries—energize! (March 21–April 19)

This Mars-ruled sign is a high-energy time of year. It's time to step up the intensity of your workouts, so you'll be in great shape for summer. Aerobics, competitive sports, activities that burn calories are all favored. Try a new sport that has plenty of action and challenge, like soccer or bike racing. Be sure you have the proper headgear, since Aries rules the head.

Healthwise, if you've been burning the candle at both ends or repressing anger, this may show up as headaches. The way to work off steam under Aries is to schedule extra time at the gym, take up a racket sport or ping pong, anything that lets you hit an object hard! Go into spring training with your local baseball team!

Taurus—back to nature! (April 20–May 20)

Spring is in full bloom, and what better time to awaken your senses to the beauty of nature? Planting a garden can be a wonderful, relaxing antidote to a stressful job. Long walks in the woods, listening to the sounds of returning birds, and smelling the spring flowers help you slow down and enjoy the pleasures of the Earth.

This is a month to enjoy all your senses: Add more beautiful music to your library, try some new recipes, take up a musical instrument, learn the art of massage. This pleasure-loving time can be one of the most sensual in your love life, so plan a weekend getaway to somewhere special with the one you love.

This is also a time to go to local farmers' markets and to add more fresh vegetables to your diet. While we're on the subject of food, you may be tempted to overindulge during the Taurus period, so be sure there are plenty of low-calorie treats available. If you are feeling too lethargic, your thyroid might be sluggish. Taurus rules the neck and throat area, which includes the thyroid glands and vocal cords.

Since we often hold tension in our neck area, pause several times during the day for a few stretches and head rolls. If you wake up with a stiff neck, you may be using the wrong kind of pillow.

Gemini—stay in touch! (May 21–June 20)

One of the most social signs, Gemini rules the nerves, our body's lines of communication. doing things with others is therapeutic now. Include friends in your exercise routines. Join a friendly exercise class or jogging group. Gemini-type sports require good timing and manual dexterity as well as communication with others, like tennis or golf.

If your nerves are on edge, you may need more fun and laughter in your life. Getting together with friends, going to parties, doing things in groups brings more perspective into your life.

Since Gemini also rules the lungs, this is an ideal time to quit smoking. Investigate natural ways to relieve tension, such as yoga or meditation. Doing things with your hands—playing the piano, typing, doing craftwork—is also helpful.

Those of you who jog may want to try hand weights during the Gemini months, or add upper-body exercises to your daily routine.

Cancer—create a healthy home! (June 21–July 22)

Good health begins at home, and Cancer is the perfect time to do some healthy housekeeping. Evaluate your home for potential toxins in the water or building material. Could you benefit from air and water purifiers, undyed sheets and towels, biodegradable cleaners? How about safer cooking utensils of stainless steel or glass?

This is also a good month for nurturing others and yourself, airing problems and providing the emotional support that should make your home a happier, more harmonious place to live.

Cancer rules digestive difficulties, especially gastric ulcers. Emotionally caused digestive problems—those stomach-knotting insecurities—can crop up under Cancer. Baby yourself with some extra pampering if you're feeling blue.

Boating and all water sports are ideal Cancer-time activities. Sometimes, just a walk by your local pond or sitting for a few moments by a fountain can do wonders to relieve stress and tension.

If you've been feeling emotionally insecure, these feelings may be sensitized now, especially near the full moon. Being with loved ones, old friends, and family could give the support you need. Plan some special family activities that bring everyone close together.

The breast area is ruled by Cancer, a reminder to have regular checkups, according to your age and family history.

Leo—heart and spine time! (July 23–August 22)

We're now in the heart of summer, the time when you need to consider your relationship to Leo's ruler, the sun. Tans look great, but in recent years we've all been cautioned about the permanent damage the sun can do. So don't leave home without a big hat or umbrella, and some sunblock formulated for your skin type.

If you've been faithful to your exercise program, you probably look great in your swimsuit. If not, now's the time to contemplate some spot-reducing exercises to zero in on problem areas. This is prime time for outdoor activity—biking, swimming, team sports—that can supplement your routine. Leos like Arnold Schwartzenegger and Madonna have profited immensely from weight training. Since this is a time to glorify the body beautiful, why not consider what a body-building regime could do for you?

Leo rules the upper back and heart, so consider your cardiovascular fitness and make your diet healthier for your heart. Are you getting enough aerobic exercise? Also, step up exercises that strengthen the Leo-ruled upper back, like swimming.

If you have planned a vacation for this month, make it a healthy one, a complete change of pace. Spend time playing with children, expressing the child within yourself. The Leo time is great for creative activities, doing whatever you enjoy most.

Virgo—analyze! (August 23–September 22)

Virgo rules the care and maintenance of the body in general, and the abdomen, digestion, lower liver and intestines in particular. This is a troubleshooting sign, the perfect time to check your progress. Schedule medical exams and diagnostic tests, and generally evaluate your health. If you need a change of diet, supplements, or special care, consult the appropriate advisers.

It's also a good time to make your life run more efficiently. It's a great comfort to know that you've got a smooth organization backing you up. Go through your files and closets to eliminate clutter; edit your drawers and toss out whatever is no longer relevant to your life.

In this back-to-school time, many of us are taking self-improvement courses. Consider a course to improve your health—nutrition, macrobiotic cooking, or massage, for example.

Libra—balance your life! (September 23–October 22)

Are your personal scales in balance? If you're overdoing in any area of your life, Libra is an excellent time to address the problem. If you have been working too hard or taking life too seriously, what you may need is a dose of culture, art, music, or perhaps some social activity.

If your body is off balance, consider yoga, spinal adjustments, or a detoxification program. Libra rules the kidneys and lower back, which respond to relaxation and tension-relieving exercises. Make time to entertain friends. Be romantic with the one you love. Harmonize your body with chiropractic work. Cleanse your kidneys with plenty of liquids.

Since this is the sign of relationships, you may enjoy working out with a partner or with loved ones. Make morning walks and weekend hikes family affairs. Take a romantic bicycle tour and picnic in the autumn countryside. Put more beauty in all areas of your life.

Libra is also the sign of grace, and what's more graceful than the dance! If ballet is not your thing, why not swing to a Latin or African beat? Dancing combines art, music, romance, relaxation, graceful movement, social contact, and exercise—what more can you ask?

Scorpio—transformation! (October 23–November 21)

If you have been keeping up an exercise program all year, you should see a real difference now, if not a total transformation. Scorpio is the sign to transform yourself—try a new hair color, get a makeover, change your style. Eliminate what's been holding you back, including self-distructive habits—Scorpio is a sign of willpower and determination.

This sign rules the regenerative and eliminative organs, so it's a great time to turn over a new leaf. Sexual activity comes under Scorpio, so this can be a passionate time for love. It's also a good time to examine your attitudes toward sex and to put safe sexual practices into your life.

It's no accident that this passionate time is football season, which reminds us that sports are a very healthy way to diffuse emotions. If you enjoy winter sports, why not start preparing for the ski slopes or ice skating? Scorpio loves intense life-or-death competition, so be sure your muscles are warmed up before going all out.

Sagittarius—set goals! (November 22–December 21)

Sagittarius, ruled by jovial Jupiter, is holiday time, a time to kick back, socialize with friends, and enjoy a whirl of parties and get-togethers. High-calorie temptations abound, so you may want to add an extra workout or two after hitting the buffet table. Or better yet, head for the dance floor instead of the hors d'oeuvres. Most people tend to loosen up on resolve around this time of year; there's just too much fun to be had.

If you can, combine socializing with athletic activities. Local football games, bike riding, hikes, and long walks with your dog in tow are just as much fun in cooler weather. Let others know that you'd like a health-promoting gift—sports equipment, a gym membership, or an exercise video—for Christmas. Plan your holiday buffet to lessen temptation with plenty of low-calorie choices.

In your workouts, concentrate on Sagittarius-ruled areas with exercises for the hips, legs, and thighs. This is a sports-loving sign, ideal for downhill or cross-country skiing, ice skating or roller blading, and basketball.

You may find the more spiritual kinds of exercise, such as yoga or tai chi, which work on the mind as well as the body, more appealing now. Once learned, these exercises can be done anywhere. Yoga exercises are especially useful for those who travel, especially those designed to release tension in the neck and back. Isometrics-type exercises, which work one muscle group against another, can be done in a car or plane seat. If you travel often, investigate equipment that fits easily in your suitcase, such as water-filled weights, jump ropes, elastic exercise bands, and home-gym devices.

This sign of expansiveness is the ideal opportunity to set your goals for next year. Ask yourself what worked best for you this year and where you want to be at the end of 1996. Most important, in holiday-loving Sagittarius, go for the health-promoting sports and activities you truly enjoy. These are the best for you in the long run, for they're the ones you'll keep doing with pleasure.

CHAPTER 14

Your Taurus Personal Life—Including Your Decision Maker

The Taurus Man: Well Grounded

You're interested in real, tangible things and you'll work hard to provide yourself and your loved ones with material comforts. Born under a fixed, earth sign, you like solid, secure ground under your feet. Each step is carefully considered before you make your move. Slow to commit and equally slow to let go, you are known for physical and emotional endurance, which is an asset in business, where you are an excellent judge of whether something will have lasting value.

Gifted with stamina and persistence, your focused approach usually moves you steadily toward your goal, like the strong, silent-type hero portrayed by Gary Cooper, rather than the swashbuckling extrovert on the fast track. You stick to your guns, rarely changing horses in midstream. Once committed, no one robs you easily of your rightful possessions or position. Taurus has so much patience that it takes a lot of pushing to make you angry, but one sure way of turning you into a raging bull is to threaten your well-established territory or your material security.

Taurus is usually uncomplicated in your wants and needs. What you see is what you get with Taurus. You are usually quite predictable and take life literally, preferring to think in terms of what you can experience with your senses, rather than in abstract concepts. Not one for a spartan lifestyle, Venus-ruled Taurus likes to enjoy the fruits of your labors. You're susceptible to physical comfort, if not outright luxury—tables laden with delicious, substantial food; the smell of full-blown roses (or a simmering pot on the kitchen stove); beautiful fabrics that are nice to touch. Overall, the atmosphere of plenty appeals to Taurus most. (Even the most pared-down Taurus lifestyle has comfort, sensual texture, and carefully chosen objects.)

Because you love to be surrounded by comfort and beauty, you may overindulge in good food, or pile up collections of objets d'art. You love your home and devote much time and effort to making it as comforting and welcoming as possible. In fact, it may be very difficult to lure you away from your well-feathered nest. You prefer to entertain at home, remaining on your own secure, comfortable turf, where you can enjoy your treasures and pleasures to the fullest in familiar surroundings, rather than venturing out to explore new territory.

In a Relationship

The physical side of a relationship is high priority for sensual Taurus men. You need to be touched, held, and hugged. You love to look at the beauty of the human form. Romantically, you'll tumble hard and fast for physical beauty, especially if combined with a voluptuous, well-sculpted body. The combination of sensuality and endurance makes Taurus one of great lovers of the zodiac, though your outward appearance is more wholesome and easygoing, like the Taurus movie heros of the thirties and forties: Jimmy Stewart, Bing Crosby, James Mason, and Gary Cooper.

Letting go of anything, whether it's a threadbare, once-beloved old sweater or your first love, is especially difficult for you. You can carry the torch for years after a romance has faded, sometimes staying in an unhappy or abusive relationship long after another sign would have departed. In the extreme, this becomes an obsession—Taurus never seems to forget, especially a promise that was broken.

You can be one of the most devoted husbands once you have established a loving, cozy, secure home base. You're happiest with a rather domestic, earth-mother type woman who is interested in providing these things and won't interfere in your equally comfortable work routines. Before that time, however, you experiment with different erotic adventures. Such is your fondess for beauty of all kinds that you could easily fall for a flirtatious charmer or an independent beauty. However, ultimately, you'd prefer having your wife nearby—a partner who is too independent and self-sufficient will either send you off to greener pastures or make you see red. Since you have such a long memory for discomfort or grief, you may let grievances accumulate until you are pushed too far, then end the relationship with an explosion. However, when you do find a compatible mate, you can be the stable, secure, and sensual husband of most women's dreams.

The Taurus Woman: Soft and Strong

You are the earth mother of the zodiac, an unabashed, uninhibited sensualist who revels in beauty in all its earthly manifestations. You are the animal lover and the green-thumbed gardener who sees divinity in nature and responds almost spiritually to physical beauty in all its forms. You're also conscious of what these things cost, both in terms of talent and cold cash (no one can tell the "real thing" from the fake as well as you can). Nature-loving Taurus takes an especially protective attitude toward the environment and the welfare of animals (you're sure to have at least one beloved pet).

Your other pronounced trait is stubbornness. When a Taurus woman sets her mind to something, there is no stopping her. With blinders on, you'll bulldoze ahead until you get what you want, disregarding public opinion or advice to the contrary. When you undertake something, you'll wait until your infallible instincts tell you the time is right to take action. Once on track, you won't be derailed by other options.

Taurus is slow to make changes, even in a situation that you know won't work out. On the other hand, you'll stick to a particular style or an image that works for you and make it your own. That is why so many Taurus women in show business stand out for their special style, which many try to copy but few can imitate. Think of Audrey Hepburn, Katharine Hepburn, Carol Burnett, Barbra Streisand, Cher, and Candice Bergen, who are unique, memorable, and much imitated. Yet they have had amazing professional longevity. While other stars fade, talented Taureans go from strength to strength, only improving with age and experience.

One of your greatest gifts is your common sense. You're a realist who brings ideas down to earth. Though you may be less gifted in judging the complexities of people, you understand functional relevance: what really works. You drive a hard bargain, and you're the least likely of any sign to fall for a puffed-up sales pitch.

You'll also hold other people to their commitments, with little regard for those who change their minds or promise what they cannot deliver. Therefore, many fire (Aries, Sagittarius, Leo) and air (Gemini, Libra, Aquarius) signs will present special difficulties for you, Taurus. Though you love the glamour and dash of more flashy types, you're not always willing to grant the flexibility these signs demand, or to leave your comfortable abode to accompany them to more exciting places (many Tauruses have "fear of flying," of losing control of their environment). You'll also give short shrift to the playboy who changes his mind and his women frequently and to the loser who doesn't produce.

In a Relationship:

You rarely marry on a whim, and many of you give special consideration to a man's ability to provide the lifestyle you dream of (or to create it with you). Because of your dislike of change or instability, you tend to stick with a marriage even after it has deteriorated. The most successful Taurus relationships are those where both partners have similar goals and a mutual appreciation of talent and luxury, such as the Taurus actress with the director who helps develop her talent or the Taurus fashion designer with the entrepreneur who backs her in business or provides her with a beautiful home. You often make a particularly good partner for a sensitive, artistic man, who appreciates the warm, stable, nurturing atmosphere you provide.

You're usually a talented homemaker (though you may delegate some or most of the chores to others), who prizes your secure home turf and family life above all. Whether you stay rooted in the same place for decades or, like Cher, change homes on a whim, each nest will be beautifully and comfortably, if not luxuriously, appointed. You'll hold the fort, giving your partner a welcoming, pampering environment.

A wizard with money, you have a talent for budgeting, investing, and finding a bargain. You'll be a full-time mother, if necessary, preferring to devote time and attention to your brood (though you may run a little business from your home).

The Taurus Family

The Taurus Parent

Taurus is one of the natural parents of the zodiac, especially for young children, who benefit most from your patient, nurturing qualities; the firm foundation of love, and the stable family atmosphere you provide. Your heart goes out to children who do not have a stable family or who are growing up in difficult circumstances, and you can be a tireless worker in their behalf. Audrey Hepburn's wonderful work for UNESCO and Cher's work with disabled children come to mind.

Your demonstrative, affectionate nature seems designed to give the child a sense of security. Later, as the child grows more independent, it may be difficult for you to let go. (You may find it especially difficult to deal with the more individualistic, rebellious teenager who also has a stubborn streak.) Indeed, many Taurus children remain in the Taurus family nest into adulthood. A Taurus mom is a tough act to follow, as many young wives have discovered! And there is no one as protective as a Taurus dad.

The song, "There's No Place Like Home," was surely written by a Taurus. Images of Mother baking chocolate-chip cookies in the kitchen and Daddy comfortably lodged in his "Papa Bear" chair with his favorite dog lounging at his feet are Taurus stereotypes. However, though few Taureans can manage the Norman Rockwell fantasy in today's world, that is the image closest to Taurus hearts, and rare is the Taurus who doesn't long for a place in the country with swings on the trees and a fragrant rose garden.

The Taurus Stepparent

Your steady, calm nature can be reassuring to stepchildren longing for a stable atmosphere. Patiently, you'll wait for the children to come around when they become accustomed to the new family structure. When they do, you'll be warm and affectionate. However, when you must assert your disciplinary authority, do so with calm control, understanding that others with strong wills may resent your power. Stepchildren will teach you to develop flexibility and can expand your horizons if given the chance. Be open to an extended family situation that may not follow the traditional rules. Children will appreciate your allowing them time alone with their parent to share mutual interests and strengthen bonds.

The Taurus Grandparent

In spirit, Taurus grandparents are picture-book elders of Norman Rockwell paintings, even if they look as glamorous as Cher. By this time, you've established a warm, comfortable home and are contented to gather all the family 'round. The Taurus grandma is the archetypal earth mother with a large brood to nurture, whether they are your own or other children in need. Taurus is concerned about the children's future and may provide a trust fund or nest egg to finance their education. As the years go by, you'll keep family ties close by planning family gatherings, sending thoughtful notes, and making frequent phone calls. Taurus teaches grandchildren the true meaning of family traditions by providing them with a strong sense of their roots.

Your Taurus Decision-Maker!

Astrology can help you with all kinds of daily decisions, from what kind of clothes to wear to what color to paint your room. Here are some of the ways you can use the stars to find the style that suits you best.

How Should I Furnish My Home?

Go back to nature for your ideal environment. You're the earth mother (or father) who makes everyone feel instantly at home. Flower prints (or gutsy earth tones), windows full of plants (even indoor trees), and plenty of light are Taurus musts. Your furniture should be roomy and comfortable, upholstered in a natural, touchable fabric. You are a collector who is sure to accumulate possessions and display them beautifully. Collections of pottery or delicate porcelain, artworks, sculpture, records, jewelry, and antiques vie for attention in your environment. Taurus usually likes the luxurious, comfortable look of English or French country houses. Since you love good food and you entertain at home, you'll want a beautiful, well-equipped kitchen. Your animal companions should be well provided for, with spaces to roam and places to roost.

What Music Puts Me In A Good Mood?

Rich, sensual sounds of all kinds appeal to you, one of the most musical and creative signs. You are sensitive to the slightest distortion in tone, so invest in an excellent sound system. Since Taurus rules the voice, you may collect the great vocalists like Streisand, Cher, Willie Nelson, and Ella Fitzgerald. Or rock to Janet Jackson, Stevie Wonder, and David Byrne. Taurus songwriters like Burt Bacharach, Oscar Hammerstein, and Irving Berlin created sensuous sounds that glorify the human voice.

Where Should I Go On Vacation?

When traveling, comfort comes first for Taurus. Female Tauruses adore shopping and bargain hunting, so be sure there's enough time to shop, as well as to explore art museums. If you are booking a tour, let it be one that also explores the fine cuisine and antiques marketplaces of each region. You might also enjoy a vacation apprenticeship with a famous French or Italian chef.

Minimize the discomforts of travel by packing a tiny inflatable pillow. Since food on the run is never your style, get a small insulated bag to carry your own favorite gourmet comfort foods, rather than relying on airline fare. A portable stereo with your favorite sounds relaxes you on the trip and blots out unwelcome noise. Bring along a scented candle for instant ambience in your hotel room, as well as a few photos of loved ones to remind you of home.

Cancer and Pisces are wonderful traveling companions to share sunsets and moonlit walks along the shore. Scorpio and Capricorn will help you combine business with pleasure (and help you find a way to write off that trip as a tax deduction). Libra and Leo share your love of beauty and luxury (but will also want to travel first class all the way).

What Colors Look Best On Me?

Your colors are the soft floral tones of 18th-century painters or the woody, natural earth tones. Too many dark colors may depress you, and vibrant brights may disturb your tranquillity. You'd prefer the lush romance of an English garden or the mossy neutrals of a woodland glade.

What Kind Of Clothes Should I Wear?

Once Taurus finds your "look," you stick with it, whether it's as elegant and classic as Fred Astaire, Audrey Hepburn, and Candice Bergen or as far-out as Cher. Your aim is to be distinctively and consistently "you." You'll create your own styles, rather than latch onto a trend for the sake of being in. Play up your femininity with perfume (all three of the above ladies have their own signature scent) and with beautiful, luxurious fabrics. Taurus women have an especially lovely neck and throat. Play it up with necklaces (you probably have a lovely jewelry collection) and off-the-shoulder styles.

What Fashion Designers Suit My Sign?

The late, great designer Halston epitomized Taurus style, with luxurious fabrics and simple, sensuous lines. Carolyne Roehm makes elegant, feminine gowns that are the height of luxury. Christian La Croix is inspired by the costumes of the French countryside to create whimsical yet very luxurious clothes. Jean-Paul Gaultier shows the sexy side of

Taurus in his avant-garde clothes for rock stars like Madonna.

What Should I Have For Dinner?

Never a picky eater, you can consume food in megaportions. Often you'll obsess about one type of food—one flavor of ice cream, for instance—and secretly gorge on it. If problems send you running to the refrigerator, find a weight-watching group to give you support and encouragement, as well as a sensible diet program. You derive so much pleasure from delicious food that you could easily feel deprived on a strict diet. Then you'll overcompensate by binging and undoing your diet. A program that helps you form a long range health-promoting relationship with food is a better alternative. On the positive side, you especially appreciate food that is fresh, ripe, and beautifully presented. Find an organic or farmer's market and get your vegetables there—you'll notice the difference—and learn to love fresh fruits and vegetables more than hearty meat and potatoes. A natural foods or macrobiotic cooking course could show you how to incorporate healthier eating habits into your life.

CHAPTER 15

Getting Together—How Taurus Pairs Up with Other Signs

Here is a lineup of your sun sign's compatibility quotient with each other sign. Remember that most successful relationships have a balance of harmonious points and challenges, which stimulate you to grow and keep you from getting bored with each other. So if the forecast for you and your beloved (or business associate) seems like an uphill struggle, take heart! Such legendary lovers as Juan and Eva Peron, President and Mrs. Ronald Reagan, Kurt Weill and Lotte Lenya, Harry and Bess Truman, Julius Caesar and Cleopatra, the Duke and Duchess of Windsor, Ruth and Billy Graham, George and Martha Washington, are among the many born under supposedly incompatible sun signs.

Taurus–Aries

Smooth Sailing. Here is someone who really needs your organization and follow-through, not to mention your patience and stamina. On the other hand, you need Aries to get you up and moving and to provide you with great new ideas. You two can move mountains together.

Rough Waters. This sign often jumps in without testing the water. You're the cautious type who goes for long-term goals. And when they get pushy, you won't budge. They want freedom; you want a cozy, secure lifestyle. Get ready for lots of compromises.

Taurus–Taurus

Smooth Sailing. You are so comfortable together that it's tempting never to move. Here is someone who loves acquiring beautiful things as much as you do. And they'll be just as faithful, passionate, and sentimental as you are. Sound perfect?

Rough Waters. They are also just as stubborn as you are. Neither of you tends to forgive and forget. And too much of the same thing could get boring. If you get bogged down together, you might look for stimulation elsewhere, just to get out of your rut.

Taurus–Gemini

Smooth Sailing. Here is the sparkle you need to inspire you to get out and about. Gemini's quick mind and charm are a turn-on for you. You share many laughs together, and you'll bring stability to their life.

Rough Waters. Gemini is not a sign to stay home by the fire for long. They love being busy, doing two things at once, having friends over. You may long for peace and tranquility. Gemini flirts; you're the faithful, possessive type.

Taurus–Cancer

Smooth Sailing. You do great things for each other. Cancer gives you tenderness and a lovely home. You give this moody sign comfort and support. You're a dynamite team in business and in pleasure.

Rough Waters. Cancer operates from an emotional, intuitive level. You like to make solid, sensible plans. You both tend to brood and withdraw. Watch out for a Mexican standoff.

Taurus–Leo

Smooth Sailing. Here is someone who thinks big and loves beautiful things, like you do. And who better to show them off? You love Leo's glamour and style and know how to make them purr with pleasure.

Rough Waters. You keep an eye on the budget at all times—accumulation is the idea. Leo believes that living well is a divine right, even if the bills aren't paid yet. Taurus is very possessive; the lion won't be caged. Since both of you hate to give in, something's got to give here.

Taurus–Virgo

Smooth Sailing. Virgo relaxes under your calm, steady hand. You bring out their sensual side, while they take care of all those details you hate and make sure you stay healthy, wealthy, and wise.

Rough Waters. Virgo's worrying, nagging, and constant criticism disrupt your tranquility. Little things seem to irritate them in a big way. Their pickiness might try your patience; then it'll be hard to keep the peace. If this situation is allowed to escalate, you could have a very uncomfortable relationship.

Taurus–Libra

Smooth Sailing. This seems to be your perfect match—at first. You could be dazzled by Libra's beauty, charm, and finesse, and by their talent for creating a lovely environment. You'll be happy to take over the burdensome decision-making and financial matters. Both of you will delight in aquiring the finer things in life together.

Rough Waters. Libra is a social being, while Taurus is a homebody. Taurus is possessive; Libra is flirtatious. Taurus likes to save; Libra likes to spend. And just when Taurus thinks a decision has been made, Libra changes its mind.

Taurus–Scorpio

Smooth Sailing. From opposite sides of the zodiac, you seem to be the perfect complements. You love those intense Scorpio passions. They can give you the total commit-

169

ment and nonstop sensuality you so desire. And Scorpio will find a tranquil oasis in your calm, steady, soothing personality.

Rough Waters. Control and power can be devisive issues here. Both of you are stubborn and like to hold the reins. And neither likes to give in. To stay in control, either may resort to manipulative tricks. Better stake out your territory early in the relationship.

Taurus–Sagittarius

Smooth Sailing. You admire their honesty and directness, and enjoy their love of the outdoors and their terrific sense of humor. And they really need the organization and solid base of operations your provide.

Rough Waters. Sagittarius is a wanderer who can't be tied down. They often have a roving eye, too. You won't have many cozy nights at home with this one. Better curb your jealousy and possessiveness.

Taurus–Capricorn

Smooth Sailing. This is an extremely comfortable situation where both of you share similar tastes and goals. You're hard workers who love beauty, quality, and tradition. You're both responsible and mature, so what you see is what you get.

Rough Waters. Climbing to the top in the business and social world is Capricorn's priority. You'd better fit into their plans, or forget it. Hopefully, you can deal with their ambitions and late nights at the office or the club.

Taurus–Aquarius

Smooth Sailing. You two could go far with your practical know-how and their originality. You give them solid grounding and they give you inspiration. You'll do things you'd never dreamed of trying before, and what's more, you'll enjoy yourself. Aquarius jolts you out of a rut and encourages you to expand your mind and think beyond your comfortable little world.

Rough Waters. You like the predictable; Aquarians love surprises. They are not security minded and will give their all—and yours—to a worthy cause. You like a close, intimate relationship, which Aquarius could find confining. Bear all this in mind.

Taurus–Pisces

Smooth Sailing. You respond happily to their deep emotional needs. In turn, they give you all the adoration and attention you want. You both love taking care of each other. And you help them market those creative ideas and bring in profits.

Rough Waters. You may think you have control of the situation, but it is only an illusion. The fish is very difficult to hook. You'll be continually frustrated if you try to tie this one down. Better get used to constant fluctuations—or swim away.

CHAPTER 16

Your Taurus Career Potential

Where to Find Your Best Career Opportunities.

Taurus needs a career that is built on a solid structure. Long-term gains are your major interest, so you'll usually take one direction and stick with it. The downside is that you may vegetate in a job that has no challenge because you value the steady income. Taurus does not like change, especially sudden changes. So look for an initial job that offers strong growth potential as well as security. A company that promotes from within would be ideal. Since Taurus is the sign of buying, appraising, and accumulating, you thrive in careers such as retailing, trading of any sort, auctions, dealing in art or collectibles, banking, or real estate. Your love of nature could lead you into farming, landscape gardening, horticulture, or animal breeding. Taurus is a nautral builder, so consider architecture, construction, or engineering. Your sensual side could gravitate to food, fashion, or jewelry design, or to perfume or the music industry.

Taurus in Charge

You are the boss with total control, which can make you a steady, wise leader, a benevolent dictator, or a tyrant. You will have the last word on each aspect of your business, making decisions that are well considered and permanent; you rarely change your mind. You are very nurturing and possessive of underlings, but you may hesitate to give them the independence they need to grow by trial and error. You tend to promote from within, working with people you have known for some time. Your attitude is to build a solid structure for your organization, and you'll value that structure rather than flashy ideas or flash-in-the-pan products. Try to be more flexible and open to new ideas. Though you can be demanding, you are usually even tempered and patient, and you value loyalty.

Taurus Teamwork

The Taurus worker is slow but steady and thorough. You are the one who comes through in a pinch; you are oriented toward seeing results, rather than speculating. You'll stay with an assignment until it is completed. You like to stay in a position once you are comfortable. Therefore, you may not be the most ambitious employee. But you are much less likely to job hop, preferring to stay in the same spot for years and steadily rise through the ranks.

You prefer surroundings that are physically comfortable. And you like to handle money so that you can see it grow. You have an innate sense of value, of being able to determine the true worth of something, as well as the best price it can get on the market.

To Get Ahead Fast

Pick a company with potential that promotes from within.
  Play up your best attributes:
- Loyalty
- Thoroughness
- Financial savvy
- Patience and perseverance
- Reliability
- Steadiness

Famous Taurus Millionaires

Study these Taurus millionaires for ideas on how you can best use your sign's talents.

William Randoph Hearst
Dr. Spock
Cornelius Vanderbilt
Aaron Spelling (television producer)
David O. Selznick
George Lucas
Ross Hunter

CHAPTER 17

Taurus Astro-Outlook for 1995

Throughout this year your position will be both unique and powerful. You'll not only recognize the problems but also find the solutions. During 1995, you'll have much to do with Capricorn and Cancer who are likely to have names with these letters: H, Q, Z.

One of your gifts this year will be organization, your ability to bring order out of chaos. In 1994, on more than one occasion, you felt the empty feeling of being abandoned and lost. This year, a healing process gets under way—in 1995 you are not only capable of lifting yourself above a sea of mediocrity, you also help others, inspire them, and get them going on their own. Once again, you display strength from your inner being to the outside or material world.

If you're single, marriage is strongly indicated this year. If you are married, there could be an addition to your family. Married or single, you're likely to be in business for yourself. You'll take risks or you'll be an entrepreneur.

During the first month of this year, you reach beyond your previous limitations and you could be an active participant in import–export activities. A burden is lifted; you'll be free of an emotional weight you should not have carried in the first place. January will feature travel, publishing, advertising, communicating, and gaining universal appeal. If you are not in love during January, it just will have to do until something better comes along.

You'll make a fresh start in a new direction during February. Almost as if by magic, events transpire to bring you closer to your desired goal. You'll have luck during February in matters of speculation by sticking with the number 1. Leo and Aquarius figure prominently in your February scenario.

During March, you might be convinced that angels really do exist. Your intuitive intellect is prominent; you'll win an amazing victory by following a hunch and heeding your inner feelings. Most memorable days: 6th, 15th, 24th.

April: What at first appears to be a loss will boomerang in your favor. You'll have reason to celebrate; you'll participate in a secret arrangement. You'll feel you are pulling strings in connection not only with your own life, but also in the events affecting the lives of others. Memorable days: 5th, 14th, 23rd.

May: It is extremely important that you study your day-by-day forecast in the following pages throughout the year. As your cycle moves up this month, you'll replace outworn methods and machinery with the new and improved. Your judgment and intuition will be on target. Memorable days: 4th, 13th, 22nd, 31st.

June: You might be musing, "I wish every month could be this way!" The spotlight is on change, travel, variety, and romance. You have a legitimate opportunity to hit the financial jackpot. These days prove powerful: 3rd, 12th, 21st, 30th.

July: Another Taurus figures prominently, along with Libra and Scorpio. A major domestic adjustment is featured, which could include a change of residence or marital status. Special days: 2nd, 11th, 20th, 29th.

August: You'll be gifted with second sight, which means you'll be psychic. The fact that you possess extrasensory perception will be obvious and wondrous. Decisions will be reached in connection with the sale or purchase of your home or property. Your marital status also plays a significant role.

September: This will be the most memorable, productive month of 1995. The emphasis is on style, creativity, a variety of sensations, physical attraction, sensuality, and sex appeal. If you're married, you could be anticipating an addition to your family. Check carefully your daily predictions for this month. Read the indications for the 9th, 18th, and 27th.

October: Attention revolves around employment, pet ownership, fitness, and basic issues. You have a special ability to fix things, including mechanical devices. Give more than usual attention to your car, including payments, and repairs. A long-distance communication relates to travel and your ability to recognize true love.

November: You'll make a new start. You'll be dealing with Leo and Aquarius likely to have names with these letters or initials: A, S, J. In matters of speculation, stick with the number 1. These days will be most memorable: 7th, 16th, 25th.

December: Via these forecasts, you have traversed the entire year knowing your daily and monthly diary in advance. During December, you extricate yourself from a family dispute relating to who owns what, who did most, who should get the money. Refuse to be cajoled into playing the role of referee. You'll learn more about a possible inheritance. The financial status of someone close to you will be clearly revealed. Special days: 6th, 15th, 24th.

Happy New Year!

CHAPTER 18

Eighteen Months of Day-by-Day Predictions—July 1994 to December 1995

JULY 1994

Friday, July 1 (Moon in Aries)   A relative wants to tell you something but doesn't know just how to express it. Emphasize diplomacy and be sympathetic without compromising your principles. It turns out that what is revealed is something you already knew. Libra, Scorpio, and another Taurus are featured.

Saturday, July 2 (Moon in Aries to Taurus 10:23 a.m.) Don't equate delay with defeat—a telephone call reveals that a deal is successful and money will be on the way. Protect your possessions, refusing to give up something of value for nothing. Get your emotional second wind. Pisces and Virgo are represented. Your lucky number is 7.

Sunday, July 3 (Moon in Taurus)   Focus on organization, timing, showmanship, personality, and shades of your special colors—blue, indigo, and purple. You'll be at the right place at a crucial moment. By tonight, circumstances will take a sudden turn in your favor. You'll be on a winning team. A Cancer plays an important role.

Monday, July 4 (Moon in Taurus to Gemini 11:12 p.m.) A major project can be completed—however, don't stay too long at the fair. Your popularity increases. A communication from overseas relates to a possible future journey. Focus on universal appeal, romance, and your search for your soulmate. A holiday celebration synchronizes with a love relationship.

Tuesday, July 5 (Moon in Gemini) The answer to a question: Affirmative. A new start is necessary, so let go of the past. A relationship could be running its course. Imprint your own style, emphasizing independence of thought and action. A special note: Avoid heavy lifting. Leo and Aquarius figure in today's dynamic scenario.

Wednesday, July 6 (Moon in Gemini) Lucky lottery: 2, 3, 5, 13, 50, 1. At the track: post position special—number 5 P.P. in the seventh race. Pick six: 8, 5, 3, 2, 8, 7. Check these letters or initials in the names of horses or jockeys: B, K, T. A Cancer advocates a business partnership. It pays to play the waiting game.

Thursday, July 7 (Moon in Gemini to Cancer 10:17 a.m.) Today you'll be celebrating a reunion or a unique social affair. You may receive an addition to your wardrobe. The financial picture continues brighter than expected less than three weeks ago. You'll locate a lost, missing, or stolen article. Sagittarius is involved.

Friday, July 8 (Moon in Cancer) The new moon occupies the area of your solar horoscope relating to trips, visits, relatives, and ideas that can be developed into viable concepts. You'll encounter Taurus, Leo, and Scorpio persons with these initials or letters in their names: D, M, V. Your lucky number is 4.

Saturday, July 9 (Moon in Cancer to Leo 6:43 p.m.) Lucky lottery: 5, 20, 4, 12, 22, 23. People will say, "You do have a way with words!" The emphasis falls on investigation, exploration, flirtation, and a clash of ideas with someone of the opposite sex who is drawn to you. Gemini, Virgo, and Sagittarius play meaningful roles. You gain via the written word.

Sunday, July 10 (Moon in Leo) Attention revolves around your home and children, and focuses on challenge, variety, and the excitement of a discovery. A domestic adjustment relates to your residence, marital status, or income potential. You might be seriously considering the purchase of an art object or a luxury item. Leo, Scorpio, or another Taurus have much to say.

Monday, July 11 (Moon in Leo)   Separate fact from illusion—you now have the chance to define terms, streamline procedures, and get rid of excess clutter. Get down to fighting trim! Focus on land, real estate, and mineral rights. A confidential meeting relates to a profitable arrangement. Virgo is involved.

Tuesday, July 12 (Moon in Leo to Virgo 12:48 a.m.)   The emphasis continues on investment, including your time, money, and organization. You'll meet a challenge, a deadline exists, and you'll get the funding to get the ball rolling. An older male Capricorn lends the benefit of experience and gives moral support. Your lucky number is 8.

Wednesday, July 13 (Moon in Virgo)   Lucky lottery: 13, 9, 6, 5, 22, 33. At the track: post position special—number 8 P.P. in the first race. Pick six: 8, 1, 5, 3, 3, 4. In choosing winning horses and jockeys, look for these letters or initials: I and R. A long-standing obligation is fulfilled, and you gain added recognition as result.

Thursday, July 14 (Moon in Virgo to Libra 5:15 a.m.)   You'll decide, "It is time for fresh start in a different direction." If a love relationship is providing more pain than joy, drop it like a hot potato! Emphasize independence and self-reliance, and have the courage of your convictions. Leo and Aquarius persons play outstanding roles. Your lucky number is 1.

Friday, July 15 (Moon in Libra)   The lunar position highlights employment, health, pets, fitness, and self-esteem. The emphasis also falls on partnership, publicity, reliability, credibility, and marital status. You'll obtain inside information that enables you to participate in a profitable enterprise. Capricorn is in the picture.

Saturday, July 16 (Moon in Libra to Scorpio 8:35 a.m.) Your forces tend to be scattered—focus on the big overall picture. Leave details for another day. Stress curiosity, experimentation, and color coordination. An agreement relates to a social affair. You'll add to your wardrobe, you'll be more pleased with your image. Lucky lottery: 3, 16, 7, 6, 45, 53.

Sunday, July 17 (Moon in Scorpio) Focus on legalities, legal rights and permissions, cooperative efforts, public image, and your marital status. Check the fine print, read between the lines. What was wisely put off yesterday will surface now and you'll handle questions and problems with aplomb. Leo, Scorpio, and another Taurus figure in today's activities.

Monday, July 18 (Moon in Scorpio to Sagittarius 11:09 a.m.) You'll feel free to travel, create, write, make necessary changes, and renovate your personal affairs. This is just the kind of day you've been anticipating with glee. Get your thoughts on paper. Express your feelings creatively. Gemini, Virgo, and Sagittarius are encouraging.

Tuesday, July 19 (Moon in Sagittarius) Attention revolves around expenditures relating to music, art, and luxury. You'll beautify your surroundings. A domestic adjustment takes place and you'll be happier at home. The key is diplomacy—if you attempt to force issues, you'll fail. The choice is simple, so act accordingly.

Wednesday, July 20)Moon in Sagittarius to Capricorn 1:30 p.m.) What appeared to be lost will boomerang in your favor. In your high cycle, you'll know where to look and you'll be at the right place. A relationship that recently went off track will be restored. Define your terms, outline your boundaries, and get rid of excess baggage. Pisces plays a significant role.

Thursday, July 21 (Moon in Capricorn) It's an excellent day for reaching for what had been out of reach. This means dreams can become realities, as your talents are used for the greatest benefit. Specifically, outline your boundaries and elucidate your goals. A powerful ally appears almost as if by magic. Capricorn and Cancer play major roles.

Friday, July 22 (Moon in Capricorn to Aquarius 4:38 p.m.) The full moon accents communication, giving you the ability to get your message across in a meaningful, dynamic way. Focus also on idealism and a journey of the mind. You'll be free of an obligation actually belonging to someone else. The lunar emphasis is also on the higher mind, education, and spiritually.

Saturday, July 23 (Moon in Aquarius) Lucky lottery: 1, 11, 12, 7, 2, 5. At the track: post position special—number 7 P.P. in the third race. Pick six: 5, 1, 7, 6, 8, 4. In choosing winning horses or jockeys, consider these initials or letters in names: A, S, J. Leo and Aquarius persons share your activities.

Sunday, July 24 (Moon in Aquarius to Pisces 9:56 p.m.) Focus on a partnership and your emotional responses. Evaluate your goals to determine which are real and which are merely speculative. This meaning becomes crystal clear during the early evening hours. A reunion with a relative is featured, along with gourmet dining. A Cancer figures prominently.

Monday, July 25 (Moon in Pisces) What appears frivolous to others could be meaningful to you. Know it and respond accordingly. The lunar position accents career, business, your standing in the community, and your participation in a charitable or political drive. Your leadership role requires you to set the policy. Gemini is involved.

Tuesday, July 26 (Moon in Pisces) You'll meet those who help you get rid of red tape and obtain proper forms and credentials. Taurus, Leo, and Scorpio are helpful. Many could have these initials or letters in their names: D, M, V. Tonight you'll know that many of your aspirations are going to be fulfilled.

Wednesday, July 27 (Moon in Pisces to Aries 6:31 a.m.) Lucky lottery: 12, 7, 5, 24, 33, 18. The emphasis is on the written word—you'll be notified that the changes you requested will be fulfilled. The spotlight falls on character analysis, discovery, variety, exploration, and a clash of ideas. A chance meeting and a flirtation could result in a serious relationship.

Thursday, July 28 (Moon in Aries)   Information previously withheld comes to light. The key is to be diplomatic, to realize how much a special relationship is worth, and to consider the financial aspects of a proposal. The moon position highlights hospitals, institutions, and museums. A special tour could be arranged for you. Libra is in the picture.

Friday, July 29 (Moon in Aries to Taurus 6:13 p.m.)   Today's scenario features mystery, intrigue, and glamour, but the need for discretion becomes obvious. By telling all, you merely will be sharing guilt. Know it, and don't make others unhappy merely to let yourself feel honest. Get your second wind by dealing with a Pisces who does care for you.

Saturday, July 30 (Moon in Taurus)   In matters of speculation, stick with the number 8. You'll be dealing with older individuals willing to lend the benefit of experience, perhaps to help you obtain funding. With the moon in your sign, you'll be at the right place as events transpire to help you reach your goal and circumstances take a sudden, dramatic turn in your favor.

Sunday, July 31 (Moon in Taurus)   Memories blend with future prospects—focus on idealism, travel consideration, and spirituality. The emphasis is also on personality, inventiveness, originality, and the ability to get to the heart of matters. Someone of the opposite sex can't seem to stay away.

AUGUST 1994

Monday, August 1 (Moon in Taurus to Gemini 7:05 a.m.)   You wake up with the answers, as your psychic impressions prove accurate. Some persons will actually say,

"You seem to know what I am thinking and what I am going to say before I say it!" Regard this as a gift—your intuitive powers are being "awakened." Your lucky number is 7.

Tuesday, August 2 (Moon in Gemini)   The key is organization—you get things arranged in their proper order. Your financial cycle is high, making this a good time to study legitimate investment opportunities. An article recently lost, missing, or stolen could be voluntarily returned. A love relationship continues to be controversial but is also fulfilling.

Wednesday, August 3 (Moon in Gemini to Cancer 6:22 p.m.)   You appear you have the secret of universal appeal. You'll finish what you start and the memory of the past surges to the forefront, enabling you to tell what the immediate future holds in store. You'll meet some aggressive individuals likely to be Aries and Libra and to have these initials or letters in their names: I and R.

Thursday, August 4 (Moon in Cancer)   What had been source of fear, doubt, and suspicion will be eradicated. The emphasis is on independence, creativity, freedom, style, and courage. A love relationship survives a series of accusations including mostly canards. Be direct, get to the heart of matters.

Friday, August 5 (Moon in Cancer)   Attention revolves around your home, family, food, survival, and income. You'll be saying, "At last I know where I am going and my sense of direction has returned!" The moon position highlights excursions, investigations, intellectual curiosity, and a meaningful dialogue with a relative.

Saturday, August 6 (Moon in Cancer to Leo 2:31 p.m.)   You'll be active and some will comment, "You inspire confidence!" Persons who play significant roles are likely to be Gemini or Sagittarius with these initials or letters in their names: C, L, U. You recently asked for additional space—this request will be granted. Your lucky number is 3.

Sunday, August 7 (Moon in Leo)   The new moon position represents verification of views, guaranteeing that goods and household products are durable. Being with your loved ones elevates the spiritual qualities of today's scenario. Check references, being aware of past performances. Love plays a major role—you'll be passionate, creative, dynamic, and vigorous.

Monday, August 8 (Moon in Leo to Virgo 7:42 a.m.)   Be ready for change, variety, discovery, and a flirtation that lends spice to your life. The moon in your fourth sector coincides with the finish of negotiations over the sale or purchase of a car. A relative talks seriously about their marital status or home.

Tuesday, August 9 (Moon in Virgo)   Today's emphasis falls on home, employment, fitness, and pets. Persons most likely relatives who rely upon your care and generosity demand your attention. There's music in your life tonight, and you'll be complimented on your taste in literature and the lively arts. Your lucky number is 6.

Wednesday, August 10 (Moon in Virgo to Libra 11:07 a.m.)   An aura of creativity is featured—you'll exude a quiet, discreet kind of sensuality. Someone close to you might wish to fathom what is really inside of you. A secret meeting tonight helps you perceive where you stand and why and your future role.

Thursday, August 11 (Moon in Libra)   At the track: post position special—number 9 P.P. in the eighth race. Pick six: 3, 6, 7, 8, 9, 5. In choosing winning horses or jockeys, watch for these initials or letters in names: H, Q, Z. You'll be called upon to organize, to meet a deadline, and to make a decision about a special relationship.

Friday, August 12 (Moon in Libra to Scorpio 1:56 a.m.)
Those who claimed you could not live up to their standards will be dining on crow tonight—exult in it! You'll complete a mission. Your message gets across in a dramatic, dynamic, informative way. Focus on universal appeal, distance and

185

language, and a positive love relationship. Your lucky number is 9.

Saturday, August 13 (Moon in Scorpio)   Today's scenario features new experiences, and the restoration of your vitality and enthusiasm. Focus on credibility, cooperative effort, public image, and the discerning of legal rights and permissions. Married or single, you'll be in love, you'll be anticipating adventure, and you'll be grateful that you once again feel alive.

Sunday, August 14 (Moon in Scorpio to Sagittarius 4:53 p.m.)   The emphasis is on family relationships. You may be seriously considering buying or selling your home or property or a large household product. The moon position illuminates public appearances, participation in a commercial enterprise, and the state of your marriage. Your lucky number is 2.

Monday, August 15 (Moon in Sagittarius)   Those you helped in the recent past will now acknowledge your contributions. You'll remember this as your lucky Monday. Focus on expansion, communication, popularity, and participation in a charitable or political campaign. Gemini and Sagittarius are on your wavelength.

Tuesday, August 16 (Moon in Sagittarius to Capricorn 8:18 p.m.)   The emphasis is on accounting, inventory, and knowledge relating to tax and license requirements. What appeared to be cut and dried could suddenly burst. Be open to the unorthodox, expect the unexpected. Review, revise, remodel, and rebuild. Scorpio is involved.

Wednesday, August 17 (Moon in Capricorn)   Investigate, analyze, delineate, and have a discussion with someone of the opposite sex who is genuinely concerned about your welfare. Today's scenario features the excitement of discovery, a variety of interests, and a trip involving a relative. A chance meeting or flirtation could become more serious than you originally thought.

Thursday, August 18 (Moon in Capricorn)   A domestic adjustment is featured. Long-distance communication relates to the lively arts. Those who exert influence on you today are likely to be born under Taurus, Libra, or Scorpio and could have these initials or letters in their names: F, O, X. Your lucky number is 6.

Friday, August 19 (Moon in Capricorn to Aquarius 12:34 a.m.)   Be sure meanings are clear—find out exactly what is expected from you and what you can anticipate as a result of your contributions. See places, situations, and people in a realistic light. Pisces and Virgo figure prominently and could have these letters, initials in their names: G, P, Y.

Saturday, August 20 (Moon in Aquarius)   Lucky lottery: 8, 22, 11, 2, 1, 5. You'll be called upon to organize a charity or a political campaign. You'll be designated an official fund raiser. On a personal level, a romantic relationship can get hot and heavy. Capricorn and Cancer play dominant roles. Stand tall!

Sunday, August 21 (Moon in Aquarius to Pisces 6:28 a.m.)   The full moon emphasizes pride, promotion, leadership, and spirituality. Rules bend in your favor, so reach beyond previous expectations. Today features universal appeal, love, and the ability to bridge distance and language barriers. Your mission will be completed by 9 p.m. Lucky triple play: 3, 6. 9.

Monday, August 22 (Moon in Pisces)   On this Monday you might be saying, "This is not only a new day but I feel as if I'm a new person!" Lunar and numerical cycles accent independence, a fresh start, and the ability to win friends and influence people. The emphasis is on style, creativity, originality, and the expression of your true feelings.

Tuesday, August 23 (Moon in Pisces to Aries 2:55 p.m.)   You recently asked, "Is there someone for me?" Married or single, you'll feel that love is what makes life worthwhile. Today's scenario features a reunion, your home, security, and marital status. Capricorn and Cancer play significant roles. Your lucky number is 2.

Wednesday, August 24 (Moon in Aries)   Lucky lottery: 3, 1, 9, 12, 18, 33. The spotlight is on social activities, popularity, and the ability to keep plans flexible. As your routine changes, you'll entertain and be entertained. The lunar position accents your eagerness to see the light. Gemini and Sagittarius figure in today's agenda.

Thursday, August 25 (Moon in Aries)   Your attention revolves around philosophical concepts, methods of achieving a goal and the need to be discreet. You'll be provided with information previously kept from you. You'll know where you stand and knowing that truth will make you strong. Leo, Scorpio, and another Taurus represented.

Friday, August 26 (Moon in Aries to Taurus 2:13 a.m.)   Events occur that coincide with movement, change, variety, and greater freedom of thought and action. Friends who are creative and who have writing talents will play roles in your life. Gemini, Virgo, and Sagittarius help fill the emotional vacuum. Your lucky number is 5.

Saturday, August 27 (Moon in Taurus)   Lucky lottery: 6, 20, 2, 14, 19, 17. Today features a domestic adjustment. You excel at color coordination, with greater awareness of fashion trends and real estate cycles. You may decide to buy or sell an art object or a luxury item. Libra and another Taurus play featured roles.

Sunday, August 28 (Moon in Taurus to Gemini 3:08 p.m.)   Spiritual values surface, as your lunar cycle moves up. You'll notice a dynamic shift of emphasis now. If you look behind the scenes or meditate, you will wake up with answers. Define your terms, and be sure to get rid of unnecessary expenses. Pisces and Virgo play outstanding roles. Your lucky number is 7.

Monday, August 29 (Moon in Gemini)   Focus on organization and the ability to meet a deadline and to locate an article that had been lost, missing, or stolen. An appraisal of your personal possessions reveals you are more affluent than you thought. A romantic relationship is intense, but possibly controversial. Cancer is involved.

Tuesday, August 30 (Moon in Gemini)   You gain proper perspective as you realize your influence extends beyond previous limitations. Focus on enthusiasm, zeal, and the determination to be rid of a burden not your own. The lunar position highlights your income potential and your ability to wipe out debts. Aries and Libra will play featured roles.

Wednesday, August 31 (Moon in Gemini to Cancer 3 a.m.)   On this last day of August, you could hit the financial jackpot by sticking with these numbers: 1, 9, and 5. You have every right to be enthusiastic and to welcome an opportunity for self-expression, independence, and romance. Leo and Aquarius could become your valuable allies.

SEPTEMBER 1994

Thursday, September 1 (Moon in Cancer)   Throughout September, you uncover secrets, clarify your goals, and come to terms with yourself. On this Thursday, the first day of the month, you prove capable of meeting deadlines and challenges, and of organizing an important project. An older relative concedes that you have a right to lead your own life.

Friday, September 2 (Moon in Cancer to Leo 11:37 a.m.)   You start this weekend with bright ideas, humor, and acclaim by peers. Focus on communication, a love relationship, or the search for your soulmate. Finish what you start, placing past memories and loves in a quieter area. Aries and Libra figure prominently. Your lucky number is 9.

Saturday, September 3 (Moon in Leo)   Lucky lottery: 1, 10, 9, 5, 50, 8. Focus on large household products and the completion of negotiations involving property, home, or durable goods. A guarantee, once denied, will be honored. Emphasis revolves around showing your independence, making a fresh start, and pioneering a project. A love relationship intensifies.

Sunday, September 4 (Moon in Leo to Virgo 3:33 p.m.) On this Sunday you'll feel, "I finally have it together because we are together!" Today's scenario features direction, motivation, reunion, and gourmet dining. Focus upon popularity and the ability to detect subtle trends. Capricorn and Cancer play meaningful roles. Your lucky number is 2.

Monday, September 5 (Moon in Virgo) No Monday blues for you! The new moon falls in an area of your solar horoscope relating to love, romance, creativity, and a wide variety of experiences. A relative imparts information that sends your morale soaring. You'll feel vital, dynamic, and confident. Virgo, Gemini, and Sagittarius figure in this scenario.

Tuesday, September 6 (Moon in Virgo to Libra 6:57 p.m.) You're provided with the key. This applies both literally and symbolically. You become aware of the modus operandi, methods, and durability of goods. Test recipes, sharpen tools, reject superficial answers. Be willing to revise, review, remodel, and to tear down for purpose of rebuilding on a more suitable base.

Wednesday, September 7 (Moon in Libra) Your wit, wisdom, and humor figure prominently. The job gets done with apparent ease. Take notes and articulate your feelings. If you're married, you rediscover your mate. If you're single, you are closer to matrimony than you originally anticipated. Today's scenario highlights children, change, travel, exploration, and discovery.

Thursday, September 8 (Moon in Libra to Scorpio 8:25 p.m.) The emphasis falls on domesticity and serious consideration relating to your residence, location, or marital status. There will be music in your life, which may indicate buying CDs or a musical instrument. Libra, Scorpio, and another Taurus play significant roles. These letters, initials could appear in names: F, O, X.

Friday, September 9 (Moon in Scorpio) You're due to break free from a situation or person who holds you back, who takes plenty while giving little or nothing in return. Separate fact from fiction. See people, places, and situations as they are and not merely as you wish they might be.

Saturday, September 10 (Moon in Scorpio to Sagittarius 10:25 a.m.)   Those who scoffed will be forced to admit you were right all along and you've proved you can handle the project. Focus on a love relationship, organization, and successful dealings with older persons, especially men. Cancer, Capricorn, and another Taurus figure prominently.

Sunday, September 11 (Moon in Sagittarius)   You'll admit to yourself, "This Sunday will mark either the beginning or the end of a relationship." Focus on legal rights, cooperative efforts, and your public image and marital status. Reach beyond previous expectations. A clash of ideas will be stimulating. Aries figures prominently.

Monday, September 12 (Moon in Sagittarius)   You'll feel invigorated, ready to tell the world you'll no longer play second fiddle. You're in charge now. The lunar position highlights examination of arcane literature and additional knowledge concerning tax and license requirements and accounting procedures. Your lucky number is 1.

Tuesday, September 13 (Moon in Sagittarius to Capricorn 1:44 a.m.)   You'll get the cooperation of someone familiar with percentages, loans, and guarantees. Your attention revolves around money being withheld, possibly in escrow. On a personal level, your attention revolves around home, property, and marital status. A Cancer plays a paramount role.

Wednesday, September 14 (Moon in Capricorn)   The lunar aspect coincides with travel, philosophy, education, and communication. Attention also revolves around diversity, different modes of transportation, experimentation, an addition to your wardrobe, and sensitivity relating to your body image. Lucky lottery: 3, 8, 10, 20, 25, 51.

Thursday, September 15 (Moon in Capricorn to Aquarius 6:42 a.m.)   At the track: post position special—number

4 P.P. in the fourth race. Pick six: 8, 5, 1, 4, 7, 7. In choosing winners, check these initials or letters in the names of jockeys or horses: D, M, V. Inhibitions concerning a relationship with someone who served as counselor will be put aside.

Friday, September 16 (Moon in Aquarius)   This weekend gets off to rousing start. Emphasis on the top part of your solar horoscope means that you gain prestige as you take charge of your own destiny. A Mercury aspect indicates a confrontation with someone who challenges and stimulates you, encouraging a clash of ideas. A Sagittarian is involved.

Saturday, September 17 (Moon in Aquarius to Pisces 1:31 p.m.)   The focus is on domestic adjustment, promotion, and the elevation of your standing in the church and community. You'll be told by one you admire, "I admit I was surprised at first but later I came to realize you have an abundance of energy, talent, and good will!" Libra, Scorpio, and another Taurus are represented.

Sunday, September 18 (Moon in Pisces)   Today's scenario features a degree of solemnity, spirituality, and the ability to make your wishes come true. The lunar position accents winning ways, speculation, romance, and the ability to win friends and influence people. You might be amazed by the cooperation received from Pisces and Virgo, who sincerely want you to succeed.

Monday, September 19 (Moon in Pisces to Aries 10:30 p.m.)   The full moon position highlights publicity and an ability to complete a diplomatic mission. You'll be fortunate in matters of speculation and romance. Caution: Take care in connection with diet and nutrition. You may be tempted to overindulge in adult beverages and rich foods.

Tuesday, September 20 (Moon in Aries)   You reach a pinnacle—you are at the top and many powerful persons are drawn to you. You'll attract those with dictatorial attitudes, some of whom take the liberty of telling you how you should live your life. This message becomes crystal clear by 11 p.m. Your lucky number is 9.

Wednesday, September 21 (Moon in Aries)   Make a fresh start. Be vulnerable to romance and receptive to an offer by Aries to provide enlightenment. Your recent moods are related to fears, doubts, and suspicions, but much apprehension will be eradicated after you are reassured that you are held in high esteem and loved.

Thursday, September 22 (Moon in Aries to Taurus 9:47 a.m.)   Focus on your home and marital status, the division of property, and a reunion with a loved one. You're being drawn in two directions—the choice should be one that involves familiarity, family, and employment. Leave wild speculation for another time and refuse to be inveigled into action based on pure impulse.

Friday, September 23 (Moon in Taurus)   Emphasize diversity, versatility, fresh starts, independence, and the courage of your convictions. The moon in your sign highlights success, timing, and the ability to get to the heart of matters. By mid-afternoon, circumstances take a dramatic turn in your favor. Your lucky number is 3.

Saturday, September 24 (Moon in Taurus to Gemini 10:41 p.m.)   Lucky lottery: 4, 20, 6, 22, 33, 5. You'll encounter Leo, Scorpio, and another Taurus—persons who will play influential roles and could have these letters or initials in their names: D, M, V. Check source material, read between the lines, and be aware of references and past performances.

Sunday, September 25 (Moon in Gemini)   On this Sunday, you'll review past, present and the potential for the future. You'll contemplate words recently read or written. Your ability as a character analyst surges to the forefront—you'll learn where you stand in a love relationship. Your lucky number is 5.

Monday, September 26 (Moon in Gemini)   A remark made by family member yesterday should not be taken out of context. Your current cycle highlights harmony, color coordination, beauty, flowers, and a domestic adjustment. You'll be musing that this is one unusual Monday. By late afternoon, you'll get news about the recovery of money you thought lost for good.

Tuesday, September 27 (Moon in Gemini to Cancer 11:12 a.m.)　　Individuals who play important roles in your life today are likely to be born under Gemini and Sagittarius and will have these initials or letters in their names: G, P, Y. Important: Do not equate delay with defeat. Your suggestions will be followed despite the initial reluctance of an associate.

Wednesday, September 28 (Moon in Cancer)　　Recently you questioned the solidity of a product, and tonight your answer is received. You made a good deal—the quality is sound, so you'll be pleased and so will those who rely upon your judgment. Capricorn and Cancer play key roles and could have these initials or letters in their names: H, Q, Z.

Thursday, September 29 (Moon in Cancer to Leo 8:55 p.m.)　　The lunar position highlights trips, visits, relatives, and ideas that can be developed into viable concepts. Stress universal appeal, communicate with persons overseas who are active in import-export areas. You'll learn that you no longer are held back—for you, the sky is the limit.

Friday, September 30 (Moon in Leo)　　Stress independence, style, originality, and confidence. Those who previously failed to respond to calls and requests for interviews will now be practically at your doorstep. Focus on vindication, romance, style, and added recognition. Leo and Aquarius play major roles. Your lucky number is 1.

OCTOBER 1994

Saturday, October 1 (Moon in Leo)　　On this first day of the month, you finally can be rid of emotional debris. The lunar position accents property, basic values, and a family relationship that requires the utmost care. Someone close to you has been underground. The meaning will become crystal clear by tonight.

Sunday, October 2 (Moon in Leo to Virgo 2:39 a.m.)
What you missed yesterday will be available in abundance. The lunar emphasis continues on your home, security, locked doors, and emotional restraint. By late afternoon, you'll be saying, "Enough beating about the bush—let's speak our minds and hearts!" An onslaught of emotions will be released.

Monday, October 3 (Moon in Virgo)   You'll encounter Capricorn and Cancer persons likely to have these initials or letters in their names: B, K, T. The lunar position accents creativity, variety, physical attraction, and a unique conversation with a young person, possibly your child. Property will be divided equitably.

Tuesday, October 4 (Moon Virgo to Libra 4:56 a.m.)   You might be saying, "It's not the weekend, it's only Tuesday, but I feel as if I'm celebrating!" The emphasis is on humor, diversity, and excellent news about money. The focus is also on romance, creativity, and the scrutiny of a product aimed at a wide market, especially children. Your lucky number is 3.

Wednesday, October 5 (Moon in Libra)   Lucky lottery: 2, 7, 4, 25, 52, 12. Today's cycle highlights fitness, employment, dependents, and greater self-esteem. Carry out resolutions made early this year that relate to diet and nutrition. A family member who drinks heavily needs attention, but this should not throw you off the path that fulfills your own needs and ambitions.

Thursday, October 6 (Moon in Libra to Scorpio 5:22 a.m.)   Be ready for a sudden announcement relating to a possible trip that involves a relative. Get your thoughts on paper. You'll gain via the written word. Gemini, Virgo, and Sagittarius are involved and could have these initials or letters in their names: E, N, W. The scales of justice will balance in your favor.

Friday, October 7 (Moon in Scorpio) What at first appears to be mere fantasy will prove to be solid and reliable. Details unravel toward late evening. Focus on credibility, public image, partnership, and your marital status. You'll learn more about your legal rights and permissions, and home decoration will be featured.

Saturday, October 8 (Moon in Scorpio to Sagittarius 5:47 a.m.) Define your terms, stressing quality over quantity. A relationship, although romantic and exciting, requires review. By playing the waiting game, you avoid an emotional clash and embarrassment. Pisces and Virgo figure prominently and could have these letters or initials in their names: G, P, Y.

Sunday, October 9 (Moon in Sagittarius) The emphasis is on spirituality, quiet reflection, meditation, and news about a possible journey, perhaps overseas. You'll be dealing with older people who show confidence in your capabilities. What was once considered outmoded is back in fashion—you knew it all the time.

Monday, October 10 (Moon in Sagittarius to Capricorn 7:44 a.m.) It seemed as if a cloud of fog was in relentless pursuit—today, however, there is a breakthrough. Fresh air produces clarity, blowing away fear, doubt, and suspicion. You might feel as if you have awakened from a bad dream. You're released from an obnoxious obligation.

Tuesday, October 11 (Moon in Capricorn) Focus on initiative, clarity, independence, freedom, and plans for a possible journey. A favorable lunar aspect coincides with spirituality, education, and intelligence. A love relationship is on a different, more positive level. Leo and Aquarius play meaningful roles.

Wednesday, October 12 (Moon in Capricorn to Aquarius 12:09 p.m.) You'll be dealing with Cancer and Capricorn persons, some of whom have these letters or initials in their names: B, K, T. Focus on marital status, property, security, and basic repairs. The process of survival dominates scenario. Lucky lottery: 2, 12, 20, 10, 8, 22.

Thursday, October 13 (Moon in Aquarius)   At the track: post position special—number 5 P.P. in the seventh race. Pick six: 3, 3, 5, 7, 1, 9. In choosing winning horses or jockeys, be alert to these letters or initials in their names: C, L, U. Today's scenario features experimentation, social activity, additions to your wardrobe, and sensitivity about your body image.

Friday, October 14 (Moon in Aquarius to Pisces 7:19 p.m.)   Check the details, realizing that a recent restriction was unreasonable, will be lifted by tonight. Don't be afraid to upset the applecart. You will be on more solid emotional-financial ground. Accent the surprise element. Take an unorthodox approach. Scorpio and another Taurus play major roles.

Saturday, October 15 (Moon in Pisces)   Lucky lottery: 5, 12, 52, 7, 18, 9. The focus is on the written word, exploration, and an ability to analyze character. Someone of the opposite sex could find you irresistible and say so! Keep flattery in the proper perspective. Gemini, Virgo, and Sagittarius are on hand.

Sunday, October 16 (Moon in Pisces)   Attention revolves around promoting more domestic harmony with a family gathering, music, or decoration of the home. You may receive a token of affection. Special note: It is important that you maintain discipline in connection with your diet and nutrition.

Monday, October 17 (Moon in Pisces to Aries 4:56 a.m.)   A promise made to you twenty-four hours ago will be fulfilled before 7 p.m. Attention revolves around good fortune in matters of money and love. The lunar position accents your good salesmanship, by which you can successfully influence people and events. Your lucky number is 7.

Tuesday, October 18 (Moon in Aries)   Today's key is organization and the ability to withstand pressure and threats from an antagonist. By facing the truth, you'll erase fear, doubt, and suspicion. Communicate with someone temporarily confined to the home or hospital. Capricorn and Cancer figure in today's drama. You'll have luck with the number 8.

Wednesday, October 19 (Moon in Aries to Taurus 4:34 p.m.) A project that had been dormant will again by alive and kicking due to your efforts. The full moon in your twelfth solar house coincides with a revelation, a secret meeting, or a love relationship that cannot be openly revealed. Long-range prospects are clarified. A mission will be completed. Aries is involved.

Thursday, October 20 (Moon in Taurus) Stress independence. Be willing to make a fresh start in a new direction. The transiting moon in Taurus emphasizes your personality, individuality, and sex appeal. Emerge from your recent emotional cocoon—let others be aware of your presence as you wear shades of blue, indigo, and purple.

Friday, October 21 (Moon in Taurus) You're being pulled in two directions. The family wants you to stay home. You, however, want to be more independent, to be released from a financial obligation you should not have assumed in the first place. Your own judgement and intuition prove accurate. Your lucky number is 2.

Saturday, October 22 (Moon in Taurus to Gemini 5:28 a.m.) Diversify, emphasizing your wit and wisdom. As your popularity increases, you'll star at a social affair. Your body image improves, an offer is received in connection with travel, the display of a product, or publishing and advertising. Your cycle continues high as circumstances take a dramatic turn in your favor.

Sunday, October 23 (Moon in Gemini) Many of the individuals you contact today will be born under Taurus, Leo, and Scorpio. Some of those persons, almost all of them playing positive roles, will have these initials or letters in their names: D, M, V. Your attention revolves around rebuilding, remodeling, revising, and improving safety measures.

Monday, October 24 (Moon in Gemini to Cancer 6:15 p.m.)   The emphasis is on your ability to increase your income and to locate an article that had been lost, missing, or stolen. You get at the truth through the process of elimination—analyze character and discern possible motives. What begins as a chance meeting or mild flirtation could develop into a serious relationship.

Tuesday, October 25 (Moon in Cancer)   During the late afternoon, your automobile could require a jump start. Check batteries, tires, and water pump. The emphasis falls on transportation, trips, and visits. A relative declares "What you are seeking was hidden by me and I am sorry." A major domestic adjustment could affect your lifestyle and marital status.

Wednesday, October 26 (Moon in Cancer)   Lucky lottery: 4, 7, 22, 5, 19, 50. Much that occurs will be of a quiet nature. The emphasis is on individuality, spirituality, and a revelation that being alone has absolutely nothing to do with being lonely. You'll begin to appreciate and enjoy your own company. Pisces is involved.

Thursday, October 27 (Moon in Cancer to Leo 5:05 a.m.)   The spotlight is on organization and the ability to win friends and influence people. Some will say, in connection with obtaining funding for political or charitable campaign, "You are able to perform miracles!" An older person confesses an attraction to you. Capricorn plays a dramatic role.

Friday, October 28 (Moon in Leo)   The emphasis falls on showmanship, universal appeal, and wrapping a product in colorful package. Break free from restriction—for you today, the sky is the limit. A love relationship flourishes despite a temporary separation due to a necessary journey. Aries and Libra figure in today's dynamic scenario. Your lucky number is 9.

Saturday, October 29 (Moon in Leo to Virgo 12:21 p.m.)   Lucky lottery: 29, 5, 11, 22, 33, 18. Focus on drama, showmanship, theater, and entertainment. Express yourself. Get to the heart of matters, letting the world know you will not play second fiddle. Wear shades of yellow and gold. Make personal appearances and use graphics to illustrate your meanings.

Sunday, October 30 (Moon in Virgo) (Daylight Savings Time Ends)   Today's scenario highlights change, travel, variety, sensuality, personal magnetism, and sex appeal. It is obvious: Don't hide your light under a bushel! Stress freedom, independence, originality, and a pioneering spirit. Refuse to be cajoled into remaining with the status quo. A Cancer is in the picture.

Monday, October 31 (Moon in Virgo to Libra 2:47 p.m.)   You approach the day with some apprehension, but it proves to hold fun and frolic, and you conclude it by declaring, "Once I got in the spirit of Halloween, I realized the humor, mystery, and intrigue involved and I loved it!" Gemini and Sagittarius play significant roles. Your lucky number is 3.

NOVEMBER 1994

Tuesday, November 1 (Moon in Libra)   November gets off to a dynamic start—a job application is accepted; the employment picture is bright; you imprint your own style; a love relationship regains its spark. Take the initiative, get to the heart of matters, and deal gingerly with Leo and Aquarius.

Wednesday, November 2 (Moon in Libra to Scorpio 4:19 p.m.)   People who play key roles in your life today are likely to be born under Cancer and Capricorn, and some will have these letters or initials in their names: B, K, T. Your sense of direction is regained as a love relationship heats up. Lucky lottery: 22, 5, 12, 1, 6, 52. Enjoy food!

Thursday, November 3 (Moon in Scorpio)   The new moon, solar eclipse in Scorpio, equates to the disruption of a legal pattern. The spotlight also falls on controversy involving your credibility and public image. A clash of ideas is featured, involving your partnership or marital status. Gemini, Scorpio, and Sagittarius play featured roles.

Friday, November 4 (Moon in Scorpio to Sagittarius 2:46 p.m.)   On this Friday, you'll find the missing key. Focus on the details, the small print, and a solution to a dilemma. The emphasis remains on public relations and your image and reputation. A legal agreement is reached that could involve a new partnership or marriage. Leo, Scorpio, and another Taurus figure in this scenario.

Saturday, November 5 (Moon in Sagittarius)   Lucky lottery: 3, 8, 9, 5, 16, 45. The emphasis is on self-expression, investigation, and the ability to obtain more freedom of thought and action. Your health report is good. The employment picture is encouraging. Gemini, Virgo, and Sagittarius play significant roles. You'll be told, "You have a way with words!"

Sunday, November 6 (Moon in Sagittarius to Capricorn 3:02 p.m.)   Today's scenario features travel and excellent news concerning the health of a relative recently returned from a short trip. Be diplomatic in connection with a financial dispute. A family member will make an intelligent concession. Libra, Scorpio, and another Taurus play major roles. Your lucky number is 6.

Monday, November 7 (Moon in Capricorn)   Someone who is previously reticent proves to be a staunch ally and very likely is a Piscean. Look behind the scenes, outline boundaries, and see places and people as they actually are, not merely as you wish they might be. Today's lunar aspect coincides with travel, publishing, and the ability to get your message across.

Tuesday, November 8 (Moon in Capricorn to Aquarius 5:48 p.m.)   Deal with persons who pull strings, who invest, and who are willing to lend the benefit of experience. Some who play important roles in your life today are born under Capricorn and Cancer, and some will have these initials or letters in their names: H, Q, Z. Your lucky number is 8.

Wednesday, November 9 (Moon in Aquarius) What seemed long ago and far away is actually right up front, within reach. Focus on corresponding, communication, and your ability to widen your area of influence. You'll be rid of a burden, and know the meaning of true love. Lucky lottery: 9, 10, 12, 44, 50, 1.

Thursday, November 10 (Moon in Aquarius) You're ready for a fresh start and more independence, and once again you are vulnerable to love. Today's lunar position accents leadership, promotion, production, and the elevation of your standing in your church and community. Your own policy will be put into force. Aquarian plays a role.

Friday, November 11 (Moon in Aquarius to Pisces 12:04 a.m.) Focus on your marital status, partnership, and public image. Evaluate a decision relating to the sale or purchase of property, possibly a large household appliance. Capricorn and Cancer can motivate you. This evening, there's a reunion with a family member. Your lucky number is 2.

Saturday, November 12 (Moon in Pisces) Lucky lottery: 3, 33, 12, 18, 22, 7. At the track: post position special—number 5 P.P. in the seventh race. Pick six: 3, 3, 7, 1, 4, 3. In selecting winning horses or jockeys, be aware of these initials or letters in names: C, L, U. Gemini and Sagittarius play influential roles.

Sunday, November 13 (Moon in Pisces to Aries 9:44 a.m.) The usual procedures will not work—focus on unorthodox methods, timing, and using the element of surprise. Some will claim, "You're upsetting the apple cart!" Your ideal reply, "You're right; I'm going to continue to do so!" Scorpio and another Taurus figure prominently. Your lucky number is 4.

Monday, November 14 (Moon in Aries) Reject superficial responses. Dig deep for information. The emphasis is on character analysis, methodology, exploration, and an exciting discovery. What begins as a blind date or a chance meeting could develop into a serious relationship. Gemini, Virgo, and Sagittarius are represented.

Tuesday, November 15 (*Moon in Aries to Taurus 9:44 p.m.*)   Music is in your life today—you'll attend the theater or a concert or be entertained at home. Focus on color coordination, sound, and your own style and voice. Remember a recent resolution concerning diet and nutrition—control your sweet tooth. Libra plays a paramount role.

Wednesday, November 16 (*Moon in Taurus*)   Define terms, separating fact from illusion. The moon in your twelfth house coincides with dreams, visions, clandestine arrangements, and an aura of glamour, intrigue, and mystery. Some persons beseech you, "Tell me everything!" But be discreet. It's important not to tell all.

Thursday, November 17 (*Moon in Taurus*)   At the track: post position special—number 9 P.P. in the eighth race. Pick six: 8, 5, 4, 3, 7, 2. In selecting winning horses or jockeys, be aware of these initials or letters in their names: H, Q, Z. What you started approximately one week ago will bear fruit.

Friday, November 18 (*Moon in Taurus to Gemini 10:42 a.m.*)   The full moon, lunar eclipse, in your sign represents the overthrow of the status quo. Amidst controversy, you create and originate and you'll also be rid of hindrances. Stress universal appeal as you communicate with someone at a distance, perhaps in a foreign land. Aries is involved. Your lucky number is 9.

Saturday, November 19 (*Moon in Gemini*)   You'll be asking no one in particular except yourself, "Who's afraid of the big, bad wolf?" Emphasize courage, direction, and a pioneering spirit. Spotlight initiative, originality, and the realization that a different kind of love could be on the horizon. Leo and Aquarius figure prominently.

Sunday, November 20 (*Moon in Gemini to Cancer 11:21 p.m.*)   Reach beyond previous limitations. Although it is Sunday, you'll verify an increase in income, the release of

203

money, or the voluntary return of an article that had been lost. Focus also on your home, security, psychic impressions, and marital status. Cancer and Capricorn play major roles. Your lucky number is 2.

Monday, November 21 (Moon in Cancer)   It is Monday, the first work day of the week, but it also brings excellent news about your financial prospects. What was signaled twenty-four hours ago is now reality. You'll have reason to celebrate; you'll improve your public image and be more pleased with your own physical condition.

Tuesday, November 22 (Moon in Cancer)   What appeared to be a trap turns out to be merely a legitimate reason for a temporary delay. Use this time to investigate past performance, references, facts and figures, and inventory. Someone who had been a troublemaker will do an about-face and could become your staunch, loyal ally.

Wednesday, November 23 (Moon in Cancer to Leo 10:33 a.m.)   Lucky lottery: 5, 4, 20, 13, 17, 33. The spotlight falls on relatives, trips, visits, and ideas that require further development. Some concepts are fragmented—the puzzle pieces will (very soon) fall into place. You're capable of discerning the pattern of your own destiny.

Thursday, November 24 (Moon in Leo)   The moon position, plus the astrological and numerical aspects, reveal that indeed you have the right to be thankful. Focus on family relationships, diplomacy, pleasure, and celebrating this holiday together. You'll enjoy food and festivities, and know that you do not stand alone. Another Taurus is involved.

Friday, November 25 (Moon in Leo)   Someone who initially is vindictive will change course, actually seeking your counsel. Do not exactly forgive and forget, but don't press issues to the point of crushing another's pride. This message becomes crystal clear by 4 p.m. Pisces and Virgo are involved.

Saturday, November 26 (Moon in Leo to Virgo 7:09 p.m.)   Today's scenario emphasizes the use of force, power, and authority. Relationships can be stressful. Attention also revolves around durable goods, a property settlement, and decisions of whether to buy or sell. A clash of ideas takes place with Leo, who is romantic and stubborn and could have these initials or letters in his or her name: A, S, J.

Sunday, November 27 (Moon in Virgo) Spiritual values surface. A cycle is completed—what goes around comes around. You'll be musing, "This is déjà vu!" Release yourself from a foolish obligation you should not have incurred in the first place. Plan ahead for an imminent journey. Leo continues to be prominent.

Monday, November 28 (Moon in Virgo to Libra 12:22 a.m.) Be ready for fresh start in a new direction. Assume a leadership role. Focus on initiative, originality, a pioneering spirit, and romance. A special note: Avoid heavy lifting. Get to the heart of matters, be direct, and let others know that you no longer will play second fiddle.

Tuesday, November 29 (Moon in Libra) Go slow, accenting moderation. A decision made yesterday was correct—the status quo no longer applies and you'll be more independent now that you have started the ball rolling. Get rid of superfluous material and trim down to fighting weight. Gourmet dining is on tap for tonight. Cancer is involved.

Wednesday, November 30 (Moon in Libra to Scorpio 2:22 a.m.) Today's emphasis is on pleasure, fun, frolic, diversity, and different modes of transportation. You'll add to your wardrobe and no longer will be super-sensitive about your appearance and body image. Your health report is much better than you anticipated. Lucky lottery: 3, 30, 33, 18, 19, 22. Sagittarius is represented:

DECEMBER 1994

Thursday, December 1 (Moon in Scorpio) Today's cycle highlights partnerships, being together with one whose ideas harmonize with your own. The spotlight also falls on the favorable outcome of legal affairs, especially disputes concerning property ownership. With the moon in Scorpio, the emphasis is on your seventh solar house—this coincides with your marital status.

Friday, December 2 (Moon in Scorpio to Sagittarius 2:13 a.m.) Today's new moon highlights credibility, public image, and what might be termed a new lease on life. You get the proverbial second chance. Your popularity increases. People who seemed to be out of town when you called are now back in the fold. You are vindicated!

Saturday, December 3 (Moon in Sagittarius) Lucky lottery: 4, 9, 29, 51, 6, 5. At the track: post position special—number 4 P.P. in the eighth race. Pick six: 8, 5, 4, 1, 7, 8. In choosing winning horses or jockeys, be on alert for these initials or letters in their names: D, M, V. A Scorpio is in this picture.

Sunday, December 4 (Moon in Sagittarius to Capricorn 1:42 a.m.) The lunar position accents mystery, intrigue, and the necessity for learning more about accounting procedures and hidden values. the spotlight falls on the status of someone close to you, perhaps your partner or mate. Be analytical and get your ideas on paper. Trust your own sense of quality and character. Your lucky number is 5.

Monday, December 5 (Moon in Capricorn) You'll be away from home whether or not you move an inch geographically. This means you'll be enveloped in study as your imagination soars and you become knowledgeable about foreign lands, languages, food, and mores. Attention also revolves around a domestic adjustment that definitely results in an improved family relationship.

Tuesday, December 6 (Moon in Capricorn to Aquarius 2:51 a.m.) Define terms and make travel arrangements, either for yourself or for someone who relies on your judgment. Trust a psychic impression. Today's scenario features enlightenment and an ability to see places and people as they are, not merely as you wish they might be. Pisces plays a major role.

Wednesday, December 7 (Moon in Aquarius)   Focus on organization, responsibility, productivity, and promotion. You'll be given more authority, followed by added responsibility, followed by a chance to considerably increase your income. Some will say you're lucky. You'll muse, "Funny, the harder I work, the luckier I get!"

Thursday, December 8 (Moon in Aquarius to Pisces 7:24 a.m.)   Stress universal appeal, striving to learn more about import-export activities and reaching beyond your previous limitations. Today's scenario also features idealism, romance, travel, and more self-confidence. You'll be rid of a burden you should not have carried in first place.

Friday, December 9 (Moon in Pisces)   Emphasize independence, daring, innovativeness, and pioneering spirit. The lunar position accents your ability to make your wishes come true. You'll feel more alive, vigorous, and enthusiastic. Love plays a major role. You'll be inspired by someone of the opposite sex, possibly a Leo, with these initials or letters in his or her name: A, S, J.

Saturday, December 10 (Moon in Pisces to Aries 4:03 p.m.)   Lucky lottery: 2, 12, 14, 1, 11, 22. A reunion with a loved one comes just in time for a Saturday night celebration. Today's lunar position emphasizes the ability to win friends and influence people. Turn on your Taurus-Venus charm! Cancer and Capricorn play significant roles. Check property values.

Sunday, December 11 (Moon in Aries)   Diversify, showing versatility and humor. Give full play to your intellectual curiosity. Your lunar position highlights dreams, prophesies, mysteries, and intrigue. You'll be dealing with Gemini and Sagittarius persons likely to have these initials or letters in their names: C, L, U. Your lucky number is 3.

Monday, December 12 (Moon in Aries)   As your cycle moves up, you are now on more solid emotional-financial ground. Using an unorthodox approach or method brings you closer to your ultimate goal. What had been cause for apprehension undergoes a metamorphosis, from anxiety to laughter. Leo, Scorpio, and another Taurus figure in today's dynamic scenario.

Tuesday, December 13 (Moon in Aries to Taurus 3:56 a.m.) Today's cycle highlights a variety of experiences, discovery, character analysis, flirtation that lend spice. A clash of ideas during mid-afternoon proves far more exciting than any clash of guns. Gemini, Virgo, and Sagittarius play paramount roles. Your lucky number is 5.

Wednesday, December 14 (Moon in Taurus) A domestic adjustment is featured. Your cycle is high and you'll be at the right place at a special moment. Wear your colors: shades of blue, indigo, and purple. Emphasize your personality, physical attractiveness, and ability to get to the heart of matters. The answer to your question: Yes, take the initiative!

Thursday, December 15 (Moon in Taurus to Gemini 5 p.m.) Dig deep for information; perfect your techniques and streamline your procedures. You'll be given access to information previously withheld. You learn a secret. You'll also make a discovery concerning a relationship that you learn has not been completely above board. Your lucky number is 7.

Friday, December 16 (Moon in Gemini) Focus on organization, payments and collections, and credit attributed to you that has been long overdue. A relationship intensifies; it's exciting and controversial and well worth the trouble. Married or single, you'll participate in a commercial venture that will drain time, energy, and finances but will ultimately prove profitable.

Saturday, December 17 (Moon in Gemini) Lucky lottery: 5, 14, 9, 33, 17, 18. At the track: post position special—number 3 P.P. in the second race. Pick six: 1, 3, 8, 7, 7, 5. In checking for winning horses or jockeys, be aware of these initials or letters in their names: I and R. A mission will be completed. An Aries proves to be your strong ally.

Sunday, December 18 (Moon in Gemini to Cancer 5:25 a.m.) The full moon coincides with the completion of a financial transaction. By taking the initiative, you locate an item or product that has been lost, missing, or stolen. You'll exude personal magnetism, confidence, and sex appeal. Leo and Aquarius will play meaningful roles. Your lucky number is 1.

Monday, December 19 (Moon is Cancer) Focus on your family, property, marital status, and a legitimate opportunity to be in on the ground floor in connection with the distribution or promotion of a commerical product. The accent is on home appliances, security, and written material aimed at the female population. Capricorn and Cancer figure prominently.

Tuesday, December 20 (Moon in Cancer to Leo 4:13 p.m.) Attention revolves around relatives, visits, and the expression of views in an entertaining, informative way. Don't press issues. You gain more today by being diplomatic and even by poking fun at your own foibles. Additions to your wardrobe help overcome tensions relating to the shape you're in.

Wednesday, December 21 (Moon in Leo) Be ready to tear down in order to rebuild—stress quality and insist on warranties covering the durability of goods. An older person lends the benefit of experience, especially with negotiations. Leo, Scorpio, and another Taurus play significant roles.

Thursday, December 22 (Moon in Leo) Focus on character analysis, a variety of experiences, and unique investigation. A family member asserts, "I feel house bound and I must take a trip!" A significant adjustment will be made, and you'll have reason to celebrate because the special material you submitted is accepted and rewarded.

Friday, December 23 (Moon in Leo to Virgo 1:01 a.m.) A domestic adjustment is featured that could include an actual change of residence or marital status. With the moon in Leo, attention continues to revolve around your home and security. An older family member declares confidence in you and will prove it. Libra and another Taurus are represented.

Saturday, December 24 (Moon in Virgo)   On this Christmas Eve, you'll be inspired and you'll have plenty to do with persons with young ideas, if not literally with children. The moon in Virgo represents your fifth house having to do with variety, pleasure, speculation, and the joy of giving. Pisces and Virgo are featured.

Sunday, December 25 (Moon in Virgo to Libra 7:27 a.m.)   You'll feel the full impact of this Christmas day. No matter what your religious belief, you'll sense the majesty of true meaning. Your holiday spirit will prevail. A love relationship grows close, intense, and durable. You'll be dealing with Capricorn and Cancer persons with these initials or letters in their names: H, Q, Z.

Monday, December 26 (Moon in Libra)   What had been left hanging will be completed, and loose ends will be tied. A fiery Aries, actually a secret ally, speaks in a belligerent way, but does not mean a word of it. Focus on health, fitness, organization, employment, and the ability to locate the proper personnel.

Tuesday, December 27 (Moon in Libra to Scorpio 11:17 a.m.)   What had been regarded as a lost cause will not only be revived, but will be alive and kicking. You're due to make a fresh start, to imprint your own style, and to love and be loved. Be direct as you take the initiative in getting to the heart of matters—let others know that you refuse to play second fiddle.

Wednesday, December 28 (Moon in Scorpio)   Once again, during this month, numerical and astrological aspects blend to highlight a partnership, credibility, public acceptance, or marriage. You'll have luck in matters of romance, obtaining a legitimate bargain or speculation. Lucky lottery: 2, 22, 18, 17, 19, 50.

Thursday, December 29 (Moon in Scorpio to Sagittarius 12:46 p.m.) You'll devise new ways of entertaining—you could win a contest or create a game show. Focus on a celebration, an expansion of interests, a social invitation that could include travel. You'll encounter restless, dynamic persons who test and challenge and assist you in the selection of apparel.

Friday, December 30 (Moon in Sagittarius) Be willing to revise and review, and to invest in quality products that make you feel more secure. Focus on home, property, durable goods, and large household products. You'll be tearing down in order to rebuild on a more suitable base. A close associate says, "I'm moving!"

Saturday, December 31 (Moon in Sagittarius to Capricorn 12:58 p.m.) This New Year's Eve, you will be more exciting than in previous years. You'll be with interesting, creative persons, including family members, who talk about resolutions and freely express hopes, wishes, desires, and inspirations. Gemini, Virgo, and Sagittarius are involved. Your lucky number is 5.

JANUARY 1995

Sunday, January 1 (Moon in Capricorn) On this New Years Day, you'll be in touch with people at a distance. You'll feel refreshed and renewed; you possibly might be saying, "I'm in tune with the new year!" Emphasize independence and creativity. Have the courage of your convictions and be vulnerable to love. Leo and Aquarius are involved. Your lucky number is 1.

Monday, January 2 (Moon in Capricorn to Aquarius 1:39 p.m.) A family member, apparently disoriented 24 hours ago, communicates to thank you for everything and invite you for dinner. Be receptive but be sure others know that your own feelings are sensitive. Cancer and Capricorn play major roles.

Tuesday, January 3 (Moon in Aquarius)   Reach beyond previous expectations—focus on travel, your powers of persuasion, charm, and your ability to win friends and influence people. Today's scenario features diversity, humor, and different modes of transportation. You'll add to your wardrobe, and your body image shows marked improvement. Gemini is on hand.

Wednesday, January 4 (Moon in Aquarius to Pisces 4:49 p.m.)   An obstacle which dealt with distance, language, and your ability to communicate, is removed. Focus on reviewing and revising, and on your willingness to tear down in order to rebuild on a more suitable structure. The Aquarian moon represents leadership, promotion, direction, and the possibility of flirting with fame and fortune.

Thursday, January 5 (Moon in Pisces)   Your wishes come true. You gain by writing, reading, or teaching. A flirtation, chance meeting, or blind date lends spice and could develop into something serious. The Pisces moon highlights your ability to win others over to your point of view. Gemini, Virgo, and Sagittarius play sympathetic roles.

Friday, January 6 (Moon in Pisces to Aries 11:56 p.m.)   There's music in your life tonight—you'll receive a gift representing a token of affection and esteem. The spotlight also falls on domestic adjustment and a discussion relating to decoration, remodeling, or revising. There is a possibility that you will soon change your residence or marital status. Your lucky number is 6.

Saturday, January 7 (Moon in Aries)   Lucky lottery: 7, 12, 27, 5, 47, 49. At the track: post position special—number 1 P.P. in the sixth race. Pick six: 1, 8, 7, 5, 8, 1. In choosing the names of winning horses and jockeys, keep these letters in mind: G, P, Y. As your cycle moves up, you will be provided with information previously withheld.

Sunday, January 8 (Moon in Aries)   What frightened you previously will now be regarded as nothing more than a paper tiger. Focus on organization, business enterprise, and awareness of a deadline. An older person, possibly a

Cancer or a Capricorn, gives the benefit of experience, and could even help in obtaining funding.

Monday, January 9 (Moon in Aries to Taurus 10:58 a.m.) Stress universal appeal, accenting mystery, intrigue, and showmanship. Someone who took you for granted will have serious second thoughts. Some persons will insist you have something up your sleeve. Let them ponder and wonder! Open the lines of communication as you continue the search for a soul mate.

Tuesday, January 10 (Moon in Taurus)   As your cycle moves up, circumstances take a dramatic turn in your favor. The Taurus moon highlights your personality, personal magnetism, sensuality, and sex appeal. Imprint your style, accenting leadership, independence, and the courage of your convictions. You'll be dealing with a Leo whose name is likely to have these letters: A, S, J.

Wednesday, January 11 (Moon in Taurus to Gemini 11:57 p.m.)   Lucky lottery: 2, 12, 20, 44, 13, 19. Focus on reading and preparing special, appetizing food. A Cancer figures prominently, and says, "When you join me for dinner I feel inspired!" The emphasis is on direction, motivation, and marital status. The moon in your sign continues to highlight creativity, style, panache, and sex appeal.

Thursday, January 12 (Moon in Gemini)   Do not underrate yourself! What you offer is valuable. Your presence lends prestige to a project, group, or committee. You'll be where the action is. Circumstances continue in your favor. Events transpire in an almost mysterious way to help you achieve your goal. Fun and frolic are featured tonight.

Friday, January 13 (Moon in Gemini)   This will be far from an unlucky day for you. The Gemini moon is in that area of your solar horoscope relating to funding, income, payments, and rewards for efforts. You'll have a solid base for your aspirations and enterprises. Leo, Scorpio, and another Taurus play major roles.

213

Saturday, January 14 (Moon in Gemini to Cancer 12:20 p.m.)   Shake off any tendency toward lethargy. On this Saturday, you are a mover and a shaker. Money is involved and so is communication. You'll be alive and alert and flirtatious. Tonight you might hear these words, "You're so vibrant, it's a pleasure to be with you!" Gemini, Virgo, and Sagittarius are involved. Your lucky number is 5.

Sunday, January 15 (Moon in Cancer)   Attention revolves around your home, family, and security. Focus on acquiring solid building blocks. On this Sunday, harmony is restored in family relationships. Focus also on music, gourmet dining, and developing your spiritual awareness. You'll receive a gift that adds to your wardrobe. Another Taurus plays a major role.

Monday, January 16 (Moon in Cancer to Leo 10:36 p.m.)   The full moon in Cancer activates your interest in property, durable household goods, food, and marital status., A relative confides, "I can't exactly put my finger on it, but lately I am so moody and unhappy!" Express your own feelings; be sympathetic; but, for your own good, do not become inextricably involved.

Tuesday, January 17 (Moon in Leo)   Attention revolves around a time limitation concerning payments of mortgage, car loans, insurance. The key is organization. Be willing to accept responsibility for a relationship that lately has become controversial. A short trip or a change of scene could help alleviate tensions.

Wednesday, January 18 (Moon in Leo)   Lucky lottery: 12, 9, 14, 1, 5, 33. At the track: post position special—number 8 P.P. in the first race. Pick six: 8, 5, 1, 5, 7, 3. In selecting the names of potential winning horses and jockeys, look for these letters: I and R. You'll be dealing with Aries and Libra who want to be your friends.

Thursday, January 19 (Moon in Leo to Virgo 6:39 a.m.)   New arrival—the scene features home, family, security, and a possible addition to your personal environment. You'll have more sunlight; areas of your home will

214

no longer be dark, dank, and bleak. You'll be dealing with Leo and Aquarius likely to have these letters or initials in their names: A, S. J.

Friday, January 20 (Moon in Virgo)   Get things done without delay; check plumbing and scrutinize a recent auto repair. A family member declares, "I can always count on you!" That's fine, but remind certain people that you do have a life of your own. Capricorn, and Cancer play roles, and are likely to have these letters in their names: B, K, T.

Saturday, January 21 (Moon in Virgo to Libra 12:54 p.m.)   Lucky lottery: 3, 6, 19, 39, 41, 51. There will be reason to celebrate tonight—conditions relating to employment and basic issues show a dramatic improvement. Recent concern about your body image will be eliminated with the purchase of clothing. Gemini and Sagittarius are involved.

Sunday, January 22 (Moon in Libra)   Check source material and be sure to keep resolutions about moderation, diet, and nutrition. This is rebuilding time: sharpen your tools, do some mending. Leo, Scorpio, and another Taurus play paramount roles. Someone who was previously cool toward you will warm up and might even sing a song just for you.

Monday, January 23 (Moon in Libra to Scorpio 5:32 p.m.)   A gain is indicated via the written word. You'll receive a communication relating to travel, reporting, and enlarging the scope of your experience. The Libra moon continues to emphasize basic issues, routine, pet ownership, and the general condition of a relative's health. Virgo and Sagittarius are represented.

Tuesday, January 24 (Moon in Scorpio)   At the track: Post position special—number 2 P.P. in the fourth race. Pick six: 1, 5, 8, 2, 1, 9. Attention revolves around your home, budget, flowers, music, and a unique gift representing a token of affection. Libra, Scorpio, and another Taurus play dynamic roles and could have these letters in their names: F, O, X.

Wednesday, January 25 (Moon in Scorpio to Sagittarius 8:37 p.m.)   Lucky lottery: 7, 6, 13, 14, 28, 29. Know when to draw the line, heed your inner voice, refuse to fall victim to self-deception. You might be asked to appear before the media—don't be intimidated by someone who makes subtle threats. Focus on partnership, public relations, marriage.

Thursday, January 26 (Moon in Sagittarius)   Someone with a cavalier attitude will be reprimanded by a superior. You'll be made more aware of your own legal rights and permissions. Focus on justice, responsibility, promotion, and awareness of a deadline. You've won the battle; others now insist that you take a deserved bow. Your lucky number is 8.

Friday, January 27 (Moon in Sagittarius to Capricorn 10:26 p.m.)   This cycle emphasizes travel, freedom, and the knowledge that previous rules and regulations no longer apply. The spotlight is on universal appeal, a soul mate, and your ability to reach beyond past expectations. Today's scenario highlights acclaim and flirtation with fame and fortune. Aries and Libra figure prominently.

Saturday, January 28 (Moon in Capricorn)   Express your originality, pioneering spirit, and willingness to make a fresh start in a new direction. The Capricorn moon highlights education, communication, publishing, and completion of a mission. You'll draw attractive, dynamic people, some of whom are likely to be Aquarius and Leo.

Sunday, January 29 (Moon in Capricorn)   You get down to practical matters. Attention revolves around sturdiness of goods, chairs, and accommodations for visiting relatives. A partnership, as well as participation in a commercial project and your marital status, all continue to be big priorities. Capricorn plays an outstanding role.

Monday, January 30 (Moon in Capricorn to Aquarius 12:03 a.m.)   A burden is lifted. The Aquarian new moon reveals a second chance to grab the brass ring—this time you will succeed. Emphasize diversity, intellectual curiosity, and your sense of the ridiculous. Your popularity increases as a surprise gift is received, most likely clothing. Your lucky number is 3.

Tuesday, January 31 (Moon in Aquarius)   What appeared to be a fantasy turns out to be real. Your wish comes true in an amazing way. Stick to the unorthodox. Church and community members will back you. The sound of applause will ring in your ears. Leo, Scorpio, and another Taurus play significant roles. Collect and analyze data.

FEBRUARY 1995

Wednesday, February 1 (Moon in Aquarius to Pisces 3:05 a.m.)   On this first day of February, you have the feeling that you are in sync with the world around you. Wishes are about to come true. A euphoric atmosphere pervades. You'll be saying to yourself, "I just know I'm going to be lucky this month!" On this Wednesday, news is received about a promotion, production, or prestige.

Thursday, February 2 (Moon in Pisces)   The Pisces moon accents your ability to make your wishes come true. The opportunity exists to win friends and influence people—turn on Taurus–Venus powers of persuasion. Today is your day for finance and romance. Gemini and Sagittarius play memorable roles. You'll have luck with the number 3. A gift of clothing is received.

Friday, February 3 (Moon in Pisces to Aries 9:12 a.m.) What at first might have appeared to be mere fantasy will turn out to be real and solid. You'll meet Scorpio, Leo, and another Taurus, some of whom are likely to have these letters in their names: D, M. V. Rewrite, sharpen tools, and correct mechanical defects in home appliances.

Saturday, February 4 (Moon in Aries)   This day mingles romance, mystery, and intrigue—your writing skills prove to be valuable allies. The emphasis is on variety, flirtation, experimentation, and discovery of motives. The lunar position highlights the backstage view, or a possible tour of a museum, hospital, or model home. Lucky lottery: 5, 12, 13, 14, 49, 50.

Sunday, February 5 (Moon in Aries to Taurus 7:09 p.m.) An excellent day for a family gathering, for recognizing spiritual values and participation in a community or church project. Music plays a key role. You'll also hear the sound of your inner voice. A domestic adjustment includes lifestyle, residence, and marital status. Scorpio and another Taurus play outstanding roles.

Monday, February 6 (Moon in Taurus) Those who thought you were behind schedule will be amazed when they view the record and note that you actually are at least one step ahead. Define your terms, outline boundaries, see places and people as they actually are. A psychic impression proves accurate. Pisces and Virgo figure in today's dynamic scenario.

Tuesday, February 7 (Moon in Taurus) All stops out! Despite someone who urges you to hold back, move ahead with confidence, determination. A lesson learned in the recent past—just over one week ago—can now be successfully used. The emphasis is on intensity, passion, and the ability to be at the right place at a crucial moment. Your lucky number is 8.

Wednesday, February 8 (Moon in Taurus to Gemini 7:44 a.m.) Finish what you start, refuse to be limited, reach beyond your previous expectations. Your judgment and intuition are on target—a long-distance call relates to the opening of new markets. What you imagine could become real and solid, including finding a soul mate. Lucky lottery: 9, 20, 12, 33, 32, 4.

Thursday, February 9 (Moon in Gemini) Money that had been withheld will be released. The Gemini moon represents cash on the barrelhead. Stress independence, originality, and the courage of your convictions. You'll make a fresh start; you'll also dare to dream. Take the initiative in getting to the heart of matters. An apparent loss boomerangs in your favor.

Friday, February 10 (Moon in Gemini to Cancer 8:17 p.m.)   Attention revolves around finances, personal possessions, and basic values. You'll be told about an auction, garage sale, or a legitimate bargain. Attention also revolves around the home, property, family, and marital status. Capricorn and Cancer figure in the scenario. You'll have luck with the number 2.

Saturday, February 11 (Moon in Cancer)   Lucky lottery: 11, 3, 5, 12, 18, 48. Accent versatility, diversity, and a sense of humor. You'll be complimented on your appearance, apparel, and ability to communicate in an entertaining way. A relative who previously pouted will smile, commenting, "You really are something!" Gemini is involved.

Sunday, February 12 (Moon in Cancer)   Attention revolves around solid ground, durable goods, and large household products. The emphasis is also on relatives, trips, visits, and the testing of mechanical objects. Check your car's tires, oil, and water. By tonight, you'll be relieved of a burden belonging to another. Scorpio plays a paramount role.

Monday, February 13 (Moon in Cancer to Leo 6:31 a.m.)   The cycle is high where writing is concerned. Ideas will be transformed into viable, valuable concepts. You'll have more working room; you'll be more secure and assured that you are loved. Gemini and Sagittarius figure in today's exciting scenario. A flirtation might get out of hand.

Tuesday, February 14 (Moon in Leo)   On this St. Valentine's Day, you'll be told that when you decide to be romantic, you are a world champion. At the track: post position special—number 2 P.P. in the fourth race. In selecting winning horses and jockeys, check for these letters or initials: F, O, X.

Wednesday, February 15 (Moon in Leo to Virgo 1:52 p.m.)   The full moon highlights a property appraisal that brings surprising information. A psychic impression proves accurate—follow through on a hunch. Lucky lottery: 1, 5, 10, 32, 51, 7. You'll be collared by a Leo whose name is likely to have these letters or initials: G, P, Y. Backstage!

Thursday, February 16 (Moon in Virgo)   Attention revolves around a time limitation, the necessity for organization, a decision about a relationship best described as bittersweet. You'll be dealing with Capricorn and Cancer likely to have these letters in their names: H, Q, Z. Your lucky number is 8.

Friday, February 17 (Moon in Virgo to Libra 7 p.m.)   At the track: post position special—number 8 P.P. in the first race. In selecting winning names of horses and jockeys, keep these letters in mind: I and R. You'll have luck today because a burden you should not have carried in first place will be lifted. Aries figures prominently.

Saturday, February 18 (Moon in Libra)   Lucky lottery: 1, 6, 15, 5, 27, 13. On this Saturday, enthusiasm replaces indifference. You experience a stimulating new deal. You'll be more alert, feel more alive; you'll be independent in thought and action. Today's scenario features sensuality, personal magnetism, fresh start, and sex appeal.

Sunday, February 19 (Moon in Libra to Scorpio 10:55 p.m.)   A partnership recently broken can be mended. The Spotlight falls on cooperative efforts, diplomacy, quality material, and large household products. You receive an encouraging report concerning your physical fitness. But you might also be cautioned to pay closer attention to diet or nutrition. Your lucky number is 2.

Monday, February 20 (Moon in Scorpio)   Expand your horizons. Indulge your intellectual curiosity. Thank someone who helped you obtain more working room, more space. You'll have reason to believe this is one of your most unusual Mondays. You'll feel like celebrating tonight. Gemini and Sagittarius play featured roles.

Tuesday, February 21 (Moon in Scorpio)   The emphasis is on commitment, reputation, credibility, and legal rights. You'll be tearing down in order to rebuild on a more secure base. The Scorpio moon accents partnership, public relations, and marital status. By 10 p.m. you'll agree, "Everything seems to be happening so quickly but so orderly!" Your lucky number is 4.

Wednesday, February 22 (Moon in Scorpio to Sagittarius 2:13 a.m.)   Lucky lottery: 5, 8, 22, 4, 33, 1. The emphasis is on public appearances, reputation, credibility, partnership, and marital status. By 8 p.m. you'll say, "Thank goodness, I am the winner!" Be sure to speak up. Gemini, Virgo, and Sagittarius play meaningful roles. Advertise your product.

Thursday, February 23 (Moon in Sagittarius)   Money that had been missing will be recovered. The financial status of someone close to you, perhaps your business partner or mate, will be revealed. You're due for a surprise, very likely pleasant. But avoid drawing conclusions based on rumors. A domestic adjustment proves beneficial; this involves your residence or marital status.

Friday, February 24 (Moon in Sagittarius to Capricorn 5:11 a.m.)   At the track: post position special—number 1 P.P. in the sixth race. A long-shot winner is likely to be featured in the sixth and ninth races. In making selections of winning horses and jockeys, be alert for these letters in their names: G, P, Y. See people and places in a realistic light. Pisces is represented.

Saturday, February 25 (Moon in Capricorn)   Focus on production and methodology, a deadline and an intense relationship. A favorable lunar aspect coincides with communication, publishing, advertising, and awareness of spiritual values. What seemed long ago and far away becomes part of today's events. Lucky lottery: 8, 16, 10, 44, 45, 46.

Sunday, February 26 (Moon in Capricorn to Aquarius 8:14 a.m.)   Stress universal appeal, opening lines of communication and welcoming a chance to learn a new language. A burden is lifted. You'll experience the thrill of greater freedom of thought and action. Begin making plans for exploration and travel. Aries and Libra figure in today's action.

Monday, February 27 (Moon in Aquarius) Break free from the prison of preconceived notions. Emphasize independence, originality, and the courage of your convictions. Love plays a major role. You'll feel more aware, alert, and alive. Leo and Aquarius take part in this interesting day. Special note: Avoid heavy lifting. Keep resolutions about diet, exercise, and nutrition.

Tuesday, February 28 (Moon in Aquarius to Pisces 12:16 p.m.) Attention revolves around direction, motivation, and a decision relating to the sale or purchase of property or a home. You'll receive this warning: "It now is up to you; you are in charge, the leader!" A Cancer in your life today could have a name with these letters: B, K, T.

MARCH 1995

Wednesday, March 1 (Moon in Pisces) Almost from the time you awaken, you'll sense, "This really is going to be a new day for me!" The Pisces new moon relates to fulfillment, persuasiveness, determination, and the ability to transform fantasies into realities. Focus on methodology, and the knowledge that you made the right decision and are going to prosper as a result. Your lucky number is 3.

Thursday, March 2 (Moon in Pisces to Aries 6:30 p.m.) At the track: post position special—number 4 P.P. in the fourth race. Pick six: 8, 5, 3, 4, 2, 2. Be alert for the letters D, M, V. in the names of horses and jockeys. By tonight, you'll be saying, "I only wish my luck could continue the way it has been for the past few days."

Friday, March 3 (Moon in Aries) You're drawn in two directions—to tell all or to keep quiet. The Aries moon highlights secretiveness, discretion, and a possible tour of a museum or hospital. Someone who has been out of sight communicates. Gemini, Virgo, and Sagittarius figure in today's scenario. Your lucky number is 5.

Saturday, March 4 (Moon in Aries)   Attention revolves around an unusual visit from someone who supposedly left town. Readjust your schedule—be diplomatic, but don't water down your principles. The spotlight falls on income potential, decorating, and remodeling. Accent your marital status, home, and lifestyle. Lucky lottery: 7, 16, 6, 50, 41, 42.

Sunday, March 5 (Moon in Aries to Taurus 3:50 a.m.)   The cycle moves up; what apparently was lost is due to be voluntarily returned. It won't be easy for others to fool you, but you could, unless you are careful, fall victim to self-deception. Define terms, get rid of extra material, streamline your procedures. Pisces plays a paramount role.

Monday, March 6 (Moon in Taurus)   Focus on an organization, a deadline, an intense relationship. You'll be dealing with older people, some of whom are affluent. Disregard persons who waste your time. This message becomes crystal clear by 7 p.m. Make personal appearances, wearing blue, indigo, or purple. Capricorn and Cancer figure prominently.

Tuesday, March 7 (Moon in Taurus to Gemini 3:55 p.m.)   You'll possess the secret of popularity. Previous rules and limitations no longer apply. The emphasis is on distance, language, a special communication relating to art or music, and a journey that could be overseas. You'll meet a dynamic Aries whose name has these letters: I and R.

Wednesday, March 8 (Moon in Gemini)   Take the initiative in connection with payments, collections, and investments. The spotlight also falls on emotional responses, and on a new deal where love is concerned. Stress independence, letting others, including that special person, know that you will no longer be taken for granted. Leo is represented.

Thursday, March 9 (Moon in Gemini)   On this Thursday, a decision is reached in connection with partnership,

223

cooperative efforts, reputation, image, the sale or purchase of property, or marriage. Those who thought you were left behind will be in for a rude awakening. Protect your interests; don't give up something of value for nothing.

Friday, March 10 (Moon in Gemini to Cancer 4:40 a.m.) The moon in your second house relates to a discovery that could eventually prove profitable. Stress versatility, giving full play to your intellectual curiosity. Caution: Keep your resolutions concerning diet and nutrition. Someone who attempts to demean you because of weight is jealous and mean spirited.

Saturday, March 11 (Moon in Cancer) Check the durability of goods; correct mechanical defects in your household products and your car. A relative who pays a surprise visit does not seem to care about inconveniencing you. Make clear that your private time is precious. Another Taurus is in the picture. Lucky lottery: 20, 4, 2, 12, 22, 33.

Sunday, March 12 (Moon in Cancer to Leo 3:28 p.m.) Today's scenario features questions and answers, written material, and close relatives, some of whom take you for granted. Express your feelings; get your ideas on paper. A change of scene is beneficial—welcome a variety of experiences. A chance meeting or mild flirtation could lead to something serious. Your lucky number is 5.

Monday, March 13 (Moon in Leo) Attention revolves around a domestic adjustment that could include a change of residence or marital status. Today's scenario includes music, gifts, flowers, and genuine tokens of affection and esteem. Caution: Remove fire hazards from your home. An outspoken Leo could deliberately provoke an argument. Your lucky number is 6.

Tuesday, March 14 (Moon in Leo to Virgo 10:54 p.m.) Play the waiting game. On this Tuesday, you'll realize that someone is attempting to put something over. Know when to draw the line. The spotlight is on real estate, division of property, and behind-the-scenes negotiations. Pisces and Virgo play memorable roles. The number 7 proves lucky.

Wednesday, March 15 (Moon in Virgo)   Focus on organization and the ability to bring order out of chaos. Family relationships require special attention. The green-eyed monster attempts a stranglehold—be wary, helping yourself and others to slay this vice. The emphasis is on color coordination in connection with improving the appearance of your home.

Thursday, March 16 (Moon in Virgo)   The Virgo moon trines or favorably aspects your Taurus sun. Translated, you'll be ready for a change of scene; you will be creative and sexy. You'll feel as if you've been released from bondage. Today's scenario highlights freedom of thought and action. Someone you admire will state, "You seem like a new person!" Libra figures prominently.

Friday, March 17 (Moon in Virgo to Libra 3:18 a.m.)   In celebrating the holiday, accent moderation, steering clear of heavy drinkers. The full moon coincides with impulsiveness and carelessness, especially in traffic. Take the initiative in getting to the heart of matters, especially where romance enters the picture. Face the truth as it exists. By so doing, you'll transform obstacles into stepping-stones.

Saturday, March 18 (Moon in Libra)   Lucky lottery: 2, 7, 6, 12, 40, 50. At the track: post position special—number 6 P.P. in the fifth race. Pick six: 4, 4, 3, 8, 6, 1. You'll be dealing with a Cancer likely to have a name with these letters: B, K, T. Attention also revolves around a commercial enterprise or the sale or purchase of property.

Sunday, March 19 (Moon in Libra to Scorpio 5:52 a.m.) What appeared to be an impossible task will be completed with help from a relative. Focus also on fitness, employment, pet ownership, and the ability to face and overcome obstacles. You'll be in touch with your inner feelings. Spiritual values will be much in evidence. A Sagittarian is involved.

Monday, March 20 (Moon in Scorpio)   At first you'll feel, "This is Monday and I feel it might be colored blue."

Later, however, confidence will build, as you reach more solid emotional and financial ground. Stay with the familiar; reject fantastic, get-rich-quick schemes. Protect your reputation; make a decision in connection with a marriage.

Tuesday, March 21 (Moon in Scorpio to Sagittarius 7:57 a.m.)   Be ready for a change, travel, variety, and the excitement of discovery. A gain is indicated through teaching, writing, and expressing your feelings in a dynamic, entertaining, informative way. You'll be more fully informed where legal affairs enter the scenario. Gemini, Virgo, and Sagittarius are represented.

Wednesday, March 22 (Moon in Sagittarius)   Those who thought you were behind schedule will be surprised—in fact, you are one step ahead of your competitors. Know it and proceed accordingly. Attention revolves around art objects, luxury items, income potential and a domestic adjustment that relates to your home or your marriage.

Thursday, March 23 (Moon in Sagittarius to Capricorn 10:31 a.m.)   You learn more about money, accounting procedures, hidden values, the financial status of someone who wants to be a close associate. Where love is concerned, the road is bumpy, but there is light at the end of the tunnel. You're going places, planned or otherwise. Pisces and Virgo play significant roles.

Friday, March 24 (Moon in Capricorn)   Attention revolves around organization, future prospects, spiritual values, and intense relationships. The spotlight falls on your ability to bring order out of chaos. The lunar position highlights your awareness of what's going on, when and where. Capricorn and Cancer play outstanding roles.

Saturday, March 25 (Moon in Capricorn to Aquarius 2:10 p.m.)   Look beyond the immediate, making plans for travel, a publishing venture, or a possible advertising campaign. You'll have luck in matters of speculation—you might try these lucky lottery numbers: 9, 1, 19, 44, 45, 50. A project will be completed because of your personal efforts. Aries is involved.

Sunday, March 26 (Moon in Aquarius)   Make a fresh start in a new direction—the Aquarian moon highlights leadership, promotion, production, and your ability to take greater charge of your own destiny. Don't compromise your principles—a quarrelsome person will attempt to intimidate. Leo and Aquarius figure prominently. Your lucky number is 1.

Monday, March 27 (Moon in Aquarius to Pisces 7:18 p.m.)   Focus on marital status, property, direction, and motivation. You could win a contest involving restaurants or food. A reunion with a loved one might include gourmet dining. Someone at the top acts in an eccentric way. Keep your own options open. Capricorn and Cancer figure in today's dynamic scenario.

Tuesday, March 28 (Moon in Pisces)   Diversify, experiment, ask questions, reject superficial responses. Purchase clothing, realize you do look fine despite sensitivity about your body image. A Sagittarian says, "You are the cat's meow!" As the Moon leaves Aquarius, you'll be complimented on the way you handled a recent emergency.

Wednesday, March 29 (Moon in Pisces)   By helping a Pisces, you'll be setting the stage for future cooperation and possible riches. The person in question is likely to have a name with these letters: D, M, V. Build on a solid base; give serious consideration to a change of business address. Scorpio also figures prominently.

Thursday, March 30 (Moon in Pisces to Aries 2:26 a.m.)   You'll win friends and influence people as your popularity rating soars. Suddenly you feel free to express ideas, to read and write, to learn through the process of teaching others. Romance will not be a stranger. Your creative juices stir. Pay attention to a notice enabling you to enter a contest. You might win! Your lucky number is 5.

Friday, March 31 (Moon in Aries)   On this last day of March, there is a new moon in Aries, representing your twelfth house—this means you gain enlightenment in areas previously confusing. Focus also on beautifying your surroundings. You could receive a gift representing a token of affection or esteem.

APRIL 1995

Saturday, April 1 (Moon in Aries to Taurus 11:59 a.m.) Anyone who attempts to deceive you will be caught red-handed. You'll be familiar with the axiom, "It's fun to be fooled but not to be deceived." Insist on quality, get written guarantees, replace outworn machinery. Check the oil and water in your car. Lucky lottery: 4, 40, 8, 18, 25, 1.

Sunday, April 2 (Moon in Taurus; Daylight Saving Time Begins) The cycle jumps up. You'll exercise more freedom of thought and action. The Taurus moon highlights your personality, dedication, and magnetic appeal to members of the opposite sex. You'll profit from written material. Be analytical; don't permit others to take you for granted. Your lucky number is 5.

Monday, April 3 (Moon in Taurus) You'll receive a gift during the late afternoon, which represents a token of affection. Attention revolves around your home, income potential, or marital status. You get almost everything you want if you are diplomatic, but at the same time do not compromise your principles. Libra and another Taurus play outstanding roles.

Tuesday, April 4 (Moon in Taurus to Gemini 12:49 a.m. EDT) Define your terms, outline your boundaries, check real estate advertisements. Your cycle remains high, so your judgment and intuition are on target. Make personal appearances, wearing shades of blue, indigo, and purple. Steer clear of a heavy drinker. End a relationship with someone who cannot seem to keep promises.

Wednesday, April 5 (Moon in Gemini) Lucky lottery: 8, 21, 5, 44, 49, 3. At the track: post position special—

number 8 P.P. in the eighth race. In choosing the names of potential winning horses and jockeys keep these letters in mind: H, Q, Z. An older person lends the benefit of experience, saying, "You're most important to me!"

Thursday, April 6 (Moon in Gemini to Cancer 1:40 p.m.)   The cycle is high for money, travel, communication, and awareness of spiritual values. You'll overcome barriers, including distance and language. The Gemini moon coincides with your ability to locate a product that was lost, missing, or stolen. By tonight, you'll feel like a big winner. Your lucky number is 9.

Friday, April 7 (Moon in Cancer)   Stress independence. Be willing to participate in a pioneering project. Important note: Avoid heavy lifting. A Cancer will become your valuable ally. Gratitude is expressed for a service you recently performed. You'll meet a Leo with these letters in his or her name: A, S, J.

Saturday, April 8 (Moon in Cancer)   Lucky lottery: 2, 4, 40, 12, 19, 7. Attention revolves around property values, basic issues, a reunion with a loved one. If you're single, you're serious about marriage prospects. If you are married, you might be anticipating an addition to your family. Married or single, you regain your sense of direction and motivation.

Sunday, April 9 (Moon in Cancer to Leo 1:16 a.m.) Finish what you start, encouraging a family member to go out in the world and conquer it. Emphasize fun, frolic, and intellectual curiosity. Add to your wardrobe, be proud of your body image. A link will be broken in connection with an obligation you should not have undertaken. Shout, "Free at last!"

Monday, April 10 (Moon in Leo)   Read between the lines, keep your options open, test the durability of goods. An older person says, "You have proven your point; you most certainly are capable of handling this assignment." Be willing to tear down in order to rebuild on a more suitable base. Scorpio and another Taurus figure prominently.

Tuesday, April 11 (Moon in Leo to Virgo 9:29 a.m.)   You'll have more room; you'll get your ideas on paper; you'll agree to a short trip with a close relative, mate, or colleague. Express your views, letting others know you are more than a beautiful face. Within a few days, you might be involved in a romance you had no intention of getting involved with in the first place.

Wednesday, April 12 (Moon in Virgo)   There's music in your life, as well as creative projects and luck in matters of speculation. The Virgo moon relates to personal magnetism, sensuality, style, panache, and sex appeal. Today's scenario highlights an exciting discovery, and a variety of experiences. Protect yourself in close quarters, refusing to be cajoled into an immoral act.

Thursday, April 13 (Moon in Virgo to Libra 2:20 p.m.)   Today's scenario features illusion, romance, creativity, and your ability to make your dreams come true. The spotlight falls on children, change, travel, and a variety of sensations and experiences. You'll be saying, "This is one Thursday I will not soon forget!" Be analytical about a unique relationship.

Friday, April 14 (Moon in Libra)   Refuse to be thwarted by someone who cares little for your reputation. Accent organization, credibility, responsibility, and the awareness of your potential. The spotlight is on work methods, modus operandi, employment, diet, nutrition, and fitness. Capricorn and Cancer play major roles. Your lucky number is 8.

Saturday, April 15 (Moon in Libra to Scorpio 4:13 p.m.)   The full moon, lunar eclipse in Libra, could create shake-ups in routine, employment, and dealings with dependents. Focus on travel, popularity, and investigation of import–export opportunities. Promote your talents and products. Refuse to be limited by outmoded rules and regulations.

Sunday, April 16 (Moon in Scorpio)   Light is shed on various accounts. Display courage; take the initiative in getting to the heart of matters. Focus on mystery, intrigue, and romantic attachment. This could be a day when you decide to break away from negative influences. A Leo involved could have a name with these letters: A, S, J.

Monday, April 17 (Moon in Scorpio to Sagittarius 4:51 p.m.) Your sense of direction is emphasized. The spotlight falls on motivation, cooperative efforts, public relations, and greater understanding of legal rights and permissions. The Scorpio moon emphasizes decisions relating to your marriage. Tonight features gourmet dining and a reunion with someone who recently was out of your life.

Tuesday, April 18 (Moon in Sagittarius) Keep plans flexible, options open. Someone who originally called the shots may no longer be in charge. Keep your balance, humor, and alertness. Be willing to take charge of your own fate and destiny. Gemini and Sagittarius play significant roles. Your lucky number is 3.

Wednesday, April 19 (Moon in Sagittarius to Capricorn 5:54 p.m.) Attention revolves around tax and license requirements and the possibility of legitimate savings in connection with your investments. An obstacle that involves distance and language will be overcome. You could learn more about a possible inheritance, hidden resources, or the financial status of your partner or mate.

Thursday, April 20 (Moon in Capricorn) All indications point to freedom of expression and the ability to let go of the status quo. Lunar and numerical cycles highlight communication and knowledge of language, foreign lands, and unusual customs. A flirtation tonight could lead to something more than you expected. Sagittarius is involved.

Friday, April 21 (Moon in Capricorn to Aquarius 8:38 p.m.) Protect yourself in emotional clinches. The emphasis is on permanent relationships, including marriage. Your romantic attitude is spotlighted, including the search for your soul mate. Music is in your life tonight—someone interesting pays a meaningful compliment, which sends your morale soaring.

Saturday, April 22 (Moon in Aquarius)   Lucky lottery: 10, 8, 17, 36, 12, 45. Keep your aura of mystery, realizing that if you tell all, people will lose interest. You'll feel more alive as your individual style surfaces. Check real estate opportunities, looking behind the scenes for answers. Communicate with someone confined to home or hospital.

Sunday, April 23 (Moon in Aquarius)   Others realize you do mean business—you'll be asked to organize, to work overtime, to make a commitment in connection with your career, business, or love life. Halfway measures won't do— it is going to be all or nothing. Capricorn and Cancer play memorable roles. Your lucky number is 8.

Monday, April 24 (Moon in Aquarius to Pisces 1:51 a.m.) Previous limitations no longer apply—know it and reach for brass ring. Focus on style, panache, creativity, and self-expression. A love relationship is bittersweet. What you seek will be found through cooperation by someone at a distance, perhaps from a foreign land. Aries plays a meaningful role.

Tuesday, April 25 (Moon in Pisces)   Your wishes come true in a startling way. You'll have luck in speculation, romance, and finance. The answer to your question: Being comfortable is not enough—shake loose from the prison of preconceived notions. Emphasize original thinking, courage, and getting started on a new project.

Wednesday, April 26 (Moon in Pisces to Aries 9:41 a.m.) Lucky lottery: 12, 7, 27, 33, 45, 1. Attention revolves around partnerships, business prospects, and property appraisal. Your marital status dominates part of today's scenario. By following your psychic impressions, you gain your objective. Use elements of timing and surprise. Capricorn is involved.

Thursday, April 27 (Moon in Aries)   What was fearful will become the cause of laughter. The Aries moon highlights secrets, a unique mission, and private dining with someone who compliments you on your taste, style, and sense of privacy. Accent the exclusive, insist on quality, add to your wardrobe. Gemini and Sagittarius play outstanding roles.

Friday, April 28 (Moon in Aries to Taurus 7:53 p.m.) Ride with the tide; don't force issues, for what you seek will be made available. Focus on the rebuilding process. You may develop a secret arrangement with someone who sincerely has your best interests at heart. Scorpio plays a key role, and could have a name with these letters or initials: D, M, V.

Saturday, April 29 (Moon in Taurus) The new moon, solar eclipse in your sign coincides with a fresh start, a chance to shake off lethargy, an opportunity to be freewheeling. Lucky lottery: 15, 5, 12, 27, 8, 4. At the track: post position special—number 4 P.P. in the fourth race. In choosing winning horses or jockeys, stick to the veterans. "Youngsters" simply will not have it today.

Sunday, April 30 (Moon in Taurus) Focus on music, color coordination, and a domestic adjustment that might involve your home or marital status and require a financial maneuver. Be diplomatic without diluting your principles. Another Taurus figures prominently, and could have a name with these letters: F, O, X. Your lucky number is 6.

MAY 1995

Monday, May 1 (Moon in Taurus to Gemini 7:53 a.m.) The month begins on your high cycle—this will be anything but a blue Monday. The emphasis is on a variety of sensations and experiences. The tendency is to act impulsively—give logic equal time. A friend could become a lover. On the horizon is a financial windfall. Be confident, realizing you are on the right track and will be rewarded.

Tuesday, May 2 (Moon in Gemini) Attention revolves around money, payments, collections, and a domestic adjustment that could include decorating, remodeling, or a possible change of residence. Focus also on marital status, diet and nutrition, and added information concerning recipes and food preparation. Libra and another Taurus figure in this exciting scenario.

Wednesday, May 3 (Moon in Gemini to Cancer 8:45 p.m.) The cycle is high where money is concerned— missing material will be located. Check real estate notices, find out what is expected of you and what you can anticipate in return for your efforts. Make your terms crystal clear. Lucky lottery: 7, 14, 18, 31, 50, 5. Pisces is represented.

Thursday, May 4 (Moon in Cancer) On this Thursday you'll be called upon to bring order out of chaos. A relationship grows intense; you'll be more aware of your own abilities and talents. Refuse to be taken for granted; insist on payment for contributions and efforts, and say no to whispers of sweet nothings. Cancer is involved.

Friday, May 5 (Moon in Cancer) At the track: post position special—number 8 P.P. in the ninth race. Alternate selection: number 4 P.P. in the eighth race. Pick six: 4, 7, 8, 1, 2, 5. In selecting names of potential winning jockeys and horses, check for these letters or initials: I and R. Aries and Libra play major roles.

Saturday, May 6 (Moon in Cancer to Leo 8:55 a.m.) Lucky lottery: 20, 2, 6, 1, 16, 30. You're due for a fresh start. You get the proverbial second chance. You tend now to be introspective, to hide your light under a bushel. Emerge, confront the public, show the courage of your convictions! A short trip involves a dynamic Leo. Seek counsel concerning entertainment.

Sunday, May 7 (Moon in Leo) Attention revolves around home, security, investments, partnership, and marital status. You'll be concerned with the durability of goods, quality material, and the seriousness of a relationship. Regain your sense of direction, discern motives, check with a female family member for the inside story. Your lucky number is 2.

Monday, May 8 (Moon in Leo to Virgo 6:33 p.m.) Diversify, accenting showmanship, entertainment, and drama. New clothes are featured. You'll look just fine and you'll be pleased with your image. A sense of the ridiculous surges to the forefront. You'll make people laugh, even through their tears. Gemini and Sagittarius play meaningful roles. Your lucky number is 3.

Tuesday, May 9 (Moon in Virgo) A relationship undergoes a minor crisis. That closed-in feeling is only temporary, while you revise many ideas and attitudes. You'll be capable on this Tuesday of freeing yourself from the prison of preconceived notions. A Scorpio, whose name could have these letters—D, M, V—could play an important role in your life.

Wednesday, May 10 (Moon in Virgo) You'll use your head as well as your heart today. This power commands first place, and will not permit impulsiveness to dominate. By 10 p.m. you'll be happy you listened to the voice of logic and kept emotions under control. The Virgo moon also coincides with creativity, variety, personal magnetism, sensuality, and sex appeal.

Thursday, May 11 (Moon in Virgo to Libra 12:30 a.m.) The spotlight falls on children, change, travel, variety, and domestic adjustment. There is music in your life tonight. You'll hear the sound of your inner voice. You cannot possibly go wrong by following your conscience. If you think you can get around integrity you merely ar fooling yourself. Your lucky number is 6.

Friday, May 12 (Moon in Libra) The emphasis is on health, work methods, and the ability to know when to draw the line. Some people mistakenly think you are a pushover—to their sorrow, they find out differently! Get rid of unessential material, streamlining your procedures. Be crystal clear about what you want.

Saturday, May 13 (Moon in Libra to Scorpio 2:53 a.m.) Lucky lottery: 8, 7, 6, 12, 33, 22. Attention revolves around a time limitation and extra duties. You have a chance to improve your position and to hit the financial jackpot. If you are merely playing games, move on. If you are serious, you can succeed with amazing speed. An older person has good advice—listen!

Sunday, May 14 (Moon in Scorpio) The full moon in your house of marriage indicates that a decision is made in connection with a partnership, public relations, romance, or your marital status. Have confidence; what you fear will turn out to be the proverbial paper tiger. A burden will be lifted. You gain added popularity. Correspondence from overseas could involve import–export activities.

Monday, May 15 (Moon in Scorpio to Sagittarius 2:58 a.m.) Unless you are careful, a situation could become too hot to handle. The Scorpio moon emphasizes intensity. You could have the tendency to become inextricably involved with a situation or individual. Let go of a losing proposition, and that includes stocks. It's time for the new. It's time to remove the outmoded. Your lucky number is 1.

Tuesday, May 16 (Moon in Sagittarius) You'll learn more about money and how it is earned; you'll also be surprised to learn that your possessions are worth more than you thought. Your business partner, professional associate, or mate reveals hidden resources. You'll be saying, "This is one Tuesday I won't soon forget!"

Wednesday, May 17 (Moon in Sagittarius to Capricorn 2:36 a.m.) Lucky lottery: 3, 33, 9, 6, 28, 5. Highlight versatility and humor; display wit and wisdom. You'll receive a gift during the late afternoon that relates to clothing; it could also be cosmetics or fascinating reading material. Be receptive, showing that you are capable of laughing at your own foibles. Sagittarius is involved.

Thursday, May 18 (Moon in Capricorn) A favorable lunar aspect coincides with travel, education, and participation in a unique mission. Focus also on advertising, publishing, communication, and the search for romance. You'll be dealing with lively people who are likely to have these letters in their names: D, M. V. Be thorough; check references.

Friday, May 19 (Moon in Capricorn to Aquarius 3:39 a.m.) Suddenly it's Freedom Road! This means the past is cleared of debris; you'll have more freedom of thought and action. You might also find that flirtation lends spice, but might lead to complications. You'll be dealing with a Virgo who is likely to have these letters or: E, N, W. Your lucky number is 5.

Saturday, May 20 (Moon in Aquarius) Lucky lottery: 11, 6, 20, 12, 13, 33. Attention revolves around changes in connection with your home, property, income, or marital status. The outlook is favorable, especially if you are diplomatic. Conversely, if you attempt to force issues, you could lose. The choice is your own, so act accordingly.

Sunday, May 21 (Moon in Aquarius to Pisces 8:40 a.m.) Focus on spirituality, leadership, and your ability to set the pace and the standards. Define terms, making your meanings crystal clear. Answers are found behind the scenes— the emphasis is on the subtle. Don't tell all—keep an aura of mystery, glamour, and intrigue. A Pisces will be stimulated and inspired just by being near you.

Monday, May 22 (Moon in Pisces) On this Monday you'll be saying, "I've had fair warning; I'm being tested and I intend to come through with flying colors!" Since a deadline exists, the key is to organize, to put together the puzzle pieces and come up with a complete story. Capricorn and Cancer play unique roles. Your lucky number is 8.

Tuesday, May 23 (Moon in Moon in Pisces to Aries 3:13 p.m.) Be willing to take risks in connection with love. The Pisces moon guarantees that you'll win powerful allies, using persuasiveness to fulfill your aspiration. Under this aspect, you'll make both money and love. You'll exude an aura of universal appeal—people will be drawn to you with their most intimate questions and problems.

237

Wednesday, May 24 (Moon in Aries)   Lucky lottery: 1, 10, 9, 36, 44, 45. At the track: post position special—number 7 P.P. in the third race. Pick six: 1, 5, 7, 3, 8, 4. In choosing the names of potential winning horses and jockeys, be aware of these letters: A, S, J. A Leo lends spice to your life, helping in connection with decisions relating to your property and your durable goods.

Thursday, May 25 (Moon in Aries)   The emphasis is on marital status, home, property, and family relationships. You regain motivation, sense of direction, and a desire to proceed with a project recently stopped. A secret meeting blends romance, adventure, and business. Your gift today is that you will positively relish, enjoy what you do. Wonderful!

Friday, May 26 (Moon in Aries to Taurus 1:47 a.m.)   As your cycle moves up, you might be humming, "Tonight we live!" The spotlight falls on fun, frivolity, versatility, diversification, and a different mode of transportation. A secret romance is dangerous but thrilling. This message becomes crystal clear by 11 p.m. Gemini and Sagittarius figure in today's scenario.

Saturday, May 27 (Moon in Taurus)   Lucky lottery: 4, 3, 20, 12, 18, 33, 22. The moon in your sign coincides with selectivity, your high cycle, personal appeal, independence, and progress. Judgment and intuition, strike bull's-eye. You do best on your own. You dilute your strength by listening to people who think they know best how to live your life.

Sunday, May 28 (Moon in Taurus to Gemini 2:07 p.m.)   Be ready for change, travel, variety, and the delineation of theories and complicated subjects. A roadblock is removed. There's clear sailing, if you exhibit the courage of your convictions. Scorpio and another Taurus could become valuable allies. Both could have these letters or initials in their names: D, M, V.

Monday, May 29 (Moon in Gemini)   The new Gemini moon coincides with a financial breakthrough—what appeared to be a loss will boomerang in your favor. A different approach enables you to locate the missing link. You'll be riding high, so refuse to be discouraged by someone who lacks talent and faith. Libra and another Taurus figure prominently.

Tuesday, May 30 (Moon in Gemini)   Define terms, seeing places and people in a more realistic light. You'll have access to valid investment information. Your cycle continues high, so stress independence, originality, and innovativeness. Another Taurus says, "Stop hiding your light under a bushel!" That's sound advice—heed it! The number 7 plays a mysterious role in your scenario.

Wednesday, May 31 (Moon in Gemini to Cancer 2:59 a.m.)   On this last day of May, news is received concerning insurance, mortgage, automobile payments, a deadline. A love relationship is exciting and controversial, but will prove durable. Plans become more flexible, especially in connection with money management. Lucky lottery: 30, 3, 4, 12, 17, 18.

JUNE 1995

Thursday, June 1 (Moon in Cancer)   Throughout June, your financial picture will show marked improvement. You'll be dealing with bright people who appreciate your talent and potential. Many of those persons are likely to have these letters or initials in their names: E, N. W. On this Thursday, attention revolves around home, marital status, where you live, and your lifestyle.

Friday, June 2 (Moon in Cancer to Leo 3:17 p.m.)   On this second day of June, you learn more about real estate and the durability of goods; you could also purchase large household products and be very much concerned with partnership, reputation, credibility, legal rights, and marriage. Admittedly, very busy—but you of all people can handle it! Pisces plays a paramount role.

Saturday, June 3 (Moon in Leo)   Lucky lottery: 8, 15, 14, 5, 1, 12. At the track: post position special—number 4

239

P.P. in the eighth race. Pick six: 8, 5, 4, 7, 2, 2. In selecting names of potential winning horses or jockeys, be aware of these letters in names: H, Q, Z. Cancer and Capricorn play instrumental roles in helping you achieve your goal.

Sunday, June 4 (Moon in Leo)   Finish what you start. Check guarantees and the durability of goods; make amends to a relative who feels he or she is always being left alone. You'll be dealing with a fiery Leo whose name is likely to have these letters: I and R. A long-distance communication alerts you to the possibility of a journey, perhaps overseas.

Monday, June 5 (Moon in Leo to Virgo 1:46 a.m.)   A fresh point of view is necessary in connection with a possible sale or the purchase of business or property. You'll be temporarily introspective, but the mood will change by noon. Take a bold step into the future, letting go of the status quo. Leo, Aquarius play significant roles. Your lucky number is 1.

Tuesday, June 6 (Moon in Virgo)   What had been divided will be drawn together—focus on a family reunion, romance, creativity, and marital status. The Virgo moon coincides with personal magnetism, a variety of experiences, intellectual curiosity, and physical attraction. A young person chooses you as a role model. A Cancer is involved.

Wednesday, June 7 (Moon in Virgo to Libra 9:13 a.m.) Keep your options open; plans are subject to change due to a social invitation. Romance flourishes; you'll be musing, "Now I know I am alive and glad of it!" Focus on vitality, confidence, and inspiration. Gemini and Sagittarius figure in today's dynamic scenario. Lucky lottery: 3, 5, 8, 17, 48, 6.

Thursday, June 8 (Moon in Libra)   The employment situation will be straightened out to your advantage. You'll learn the tricks of the trade. The emphasis is on locks and keys, methodology, and the ability to transform obstacles into stepping-stones toward the ultimate goal. You'll meet a challenge and a deadline with alacrity. Your lucky number is 4.

Friday, June 9 (Moon in Libra to Scorpio 1:03 p.m.)   As this weekend approaches, you'll be pleased with your appearance. You have the opportunity to set the record straight. Love will not be unrequited. The focus is on distance, language, your ability to bring a project back to life. Gemini, Virgo, and Sagittarius figure in today's interesting scenario.

Saturday, June 10 (Moon in Scorpio)   Lucky lottery: 6, 10, 12, 8, 33, 15. Attention revolves around decorating, remodeling, and a domestic adjustment that could include your home, your lifestyle and your marital status. Color coordination and music play featured roles. Your partnership proposal deserves serious consideration. Legal rights are featured.

Sunday, June 11 (Moon in Scorpio to Sagittarius 1:50 p.m.)   Spiritual values surface; hidden resources are revealed. You'll define terms and be happy as a result. See people, places, and situations as they actually are, not merely as you wish they might be. Streamline procedures, getting rid of extra material. The Scorpio moon spotlights legal affairs, public appearances, and marriage.

Monday, June 12 (Moon in Sagittarius)   Don't skip basics—check references and be aware of time limitation. Focus on a relationship that is exciting and controversial and that will ultimately prove durable. An older person lends the benefit of experience, and tells you, "I am betting on you to succeed, to be a big winner!" Capricorn plays a role.

Tuesday, June 13 (Moon in Sagittarius to Capricorn 1:05 p.m.)   The full moon position coincides with financial arrangements being handled by another, possibly your agent or business manager. A decision is reached on whether to continue along the same path or to break through to a different area that allows you more freedom of thought and action.

241

Wednesday, June 14 (Moon in Capricorn)   Lucky lottery: 1, 10, 8, 50, 45, 3. Highlight your original approach, independence, and willingness to stop hitting yourself with sledgehammer words such as "might have," "could have," and "should have." Express your own style, emphasizing your individuality. Leo and Aquarius figure in today's exciting scenario.

Thursday, June 15 (Moon in Capricorn to Aquarius 12:52 p.m.)   What seemed long ago and far away is back on center stage. Focus on durable goods, household products, and your marital status. The lunar position highlights a unique study group, communication, and the ability to enlarge your horizons. Cancer and Capricorn play outstanding roles. Your lucky number is 2.

Friday, June 16 (Moon in Aquarius)   Obstacles are removed. You'll receive direct answers to questions as contrasted to the more recent evasions. The spotlight is on versatility, diversity, and new modes of transportation. Your popularity increases; social activities accelerate. Gemini and Sagittarius figure prominently. Your lucky number is 3.

Saturday, June 17 (Moon in Aquarius to Pisces 3:13 p.m.)   Check the details, review references, know that finally you are on a more solid emotional–financial ground. A Scorpio plays a key role, and could have a name with these letters: D, M, V. Be willing to rebuild and remodel, to investigate the possibility of obtaining a different address.

Sunday, June 18 (Moon in Pisces)   Be ready for swift changes, and a variety of experiences—take notes, express ideas via the written word. A chance meeting, possibly with a Gemini, could lead to an interesting relationship. The focus is also on leadership, promotion, production, and added prestige. Virgo and Sagittarius also play significant roles.

Monday, June 19 (Moon in Pisces to Aries 9:29 p.m.)   What a Monday! Events transpire at a fast pace. The Pisces moon coincides with your ability to win friends,

242

to make wishes come true, and to exult in romance and finance. A domestic adjustment is also featured, which includes beautifying your surroundings or improving your marriage. Libra figures in today's scenario.

Tuesday, June 20 (Moon in Aries)   Focus on imagination, sensitivity, and psychic impressions. Discern the truth; avoid shams. Define terms and outline boundaries, letting others know you do mean business. Get rid of extra material and unnecessary expenses. Pisces and Virgo play outstanding roles. Your lucky number is 7.

Wednesday, June 21 (Moon in Aries)   Lucky lottery: 21, 10, 9, 7, 8, 45. An older person confides a secret plan. You might feel bowled over, but don't let it become obvious. Accent your maturity, aplomb, elan. A chance exists for promotion, additional production, a financial coup. A relationship becomes intense. A decision is made on whether or not to continue the status quo.

Thursday, June 22 (Moon in Aries to Taurus 7:35 a.m.) Finish what you start, refusing to be deterred by a belligerent person who knows the price of everything and the value of nothing. Emphasize universal appeal; break free from foolish restrictions. You'll be surprised by someone you admire, who has a personal problem and seeks your guidance.

Friday, June 23 (Moon in Taurus)   At the track: post position special—number 7 P.P. in the third race. Pick six: 1, 5, 7, 6, 8, 8. In selecting names of potential winning horses or jockeys, keep these letters in mind: A, S, J. Today's scenario features new friends, fresh concepts, and the chance to be more independent in thought or action.

Saturday, June 24 (Moon in Taurus to Gemini 8:02 p.m.)   Lucky lottery: 8, 2, 12, 6, 50, 1, 9. Focus on marital status, value of property, and ability to regain your sense of direction. You'll reunite with someone you originally felt had abandoned you. You might be saying, "My prayers have been answered!" You'll be on more solid emotional–financial ground. A Cancer is involved.

243

Sunday, June 25 (Moon in Gemini)   As your cycle moves up, your judgment and intuition prove valid. Emphasize independence, expressing your style and wearing your colors—blue, indigo, and purple. Diversify, and be sure to express opinions regarding a public figure—your views will be appreciated and you'll be complimented on your perception and humor. Your lucky number is 3.

Monday, June 26 (Moon in Gemini)   What begins as routine could become an exciting assignment. The Gemini moon highlights increased income. You can now locate the missing link. You'll be rewarded for your efforts, past and present. Tear down in order to rebuild, accenting quality, durability. Scorpio and another Taurus play significant roles.

Tuesday, June 27 (Moon in Gemini to Cancer 8:56 a.m.)   The emphasis is on dialogue, repartee, and a display of your wit and wisdom. Get your ideas on paper, be inventive and daring, confide in someone who recently expressed confidence and offered encouragement. A chance meeting or blind date could become more serious than you anticipated. Sagittarius plays a meaningful role.

Wednesday, June 28 (Moon in Cancer)   The new moon position accents trips, visits, and relatives. The numerical cycle promotes a domestic adjustment that could include a change of residence or marital status. You'll be more financially secure; you finally get credit for contributions previously overlooked. Lucky lottery: 6, 20, 2, 4, 15, 50.

Thursday, June 29 (Moon in Cancer to Leo 9:02 p.m.)   The answers are found via meditation—be quiet within, realizing that being alone has nothing to do with being lonely. You'll be reassured of love. The key is to be serene and reflective. Look behind the scenes, refusing to be intimidated by someone who is mediocre at best. Pisces plays a role.

Friday, June 30 (Moon in Leo)   On this last day of June, you'll be delighted to receive back pay, a royalty check, or a refund. A recent contact with a Capricorn proved fruitful. A long-distance call makes you realize that people do take you seriously and appreciate your efforts. A current relationship is exciting and controversial, but will prove durable.

JULY 1995

Saturday, July 1 (Moon in Leo)   A behind-the-scenes meeting relates to preparations for the upcoming holiday. This includes a relative who recently said, "I always feel left out of everything!" Define terms, perfect techniques, and get rid of unnecessary expenses and worn-out material. Pisces is involved. Lucky lottery: 7, 12, 17, 50, 25, 4.

Sunday, July 2 (Moon in Leo to Virgo 7:35 a.m.)   A family disagreement is not as serious as first indicated. Responsibility and money are involved. The spotlight is on durable goods, household products, and a decision relating to the sale or purchase of property. Someone you admire says, "You are the one who can make order out of chaos!" Cancer plays a role.

Monday, July 3 (Moon in Virgo)   Check your holiday list, including duties and invitations. Be aware of safety requirements, do research relating to the birth of this nation. You'll be dealing with a frivolous person who makes many promises and is charming, but has no concept of time. Obviously, if you want anything done, do it yourself. Your lucky number is 9.

Tuesday, July 4 (Moon in Virgo to Libra 3:55 p.m.)   On this holiday, bright lights shine. You'll be in a leadership role, as others look to you for information and inspiration. The Virgo moon plus the number 1 numerical cycle adds up to creativity, style, personal magnetism, and sex appeal. Love will not go unrequited. Leo and Aquarius figure in today's dynamic scenario.

Wednesday, July 5 (Moon in Libra)   The emphasis is on marital status, home economics, and participation in commercial enterprise spotlighting products that appeal to women. With your sense of direction regained, you'll learn more about motivation and sales promotion. A fitness report provides encouragement. Capricorn and Cancer dominate the scenario.

Thursday, July 6 (Moon in Libra to Scorpio 9:19 p.m.)   Focus on versatility, humor, and your sense of the ridiculous. You can puncture stuffed shirts. The Libra moon highlights employment, basic procedures, and pet ownership. You may hear from someone who relies upon your care and generosity. You'll shine tonight within your family circle or during a dinner date.

Friday, July 7 (Moon in Scorpio)   Check the details; be aware of the latest reference material. The spotlight continues to fall on methodology, modus operandi, and the possibility of hidden options. Put aside superfluous material—be direct, getting to the heart of matters. Leo, Scorpio, and another Taurus play meaningful roles. Your lucky number is 4.

Saturday, July 8 (Moon in Scorpio to Sagittarius 11:38 p.m.)   Lucky lottery: 5, 22, 8, 13, 3, 7. You'll be undergoing a transition period. Examine all the possibilities, analyze character, and be sure someone you deal with takes these words seriously: Honor, dedication, and integrity. Protect yourself at close quarters. Look out for the low blow! Gemini figures prominently.

Sunday, July 9 (Moon in Sagittarius)   At a family gathering, a domestic adjustment takes place. The scenario features music, harmony and a reunion with a person who was previously distant. Don't permit pride to deter your progress or eliminate a chance for happiness. Libra and another Taurus play featured roles.

Monday, July 10 (Moon in Sagittarius to Capricorn 11:44 p.m.)   Those who thought you were one step behind will be stunned by the realization that you are really one step ahead. This becomes crystal clear no later than 6 p.m. You'll know what's going on before most people are aware of these happenings. Focus on a possible inheritance, and on the financial status of your mate or partner.

Tuesday, July 11 (Moon in Capricorn)   Check time requirements; consult an older person who is willing to share the benefit of experience. You'll have intimate dealings with a Capricorn likely to have these letters, initials in his or her name: H, Q, Z. use lessons learned 8 weeks ago. Your lucky number is 8.

Wednesday, July 12 (Moon in Capricorn to Aquarius 11:21 p.m.)   The full moon in Capricorn equates to travel, romance, idealism, and communication. You could publish and advertise a unique product or mission. What some considered a half-baked idea will come to fruition. You'll be vindicated, even celebrated. Be your most charming self. On all upcoming trip, you might meet your soul mate.

Thursday, July 13 (Moon in Aquarius)   You'll see people and places in ways that are both romantic and practical. You'll be asking yourself, "Is it realistic to believe that I can actually begin again?" Focus on philosophy, poetry, or a special talent required to promote an unusual concept. Leo and Aquarius are involved, and are likely to have these letters in their names: A, S, J.

Friday, July 14 (Moon in Aquarius)   You'll be riding a double harness. This means you won't be standing alone—focus on motivation, partnership, a property sale or purchase, and your marital status. What appeared to be long ago and far away is so close you can almost touch it. Check plumbing, and get guarantees relating to the durability of goods.

Saturday, July 15 (Moon in Aquarius to Pisces 12:37 a.m.) Lucky lottery: 3, 11, 23, 7, 4, 40. On this Saturday, you'll be musing, "I am grateful for the gift I have that makes people smile, even though they might feel as if they want to cry." Deal gingerly with a Sagittarian likely to have a name with these letters: C, L, U. Double-check your schedule.

Sunday, July 16 (Moon in Pisces)   A task that seems monotonous will ultimately prove worthwhile, perhaps even exciting. The Pisces moon equates to your ability to win friends and influence people, from the low and the lonely to the high and the mighty. You'll have luck in matters of finance and romance. Scorpio figures prominently.

Monday, July 17 (Moon in Pisces to Aries 5:23 a.m.)   The spotlight falls on curiosity, your writing ability, and a flirtation or a blind date that lends spice to the scenario. You'll be saying, "This certainly is no blue Monday!" The accent is on change, travel, variety, and communication from a member of the opposite sex who confides, "I made a wrong decision, I wish I were with you!"

Tuesday, July 18 (Moon in Aries)   The focus is on home, security, a family relationship, and a possible change of residence or marital status. A secret arrangement relates to your budget, sales and purchases, and the possibility of music lessons. Someone whose opinions you respect might state, "Inside you is a talent that must surface!" Your lucky number is 6.

Wednesday, July 19 (Moon in Aries to Taurus 2:20 p.m.)   Psychic impressions prove valid, especially in matters of speculation. The number 7 will play a prominent role. Lucky lottery: 7, 17, 28, 19, 33, 22. Define terms, find out what is expected of you and what you can anticipate in return. Pisces and Virgo figure in this scenario.

Thursday, July 20 (Moon in Taurus)   Your cycle moves up; you'll be in the spotlight. You can run but you can't hide. Take the initiative in getting to the heart of matters. Wear shades of blue, indigo, and purple. Make this a power-play day—your judgment and intuition are on target. You'll beat a deadline. A relationship, recently cool, will heat up.

Friday, July 21 (Moon in Taurus)   A long-distance call gets this weekend off to a dramatic start. You'll exude sensuality and sex appeal and you'll feel that the sky is the limit. Attention revolves around a search, idealism, journey, and your soul mate. Circumstances continue to revolve in your favor. Aries and Libra figure in this turbulent scenario.

Saturday, July 22 (Moon in Taurus to Gemini 2:33 a.m.)
Lucky lottery: 12, 26, 6, 2, 50, 1. Attention revolves around courage, freedom of thought and action, and the willingness to take bold steps into future. This cycle continues to be dynamic—toss aside fear, doubt, and apprehension. Circumstances will help your cause. Leo and Aquarius figure in today's scenario.

Sunday, July 23 (Moon in Gemini)   Focus on family, and on an agreement relating to an investment, a sale, or the purchase of property. A female who is older, at times wiser, declares, "No more shilly-shallying—we are going to go in one direction until your goal is reached." Capricorn and Cancer play instrumental roles. Your lucky number is 2.

Monday, July 24 (Moon in Gemini to Cancer 3:16 p.m.)   You'll have reason to celebrate because a burden is lifted. A close relative says, "It was wrong of me to take offense—let us be like we were before!" Today's scenario highlights versatility, trips, visits, and a dazzling display of intellectual prowess. Gemini and Sagittarius prove to be valuable allies.

Tuesday, July 25 (Moon in Cancer)   At the track: post position special—number 4 P.P. in the fourth race. Pick six: 1, 4, 3, 4, 8, 5. Test recipes, mend clothes, sharpen tools, tear down in order to rebuild on a more suitable structure. Taurus, Leo, and Scorpio play significant roles. Update references.

Wednesday, July 26 (Moon in Cancer)   Attention revolves around a communication with a relative, and participation in an advertising–publicity campaign. Someone you admire declares, "You exude personal magnetism; I would say you have an abundance of sex appeal!" Realize that a mild flirtation could lead to a serious situation. Protect yourself in clinches!

Thursday, July 27 (Moon in Cancer to Leo 3:07 a.m.) The new Leo moon coincides with completion of long-standing negotiations. Attention revolves around your home, family, security, durable goods, and household products. More light shines in an area previously closed. Today's scenario features entertainment, style, and showmanship. Your lucky number is 6.

Friday, July 28 (Moon in Leo) Define terms, outline boundaries, and be aware of real estate offers and opportunities. Watch a Leo whose name is likely to have these letters: G, P, Y. Those who counted you out will be dining on crow. You not only survived but emerged a big winner. Your lucky number is 7.

Saturday, July 29 (Moon in Leo to Virgo 1:12 a.m.) You'll be relieved of an obligation that was not valid in the first place. You'll be saying, "I won't do anything that foolish again!" Attention revolves around responsibility, a deadline, and an intense relationship. You'll gain the confidence of someone who intends to back you all the way.

Sunday, July 30 (Moon in Virgo) Break free from a situation or person who constantly causes you to doubt your own capabilities. Today's scenario features long-range prospects, and a communication relating to travel, search, adventure, and a soul mate. You'll exude a subtle kind of sex appeal. Aries and Libra are involved.

Monday, July 31 (Moon in Virgo to Libra 9:23 p.m.) On this last day of July, decide to try something new. The Virgo moon highlights creativity, style, a variety of experiences, and a door that opens to romance. Attention revolves around independence, courage, and your ability to express your ideas in an original, informative way. Leo and Aquarius are in the picture. Your lucky number is 1.

Tuesday, August 1 (Moon in Libra)   On this first day of August, you'll have reason to be pleased in connection with the location of a lost article, the value of possessions, or the financial picture in general. The Virgo moon coincides with payments, collections, and greater self-esteem. Capricorn and Cancer play memorable roles.

Wednesday, August 2 (Moon in Libra)   A change of policy is announced during the early hours. You've passed the test with plenty to spare. What appeared to be a close call turns out to be mere exercise. Attention revolves around travel, speculation, communication, and the realization that your soul mate may not be so far away. Your lucky number is 9.

Thursday, August 3 (Moon in Libra to Scorpio 3:29 a.m.)   On this Thursday you receive a gift that glitters. Remember the aphorism, "All that glitters is not gold." The Libra moon emphasizes versatility, flexibility, and a sense of the ridiculous. A neighbor or associate declares, "When it comes to appreciating life, you've got it over most people!"

Friday, August 4 (Moon in Scorpio)   The competition will be caught off-guard—you'll get the legal green light, winning public favor. Attention revolves around direction, motivation, durable goods, partnership, and marriage. You'll meet a Cancer whose name is likely to have these letters: B, K, T. Your lucky number is 2.

Saturday, August 5 (Moon in Scorpio to Sagittarius 7:14 a.m.)   Answer questions, analyze the current situation, and arrive at a decision relating to your freedom, goal, partnership, or marital status. A Gemini helps you locate needed material and resolve a dilemma associated with someone of the opposite sex. Lucky lottery: 3, 12, 8, 22, 33, 5.

Sunday, August 6 (Moon in Scorpio)   The lunar position highlights additional knowledge concerning accounting procedures and tax and license requirements. Specifically, the spotlight will be on the financial status of someone close to you, including your partner or mate. Take charge of your own affairs, refusing to be intimidated by someone who exploits superstition.

Monday, August 7 (Moon in Sagittarius to Capricorn 8:52 a.m.) On this Monday, it becomes obvious that you must communicate, read and write, and learn through the process of sharing knowledge. A close relative pays a debt, throwing aside false pride and saying, "I owe you a lot more than just money!" Virgo plays a significant role.

Tuesday, August 8 (Moon in Capricorn) A long-distance communication relates to your residence and lifestyle, providing a clash of ideas in connection with political–religious beliefs. You get almost everything you want if you are diplomatic. Conversely, if you attempt to force the issues or to intimidate others, you lose in an embarrassing way.

Wednesday, August 9 (Moon in Capricorn to Aquarius 9:29 a.m.) Perfect techniques, look beyond the immediate, accent higher teaching. The Capricorn moon coincides with investigation, information, a possible journey that might take you overseas. Follow through on a hunch, celebrate the fact that you are in touch with the spiritual side of yourself. Lucky lottery: 9, 2, 12, 14, 7, 42.

Thursday, August 10 (Moon in Aquarius) The Aquarian full moon coincides with fulfillment, prestige, promotion, production, leadership, and the completion of a project. Focus also on your ability to control moods, transforming a tendency to brood into eagerness to realize your potential. A Capricorn becomes your ally and could have a name with these letters: H, Q, Z.

Friday, August 11 (Moon in Aquarius to Pisces 10:46 a.m.) You'll overcome barriers that include distance and language. You'll succeed via an unusual method or procedure. An Aquarian encourages you to reach for the brass ring. Stress universality, let others know you will not be limited or intimidated. Your lucky number is 9.

Saturday, August 12 (Moon in Pisces)   Emphasize independence, style, creativity, and the courage of your convictions. The Pisces moon coincides with your ability to win friends and influence people. Many individuals will be impressed by your determination and prescience. Today is excellent for making a fresh start, for being vulnerable to love. Your lucky number is 1.

Sunday, August 13 (Moon in Pisces to Aries 2:41 p.m.)   A family member helps fulfill your aspirations. Be diplomatic and flexible, taking care of your house, including the plumbing. You'll be the subject of conversation. Some will be fascinated by your marital status. Capricorn and Cancer, who play significant roles, might have these letters in their names: B, K, T.

Monday, August 14 (Moon in Aries)   What was hidden will be revealed—you'll be happier as a result. The Aries moon highlights secrets, confidential information, and the revelation that someone is spying on you. Focus tonight on celebration, inquisitiveness, and answers to puzzling questions. Gemini and Sagittarius are in the picture.

Tuesday, August 15 (Moon in Aries to Taurus 10:25 p.m.)   At the track: post position special—number 4 P.P. in the eighth race. Pick six: 4, 8, 3, 1, 7, 5. In choosing potential winning horses or jockeys, keep these letters in mind: D, M, V. Throughout the day, check details and references. You could discover a legal loophole. Scorpio is involved.

Wednesday, August 16 (Moon in Taurus)   Lucky lottery: 6, 51, 9, 5, 50, 4. The Aries moon relates to secret information and arrangements, and to a tour of a hospital, home, or museum. Someone who helped you in the past may now need your cooperation, and could be temporarily confined to living quarters. Open up the lines of communication, tossing aside false pride.

Thursday, August 17 (Moon in Taurus)   Those who claim to know best how to live your life should be dismissed. Take charge of your own destiny. A domestic adjustment includes the possibility that you might change your residence—attention also revolves around legal matters, co-operative efforts, public relations, and marital status.

Friday, August 18 (Moon in Taurus to Gemini 9:40 a.m.)
Look beyond the obvious—your cycle is high, a change of scene is advocated, and circumstances take a sudden, dramatic turn in your favor. Your judgment and intuition prove accurate. Define terms, outline boundaries, listen to your inner voice. Pisces and Virgo figure in today's dynamic scenario. Your lucky number is 7.

Saturday, August 19 (Moon in Gemini)   Lucky lottery: 8, 18, 5, 3, 30, 26. The Gemini moon relates to funding, appraisal of possessions, selectivity, and deciding what is to be retained and what is to be let go. The emphasis is on organization, priorities, responsibility, and an intense relationship. The chance to hit the financial jackpot could happen today.

Sunday, August 20 (Moon in Gemini to Cancer 10:24 p.m.)   You'll be asked to be patient about payments—an older woman says, "I feel as if you are one of the family!" The relationship with your mother, teacher, or counselor improves considerably. A mission will be completed. A long-distance call relates to a possible long-distance trip.

Monday, August 21 (Moon in Cancer)   Diversify, make a fresh start, accent versatility and humor. The lunar position highlights trips, visits, rumors, and the need to separate wheat from chaff. A close relative helps in the search, could come up with a missing document. Express yourself; don't follow others. Stick to your own course and your own convictions.

Tuesday, August 22 (Moon in Cancer)   Attention revolves around durable goods, large household products, security, and marital status. Don't stay too long at the fair—negotiations have actually been completed. Someone you admire says, "I'm betting on you and I will lend the benefit of my experience!" A Cancer plays a role.

Wednesday, August 23 (Moon in Cancer to Leo 10:13 a.m.)   This could be called your lucky day. In matters of speculation, stick with the number 3. You'll expand your horizons, adding to your wardrobe and being pleased with your body image. Gemini and Sagittarius play major roles. Try these lucky lottery numbers: 3, 30, 13, 22, 5, 1.

Thursday, August 24 (Moon in Leo)   Steer clear of explosives. This cycle coincides with danger connected with a speeding automobile, sharp utensils, fires, and explosives. On the positive side, you'll be inspired as you gain more solid financial–emotional ground. You'll be entertained at home, when a family member shows off some surprising talents.

Friday, August 25 (Moon in Leo to Virgo 7:50 p.m.)   On this Friday, an investigation could get under way. This kind of investigation equates to search, curiosity, and making a decision in connection with a professional associate or personal relationship. The Leo moon spotlights durable goods, quality, what is meant to last and what will disintegrate. Your lucky number is 5.

Saturday, August 26 (Moon in Virgo)   Lucky lottery: 6, 12, 18, 5, 1, 20. The emphasis is on home, charity, beauty, music, and reconciliation with a loved one. Attention revolves around romance, style, and a domestic adjustment that could include a change of residence or marital status. Libra and another Taurus play outstanding roles.

Sunday, August 27 (Moon in Virgo)   Spiritual values surface—your critical sense surges forward. You perceive potential as you see what previously was kept hidden. Define terms, outline boundaries, wake up with answers. A Pisces helps make your dreams come true, by serving as your private cheering section.

Monday, August 28 (Moon in Virgo to Libra 3:15 a.m.)   Attention revolves around creativity, style, variety, personal magnetism, and a physical attraction. The Virgo moon highlights sensuality and the stirring of creative juices. An older person takes you aside, commenting, "You are the only one I would trust for this job." Your lucky number is 8.

Tuesday, August 29 (Moon in Libra)   Finish what you start; welcome the chance to be free of a burden you did not ask for in the first place. The emphasis is on universal appeal, idealism, and participation in a humanitarian project. You'll have a meaningful encounter with an Aries likely to have a name with these letters: I and R.

Wednesday, August 30 (Moon in Libra to Scorpio 8:12 p.m.)   Lucky lottery: 1, 7, 6, 16, 42, 43. Make a fresh start, accenting independence of thought and action. Imprint style, avoid heavy lifting, be vulnerable to love, but avoid being exploited by a psychic vampire. Leo and Aquarius figure in today's dynamic scenario. A new love is on the horizon.

Thursday, August 31 (Moon in Scorpio)   You'll decide "you no longer stand alone!" The emphasis is on employment, basic issues, self-esteem, and resolutions relating to your diet and nutrition. A Cancer provides stimulating information, and could have a name with these letters: B, K, T. You regain your sense of direction, motivation, and purpose. Your lucky number is 2.

SEPTEMBER 1995

Friday, September 1 (Moon in Scorpio to Sagittarius 12:57 p.m.)   A decision is reached in connection with your reputation and credibility, and a possible appearance before the media. Your marital status also figures prominently—an agreement will finally be achieved if you combine reason with determination and a sympathetic approach regarding the opinion of someone close to you. Your lucky number is 9.

Saturday, September 2 (Moon in Sagittarius)   Lucky lottery: 1, 9, 19, 12, 3, 45. You're due for a fresh start in a new direction—on this Saturday, you might be saying, "I feel I should thank my lucky stars!" A handicap is overcome, and roadblocks that include distance and language will be swept aside. Leo and Aquarius figure in today's dynamic scenario.

Sunday, September 3 (Moon in Sagittarius to Capricorn 3:45 p.m.) A family reunion is a distinct possibility and should be encouraged. The spotlight also falls on security, home, property, excellent food, and marital status. Someone close to you, possibly a business partner or mate, confides the true financial picture. Dig deep for information, bringing references up to date. Your lucky number is 2.

Monday, September 4 (Moon in Capricorn) Attention revolves around accelerated social activities, travel plans, communication, and participation in an entertainment program relating to a political or charitable project. A Sagittarian plays an important role, and could have a name with these letters: C, L, U. Elements of luck and timing ride with you.

Tuesday, September 5 (Moon in Capricorn to Aquarius 5:47 p.m.) What begins as routine, dull, and dreary, will be transformed into an exciting project with plenty of potential. Be willing to tear down in order to rebuild on a more attractive, secure base. Leo, Scorpio, and another Taurus play representative roles.

Wednesday, September 6 (Moon in Aquarius) Be ready for challenges relating to your ability to express your ideas. Get your thoughts on paper. Be analytical. Use your inherent talent for separating fact from fiction. You'll gain via words, whether spoken or written. A Virgo states, "I'm sure you have what it takes. You have my vote of confidence!"

Thursday, September 7 (Moon in Aquarius to Pisces 8:08 p.m.) The accent is on a domestic adjustment, remodeling, decorating, filling in blanks that include music and the appreciation of the arts. You'll receive a compliment on color coordination, design, and an unusual way of expressing yourself, and on your voice as well. Leo, Scorpio, and another Taurus figure prominently. Your lucky number is 6.

Friday, September 8 (Moon in Pisces)   Define terms, look behind the scenes, accept a challenge relating to leadership and participation in a community project. A recent blow to your pride is undergoing a healing process. Someone who spreads a lie will be caught red-handed. Your views will be vindicated. Pisces plays dominant role.

Saturday, September 9 (Moon in Pisces)   The full moon in your eleventh sector reveals an opportunity for both successful romance and finance. You might be invited to go on a unique cruise. Many of your desires will be fulfilled. You'll win friends and influence people. Money that had been held back will be released in your name. Your lucky number is 8.

Sunday, September 10 (Moon in Pisces to Aries 12:14 a.m.)   You'll sense what had been lost, missing, or stolen—you'll be saying, "At last I know what I've been seeking!" Today's scenario features search, recovery, discovery, and the completion of a mission. Take special care in connection with fire, engines, and mechanical objects. Aries will figure in today's scenario.

Monday, September 11 (Moon in Aries)   Accent the unorthodox, emphasizing originality and expressing your own style. The spotlight also falls on hospitals, institutions, and a promise that close quarters will not equate with being cramped. Follow through on a hunch, letting others know that you have confidence and will act on your beliefs. Your lucky number is 1.

Tuesday, September 12 (Moon in Aries to Taurus 7:21 a.m.)   You gain allies despite controversy over land and over the division of property. Someone who had remained on the sidelines makes a commitment in your behalf. By mid-afternoon, you'll know where the money is and how best to obtain it. Capricorn and Cancer play featured roles. Your lucky number is 2.

Wednesday, September 13 (Moon in Taurus)   Lucky lottery: 3, 2, 20, 12, 6, 5. Focus on diversity and on celebration. There is a legitimate bargain in connection with clothing. You have much to do with a Sagittarian, whose name is likely to have these letters: C, L, U. Your cycle is high, and circumstances will favor your efforts. Fun is due tonight.

Thursday, September 14 (Moon in Taurus to Gemini 5:48 p.m.)   You're on solid ground. A Scorpio helps settle a legal dispute in your favor. Check references; look for source material previously unavailable. Be willing to revise, review, remodel, and tear down in order to rebuild. Another Taurus also plays a paramount role in today's exciting scenario.

Friday, September 15 (Moon in Gemini)   Today's cycle reveals your ability to fulfill your wishes, to make financial gain, to express ideas in a creative, entertaining way. If you are single, a blind date, chance meeting, or participation in a study group could result in a meaningful relationship. If you are married, a short trip involves a relative. You'll be told, "You're correct!"

Saturday, September 16 (Moon in Gemini)   Sing out regarding your own products and talents. Keep in mind this dictum: "If you don't blow your own horn, there will be no music!" Focus on sound, rhythm, style, and an important domestic adjustment relating to your home or marital status. Libra and another Taurus figure in today's significant scenario.

Sunday, September 17 (Moon in Gemini to Cancer 6:16 a.m.   Look beyond the immediate. What appeared to be a loss will boomerang in your favor. The Gemini moon highlights your financial status, investment, personal values. You'll wake up with the answers. Focus on meditation, spiritual values, and an exploration of mysticism. Your lucky number is 7.

Monday, September 18 (Moon in Cancer)   You'll be on solid ground, a Cancer helps with information concerning durable goods, insurance, and mortgage and car payments.

You'll learn more about tax and license requirements. You'll easily meet a deadline—stay close to home to preserve a relationship. Capricorn is involved.

Tuesday, September 19 (Moon in Cancer to Leo 6:19 p.m.)   At the track: post position special—number 8 P.P. in the first race. Pick six: 8, 5, 1, 3, 3, 7. In selecting names of potential winning horses and jockeys, pay attention to these letters in their names: I and R. A foreign horse is likely to upset the odds. This applies to any and all tracks. Libra is involved.

Wednesday, September 20 (Moon in Leo)   Lucky lottery: 20, 25, 5, 1, 10, 22. You'll make a fresh start in a new direction as enthusiasm replaces ennui your hopes for a new or different kind of love ride high. Express yourself. Don't follow others; let them follow you. Leo and Aquarius will play outstanding roles.

Thursday, September 21 (Moon in Leo)   The cycle is high. Wear shades of yellow and gold, make personal appearances, assert your views in a dynamic, direct way. Someone of the opposite sex is provocative and desires you physically but wants you to figure it out for yourself. Capricorn and Cancer play major roles.

Friday, September 22 (Moon in Leo to Virgo 4:01 a.m.) Reject secondhand tools and goods. Someone of the opposite sex provides inspiration and relates, "You deserve the very best, but you won't receive it until you insist on it." Focus on style, creativity, panache, and an opportunity for gain via the written word. Gemini, Virgo, and Sagittarius figure prominently.

Saturday, September 23 (Moon in Virgo)   Lucky lottery: 4, 40, 44, 5, 6, 10. On this Saturday, you'll read and write; you'll correct mechanical defects; you'll be in touch with a manufacturer whose product you recently purchased. Refuse to be swayed or dismayed by someone who is a legend in his own mind. Another Taurus is in the picture.

Sunday, September 24 (Moon in Virgo to Libra 10:50 a.m.) You recently missed an appointment, but now you make up for it and a special person says, "When you missed me, I missed you twice as much!" The new moon in Libra represents fresh opportunities in connection with employment, basic issues, and relations with dependents. Spirits are elevated by an excellent health report.

Monday, September 25 (Moon in Libra) On this Monday, you'll be saying, "I hear music!" The music is inner tranquility, a domestic adjustment that brings you together with the one you love. After 4 p.m., you'll receive a gift representing a token of affection and admiration. You'll be saying, "This Monday is certainly not blue!"

Tuesday, September 26 (Moon in Libra to Scorpio 3:20 p.m.) Look behind the scenes for answers, paying close attention to someone who discusses basic issues, domestic harmony, and the responsibility of pet ownership. Learn when to draw the line. The emphasis is on real estate and property values. Make a decision regarding a relationship—is it worthwhile or not?

Wednesday, September 27 (Moon in Scorpio) A hunch or psychic impression received 24 hours ago bears fruit and will now pay dividends. The lunar and numerical cycles highlight an intense relationship, time limitation, responsibility, reward, partnership, or marriage. You might also be anticipating an addition to your family. Your lucky number is 8.

Thursday, September 28 (Moon in Scorpio to Sagittarius 6:30 p.m.) Good news—a mission is completed! Get an agreement in writing. Remember Samuel Goldwyn's dictum: "A verbal agreement isn't worth the paper it's written on!" The emphasis is on public relations, credibility, cooperative efforts, and improved image. Marriage continues to command a portion of the spotlight. Aries is involved.

Friday, September 29 (Moon in Sagittarius) You get the proverbial second chance—you'll locate a missing item; you'll be paid in cash. An income tax problem will be resolved. An agent or representative says, "I am proud to be representing you!" Focus on creativity, style, passion, and ultimate success. Leo and Aquarius play dramatic roles.

Saturday, September 30 (Moon in Sagittarius to Capricorn 9:10 p.m.)   Focus on reunion, marital status, and the sale or purchase of a property or home. On this Saturday night, you'll be wined and dined in gourmet style. You'll have luck in matters of speculation—here is your lucky lottery: 8, 26, 17, 2, 3, 30. A Cancer figures prominently.

OCTOBER 1995

Sunday, October 1 (Moon in Capricorn)   On this Sunday, you'll be musing, "Indeed, life can be beautiful!" Your creative juices stir. A young person says, "I would be proud to make you my role model!" You'll get to the heart of matters. A love relationship is back on track. Express yourself. Leo plays a key role.

Monday, October 2 (Moon in Capricorn to Aquarius 11:59 p.m.)   Funding is made available. The lunar position highlights philosophy, theology, travel, publishing, and participation in a special mission. An aura of romance is featured. Your marital status figures prominently. You regain your sense of direction and motivation. You reunite with someone who played an important role in your life.

Tuesday, October 3 (Moon in Aquarius)   At the track: post position special—number 5 P.P. in the seventh race. Pick six: 3, 9, 6, 7, 8, 4. Keep these letters in mind when selecting potential winning horses and jockeys: C, L, U. Your popularity increases in a dramatic way. Gemini and Sagittarius play significant roles.

Wednesday, October 4 (Moon in Aquarius)   Those who thought you slipped will be startled to discover that your feet are solidly planted on firm ground. Review references, check the fine print, leave your options open. The Aquarian moon highlights leadership, promotion, production, and rapport with a superior. Your lucky number is 4.

Thursday, October 5 (Moon in Aquarius to Pisces 3:35 a.m.)   At the track: post position special—number 3 P.P. in the second race. Pick six: 1, 3, 7, 4, 8, 4. In selecting names of winning horses and jockeys, keep these letters in mind: E, N, W. Throughout the day, be analytical, get your ideas on paper. Take nothing for granted where notices and payments are concerned.

Friday, October 6 (Moon in Pisces)   Attention revolves around a sensitive family member who pleads for more attention. Focus on a domestic adjustment that could include beautifying your surroundings, an actual change or residence or marital status. A wish comes true. A Pisces declares, "I would not want to be part of any world without you!"

Saturday, October 7 (Moon in Pisces to Aries 8:41 a.m.) Lucky lottery: 9, 12, 17, 7, 6, 14. The key is to be discreet, to accent the spiritual, to be open minded but not gullible. You could be engaging in a theological give-and-take with a Pisces. Most answers relating to your personal life can be obtained via meditation.

Sunday, October 8 (Moon in Aries)   The full moon, lunar eclipse falls in the section of your chart associated with dreams, visions, theatrical productions, and secret arrangements. What supposedly was off the record could appear in bold print. Keep your options open, have faith, realize it's up to you to be in charge of your own fate.

Monday, October 9 (Moon in Aries to Taurus 4:05 p.m.)   There is no need to be limited. What held you back is removed from the scene. Focus on international outlets, and on your ability to get a better display for your product and talent. You might be participating in an overseas mission. Be aware of import–export opportunities. Aries plays a paramount role.

Tuesday, October 10 (Moon in Taurus)   Those in flirtatious moods might say, "You look as if you found a new heartthrob!" Vigor returns, smiles replace frowns, enthusiasm shoves aside boredom. Your cycle is high, and your judgment and intuition are on target—the action will be where you are. You're the main event, the hot ticket on this Tuesday.

Wednesday, October 11 (Moon in Taurus)   Lucky lottery: 2, 20, 12, 30, 33, 6. At the track: post position special—number 6 P.P. in the fifth race. Pick six: 5, 2, 1, 7, 6, 5. What you achieve will be via an unorthodox method. Money that had been withheld will be released in your name. Another Taurus is in the picture.

Thursday, October 12 (Moon in Taurus to Gemini 2:10 a.m.)   An excellent day for dining out, for recovering a lost article, for supervising an entertainment program aimed at obtaining funding for a political or charitable project. The emphasis is on charm, versatility, diversity, and the willingness to try different modes of transportation. Your lucky number is 3.

Friday, October 13 (Moon in Gemini)   This will not be an unlucky day for you! The Gemini moon highlights income, "found money," and the ability to use investment counseling successfully. On this Friday, you're on solid emotional–financial ground. This applies despite someone who knows the price of everything and the value of nothing.

Saturday, October 14 (Moon in Gemini to Cancer 2:20 p.m.)   Be ready for change, travel, variety, and the excitement of discovery. You'll receive an offer to express your views, orally or in writing, which could evolve into a profitable enterprise. Invest in your own ideas and creations. If you don't blow your own horn, there won't be any music. Your lucky number is 5.

Sunday, October 15 (Moon in Cancer)   Accent harmony, family reunion, and dialogue with someone who is bright and cares very much for you. The emphasis is on music, entertainment, and an ability to write lyrics. Laugh at your own foibles; don't be afraid to ask dumb questions. Libra, Scorpio, and another Taurus play outstanding roles.

Monday, October 16 (Moon in Cancer)   A relative says, "I agree, we must get rid of unnecessary expenses and superfluous material!" Focus also on spiritual values and the ability to streamline procedures. The Cancer moon highlights a trip in connection with a relative who says, "With you along, anything is possible!"

Tuesday, October 17 (Moon in Cancer to Leo 2:46 a.m.)   The emphasis is on challenge, gain, travel, entertainment, and a serious discussion of sexual proclivities. Get in tune with your inner feelings—be true to yourself. If you are "you" and not an imitation or robot, you simply cannot lose. A Cancer figures prominently and a Capricorn is also in the picture.

Wednesday, October 18 (Moon in Leo)   Lucky lottery: 5, 15, 9, 10, 12, 14. Previous rules no longer apply—a burden has been lifted. You're free to travel, to express, to publish, and to love. A project that had been abandoned will be revived. Someone with a reputation as a chef invites you to dine gourmet-style.

Thursday, October 19 (Moon in Leo to Virgo 11:11 a.m.) Make a fresh start; let this Thursday be a day you'll remember. The Leo moon highlights involvement with someone who is dynamic, creative, exciting, and likely to have a name with these letters: A, S, J. The key is to let go of the status quo, to take bold steps into the future. Your lucky number is 1.

Friday, October 20 (Moon in Virgo)   Attention revolves around your home, security, a decision relating to the sale or purchase of property. A family member proves instrumental in helping you gain your sense of direction and motivation. If you are single, you decide on whether to remain in that state. If you're married, you might be interested in going into business for yourself.

Saturday, October 21 (Moon in Virgo to Libra 8:15 p.m.)   The Virgo moon highlights a stirring of creative juices. You'll be saying, "What a Saturday night!" Focus on diversity, creativity, change, challenge, and a variety of sensations and experiences. Someone you are much attracted to counsels, "Let's slow down; let's be a bit more analytical!"

Sunday, October 22 (Moon in Libra) Attend to details without neglecting basic issues—it's an excellent day for making repairs, testing recipes, and communicating with someone who recently expressed doubt about personal value. You'll break free from the prison of preconceived notions. Leo, Scorpio, and another Taurus figure in the unique scenario.

Monday, October 23 (Moon in Libra) Take nothing for granted; ask questions; let a loved one know, "I do care and I am so much more alive when I'm near you!" A gain is indicated via the written word—take notes and sharpen your reportorial skills. A Virgo offers encouragement and could have a name with these letters: E, N, W.

Tuesday, October 24 (Moon in Libra to Scorpio 12:07 a.m.) The new moon, solar eclipse in the area of your chart is associated with legal regulations, credibility, reputation, a partnership proposal, and marriage. Play the waiting game, collecting additional information as different source material becomes available. Advise someone close to you to take special care in handling sharp objects and when driving.

Wednesday, October 25 (Moon in Scorpio) Lucky lottery: 7, 25, 8, 22, 33, 18. Attention revolves around your reputation, prestige, and ability to express yourself clearly. The Scorpio moon continues to spotlight your ability to win public support, as well as cooperative efforts and your marital status. Pisces and Virgo play significant roles. Perfect your skills.

Thursday, October 26 (Moon in Scorpio to Sagittarius 1:56 a.m.) The emphasis is on organization, responsibility, and a chance to display wares and talents. Someone who invests and is knowledgeable about money matters could become your ally. The Sagittarius moon relates to the financial structure of your partner or mate. A Cancer figures prominently. Your lucky number is 8.

Friday, October 27 (Moon in Sagittarius)   Refuse to be taken for granted; continue your search for a soul mate. The emphasis is on inspiration, distance, language, and the opportunity to expand your personal or professional horizons. You'll meet an Aries whose name has these letters: I and R. You could have luck with the number 9.

Saturday, October 28 (Moon in Sagittarius to Capricorn 3:15 a.m.)   Lucky lottery: 28, 10, 12, 8, 5, 51. Attention revolves around newfound confidence. Express yourself, become vulnerable to love. A showy Leo helps promote your cause, elevates your morale and could have a name with these letters: A, S, J. Let go of the status quo. Refuse to be placed in any one category.

Sunday, October 29 (Moon in Capricorn; Daylight Saving Time Ends)   A family gathering proves beneficial. Open lines of communication and investigate the possibility of a journey, perhaps overseas. The emphasis is on spirituality, completion of a project, or a declaration of love. A rare opportunity exists to write your own script, to carve out your own destiny.

Monday, October 30 (Moon in Capricorn to Aquarius 4:23 a.m.)   The work week gets off to an interesting start. The Aquarian moon highlights leadership, promotion, and elevation of your standing in your community, church, or profession. Tonight, you'll celebrate the fact that money is coming from a surprise source. Your popularity increases and you receive a gift that improves your wardrobe.

Tuesday, October 31 (Moon in Aquarius)   On this Halloween, you could be regaled with tales of ghosts, spirits, and the possible return of Houdini. Check your source material, look for an opportunity to be on stage. Events happen that cause you to declare, "This must be déjà vu!" Your lucky number is 4.

Wednesday, November 1 (Moon in Aquarius to Pisces 8:17 a.m.) You're on the brink of a cycle that could bring happiness and wealth. Attention revolves around public acclaim, partnership, cooperative efforts, and the ability to put your product and talents across in a big-time way. Deal with people who are knowledgeable about distribution and advertising. Make a special appeal to women.

Thursday, November 2 (Moon in Pisces) At the track: post position special—number 5 P.P. in the seventh race. Pick six: 2, 3, 7, 8, 1, 5. In choosing the names of potential winning horses and jockeys, keep these letters in mind: C, L, U. A burden will be lifted: as your popularity increases, it is likely that tonight you will be wined and dined.

Friday, November 3 (Moon in Pisces to Aries 2:21 p.m.) Be willing to tear down in order to rebuild on a more suitable structure. The Pisces moon coincides with your ability to win friends and influence people and to use powers of persuasion. You'll be introduced to people who could prove valuable in connection with your career, personal activities, or romance.

Saturday, November 4 (Moon in Aries) Lucky lottery: 5, 9, 14, 12, 1, 10. At the track: post position special—Number 3 P.P. in the second race. Pick six: 8, 3, 2, 2, 5, 8. Today's scenario highlights elements of timing and surprise. You'll add to your wardrobe. You'll also participate in a social activity enabling you to express ideas in a charming, entertaining way.

Sunday, November 5 (Moon in Aries to Taurus 10:35 p.m.) Attention revolves around family and tradition. A gift received is likely to be a luxury item or an art object. the Aries moon coincides with the need to be discreet. Focus on a possible tour of a hospital or museum. The spotlight is on lifestyle, music, gourmet dining, and marital status. Your lucky number is 6.

Monday, November 6 (Moon in Taurus)   You'll be involved in an activity or project requiring creativity, imagination, and faith. The key is to see clearly in connection with your potential. A psychic impression proves accurate. You'll have a view from backstage. Pisces and Virgo figure in this unusual scenario. Your lucky number is 7.

Tuesday, November 7 (Moon in Taurus)   You'll be saying, "This is one Tuesday I'll not soon forget!" The full moon in your sign combines with the number 8 astrological and numerical cycle to represent power, authority, an intense relationship, commitment, and knowledge of a time limitation. You'll imprint your style, and your efforts will be rewarded.

Wednesday, November 8 (Moon in Taurus to Gemini 8:55 a.m.)   A long-distance communication relates to universality, romance, and a possible journey. Your cycle is high as circumstances turn in your favor. Emphasize personality, originality, and innovativeness. The old rules don't apply—set your own pace, create new standards. Lucky lottery: 9, 20, 2, 6, 14, 50.

Thursday, November 9 (Moon in Gemini)   Make a fresh start, get your ideas on paper, realize that a current activity could lead to considerable profit. Stress independence. Have the courage of your convictions. Be willing to take a risk. Leo, Gemini, and Aquarius can be supportive now. Love plays a surprise role.

Friday, November 10 (Moon in Gemini to Cancer 8:57 p.m.)   Gather facts and figures—money rests on the outcome of diligent research. The spotlight is on direction and motivation. A decision is made relating to property, basic issues, partnership, and marriage. You could have a gourmet appetite but watch out for minor digestive problems, unless the word moderation is emphasized.

Saturday, November 11 (Moon in Cancer)   Lucky lottery: 11, 3, 30, 5, 18, 12. The key to happiness on this Saturday is diversification, a sense of humor, and the ability to laugh at your own foibles. A Sagittarian plays a significant role and could have a name with these letters: C, L, U. By tonight, you'll pull victory from the jaws of defeat. Applause!

Sunday, November 12 (Moon in Cancer)   A relative is serious about losing weight. Don't be overly critical. The spotlight is on image, reputation, fitness, and willingness to travel to complete an assignment. The lunar position highlights relatives as well as ideas that can be developed into viable concepts. Scorpio plays a major role.

Monday, November 13 (Moon in Cancer to Leo 9:37 a.m.)   Get your thoughts on paper—ideas flow once you get started. What begins as a mild flirtation could get out of hand. Protect your assets; don't give up something of value for mere cheap thrill. The message becomes crystal clear. Gemini, Virgo, and Sagittarius are represented.

Tuesday, November 14 (Moon in Leo)   At the track: post position special—number 2 P.P. in the fourth race. Pick six: 1, 3, 5, 2, 8, 8. The emphasis is on music, flowers, charm and a reunion with a loved one. A domestic adjustment figures prominently, and could involve an actual change of residence or marital status. Libra is in the picture.

Wednesday, November 15 (Moon in Leo to Virgo 9:02 p.m.)   Lucky lottery: 7, 50, 1, 5, 8, 44. The emphasis is on power, authority, deadline, and an intense relationship. Define terms, outline boundaries, see people and places in a realistic light. A real estate opportunity might present itself before 4 p.m. A relative says, "I want to discuss my future!"

Thursday, November 16 (Moon in Virgo)   An aura of intensity is present—many will be drawn to you; others will fear you; no one will ignore you. Step into the limelight, state your case, have confidence, because you will win. A love relationship proceeds with some thorns among the roses. A special person confides, "I intend to leave home!"

Friday, November 17 (Moon in Virgo)   Finish what you start. Love that had been absent is back; you'll be saying, "I feel alive again!" Get involved, refuse to sit on the sidelines. Your contributions are valuable and should not be withheld. You'll exude universal appeal. Aries and Libra figure prominently.

Saturday, November 18 (Moon in Virgo to Libra 5:18 a.m.)   Lucky lottery: 18, 6, 5, 12, 33, 1. Stress independence and originality. Be willing to participate in a pioneering project. Don't follow others—let them follow your lead. The Virgo moon highlights your personality, attractiveness, sensuality, and sex appeal. You'll be dealing with a dynamic Leo whose name has these letters: A, S, J.

Sunday, November 19 (Moon in Libra)   You'll decide on direction, motivation, and marital status. The Libra moon highlights cooperative efforts and restoration of harmony at the workplace and on the home front. A Cancer, who helps restore your faith, could have a name with these letters: B, K, T. A Capricorn also plays a paramount role.

Monday, November 20 (Moon in Libra to Scorpio 9:40 a.m.)   On this Monday, you'll be saying, "I feel good. No blue Monday! I'm going to laugh and bring joy to others, too." The emphasis is on versatility, diversification, different modes of transportation, and additions to your wardrobe. You'll be more pleased with your body image than in the recent past. Your lucky number is 3.

Tuesday, November 21 (Moon in Scorpio)   Accept a challenge, stand tall for your principles. The lunar position highlights subtle legal nuances—you might be calling for a "Philadelphia lawyer." The Scorpio moon accents public appearances, a clash of ideas, and your marital status. Check references; read the fine print.

Wednesday, November 22 (Moon in Scorpio to Sagittarius 10:56 a.m.)   The new moon in Scorpio activates hopes and wishes in connection with publicity, acclaim, partnership, and marriage. You'll look different to the world, which will have new dimensions for you. Get your ideas on

271

paper. Emphasize a variety of experiences and sensations. Your lucky number is 5.

Thursday, November 23 (Moon in Sagittarius) A family gathering on this Thanksgiving buoys spirits, restores harmony, and is an excellent setting for breaking the news—"I'm going to get more money." Attention revolves around the home. An atmosphere coincides with your holiday spirit. A Sagittarian could be a surprise guest. Another Taurus is also in the picture.

Friday, November 24 (Moon in Sagittarius to Capricorn 10:48 a.m.) The lunar position highlights practical financial affairs that include tax and license requirements. You gain additional knowledge relating to accounting, credits, and debits. Someone who is usually secretive blurts out information that had been kept secret. Use the information in a constructive way.

Saturday, November 25 (Moon in Capricorn) Lucky lottery: 8, 16, 17, 10, 33, 18. This could be your power play day! You'll meet a deadline. You'll be praised by your superiors and peers. A love relationship is intense and controversial but worth the trouble and pain. By 8 p.m. you'll be assured, "You are the main event!"

Sunday, November 26 (Moon in Capricorn to Aquarius 11:15 a.m.) A long-distance communication relates to a unique invitation that could include travel. Today's scenario features spiritual values, philosophy, theology, and your ability to put across your program. The Capricorn moon coincides with a solid foundation for future plans and prospects. You'll get money and love.

Monday, November 27 (Moon in Aquarius) Make a fresh start. Refuse to be held back by someone who is envious and lacks inspiration. Express yourself. Take on a leadership role. A special note: Avoid heavy lifting. A new enthusiasm or a new love could be on the horizon. Be independent without being arrogant. Leo and Aquarius are in the picture. Your lucky number is 1.

272

Tuesday, November 28 (Moon in Aquarius to Pisces 1:59 p.m.) As November draws to a close, you feel more secure about your legal position, marital status, and income. The Aquarian moon coincides with a promotion, production, time limitation, or a strong love relationship. Those who said "It can't be done" will have red faces. Capricorn is involved.

Wednesday, November 29 (Moon in Pisces) Forces tend to be scattered, but the puzzle pieces will fall into place. You'll win friends and influence people as wishes will be granted in amazing ways. Use your powers of persuasion; be determined to win. You are on the right track and will gain valuable allies. Lucky lottery: 12, 7, 22, 33, 18, 5.

Thursday, November 30 (Moon in Pisces to Aries 7:51 p.m.) Those who thought you were being impractical are proven wrong. You get what you asked for; your wishes were not out of reach. The Pisces moon coincides with your ability to convince others that your goals are worthwhile and within reach. Libra, Scorpio, and another Taurus play outstanding roles.

DECEMBER 1995

Friday, December 1 (Moon in Aries) What a way to begin December! The Pisces moon accents your ability to win friends, to be popular, to shine in areas of finance and romance. The pleasure principle is highlighted—you might be saying, "This may be too much of a good thing too soon!" A Pisces figures prominently, and could have a name with these letters: C, L, U.

Saturday, December 2 (Moon in Aries) Lucky lottery: 4, 1, 9, 10, 44, 7. At the track: post position special—number 4 P.P. in the fourth race. Pick six: 3, 8, 1, 4, 7, 7. In selecting names of potential winning horses or jockeys keep these letters in mind: D, M, V. A secret meeting tonight will prove fascinating.

273

Sunday, December 3 (Moon in Aries to Taurus 4:40 a.m.)
Read and write, communicate your ideas, get permission to tour a library, museum, or hospital. Give full rein to your intellectual curiosity. You'll profit from the written word. A flirtation tonight lends spice, but don't let it get out of hand. Gemini and Virgo are involved. A missing document will be located by 8 p.m.

Monday, December 4 (Moon in Taurus) Attention revolves around money, payments, collections, and a domestic adjustment that might include a possible change of residence or marital status. Although it is Monday, it will not be dull or blue. There's music in your life tonight, a possible celebration, and reassurance that your love is not unrequited.

Tuesday, December 5 (Moon in Taurus to Gemini 3:35 p.m.) Define terms, perfect techniques, take the initiative in getting to the heart of matters. The moon in your sign emphasizes originality and the ability to be at the right place at the crucial moment. Your judgment and intuition are on target—circumstances take a dramatic turn in your favor. Your lucky number is 7.

Wednesday, December 6 (Moon in Gemini) Lucky lottery: 8, 3, 50, 5, 13, 22. Focus on organization, responsibility, and an overtime assignment. There's a chance to hit the financial jackpot, to win a contest or lottery. You'll be dealing with older people who do have your best interests at heart. Capricorn is featured, and might have a name with these letters: H, Q, Z.

Thursday, December 7 (Moon in Gemini) The full moon in your second house represents memories, collections, and reasons for being thankful. You'll recall that "Day of Infamy" with appropriate sadness. However, it is best to take steps into the future, rather than brood about the past. A project will be completed. A long-distance call relates to a journey or to romance.

Friday, December 8 (Moon in Gemini to Cancer 3:44 a.m.) Emphasize independence, get rid of self-doubt, realize you'll gain financially and otherwise with the use of wit and wisdom and words. Get your ideas on paper—review copyright procedures. A bargain property or product that seemed to vanish will again be available, no later than tomorrow.

Saturday, December 9 (Moon in Cancer)   Lucky lottery: 2, 8, 12, 13, 14, 19. Focus on food, language, geography, credibility, public relations, and marriage. Plainly, it would not be wise trying to do too much at one time. A relative who once asserted, "I don't think we ever will get along!" will now be eating out of your hands.

Sunday, December 10 (Moon in Cancer to Leo 4:24 p.m.)   Refuse to become engulfed in trivia. Stick to basic issues, give sound advice to a relative who admits, "I took the wrong path, I talked when I should have listened!" Reach beyond previous limitations—accent humor, curiosity, and the healing process. Your lucky number is 3.

Monday, December 11 (Moon in Leo)   A roadblock undergoes a metamorphosis, and is transformed into a stepping-stone toward your ultimate goal. Use showmanship, advertising, music, color, and entertainment to get your product or talent across. You'll meet a powerful Scorpio likely to have a name with these letters: D, M, V.

Tuesday, December 12 (Moon in Leo)   Keep plans flexible. Someone previously in charge could be absent without notification. It's necessary to guide your own fate and destiny. A love relationship flourishes, despite some thorns among the roses. Today's scenario features bright lights, change, and meetings with creative people who say, "You could outdo all of us!"

Wednesday, December 13 (Moon in Leo to Virgo 4:26 a.m.)   Lucky lottery: 1, 10, 6, 16, 15, 33. A love relationship, despite being temporarily off track, will endure. By tomorrow you'll be saying, "I'm glad I waited and didn't do anything rash!" Focus on home, security, income, legal agreement, and marital status. Another Taurus is involved.

275

Thursday, December 14 (Moon in Virgo)   Be ready for change, travel, variety, and the excitement of discovery. The Virgo moon represents the stirring of creative juices. You'll exude sensuality, personal magnetism, and sex appeal. If you are single, you could fall madly in love. If you're married, the spark that brought you together is reignited.

Friday, December 15 (Moon in Virgo to Libra 2:09 p.m.)   The emphasis is on a business proposition, organization, intensity—don't do anything halfway, at the risk of taking a serious loss. You win big if you are sincere and dedicated—love will not be a stranger. An older person lends the benefit of experience, declaring, "You have the makings of a champion!"

Saturday, December 16 (Moon in Libra)   A project that had been abandoned will be reactivated—largely through your efforts. Focus on distance, language, and romance. A burden is lifted. An obligation you should not have assumed in the first place will no longer be of concern. Strive for balance, review basic procedures, and evaluate your job picture.

Sunday, December 17 (Moon in Libra to Scorpio 8:07 p.m.)   Spiritual values shine—you could inspire someone who recently suffered a loss. Express yourself, take the initiative, highlight originality and pioneering spirit. A special note: Avoid heavy lifting! A dynamic Leo, who helps your cause, could have a name with these letters: A, S, J.

Monday, December 18 (Moon in Scorpio)   You've been concerned, meditating on questions relating to partnership, cooperative efforts, a legal decision, and marriage. By tomorrow, many of your queries will be answered. A relative wants to prepare a gourmet dinner tonight. Accept the invitation. Accept an apology without making the other person crawl.

Tuesday, December 19 (Moon in Scorpio to Sagittarius 10:13 p.m.)   This could be a bountiful day—indecision, however, is part of the scenario. This might be a result of too much of a good thing. Attention revolves around the elements of luck, popularity, and inquisitiveness. The lunar position highlights your reputation, public image, cooperative efforts, and marital status.

Wednesday, December 20 (Moon in Sagittarius)   Play the waiting game; check references and legal ramifications. Build on a solid base, giving serious consideration to the possibility of moving your business enterprise. A close associate advocates a change of address. The seventh house moon coincides with publicity and possible acclaim.

Thursday, December 21 (Moon in Sagittarius to Capricorn 9:46 p.m.)   Today's scenario highlights philosophy, theology, character analysis, and the ability to crack codes. You'll read, write and learn through the process of teaching others. There is plenty of action due to a flirtation or a chance meeting that could develop into something serious. Gemini, Virgo, and Sagittarius are involved.

Friday, December 22 (Moon in Capricorn)   The new moon in Sagittarius highlights mystery, intrigue, and awareness of the upcoming holidays. Budget leaks—the financial status of someone close to you, are relative, including your partner or mate. You'll be more fully informed in connection with tax and license requirements. Your lucky number is 6.

Saturday, December 23 (Moon in Capricorn to Aquarius 8:52 p.m.)   Spiritual values play a major role—as the holiday approaches, you'll be musing, "Maybe for the first time, I am aware of the meaning of Christmas." Your psychic impressions prove accurate. Terms will be clearly defined. Get rid of extra material. Lucky lottery: 7, 16, 25, 40, 13, 50.

Sunday, December 24 (Moon in Aquarius)   On this Christmas Eve, you'll receive communications from near and far. The number 8 astrological, numerical cycle represents power. The moon in your ninth house symbolizes the spiritual values of a possible journey. You have good reason for belief in a soul mate. Capricorn and Cancer play distinguished roles.

Monday, December 25 (Moon in Aquarius to Pisces 9:45 p.m.)   It is Christmas Day. You are not imagining it—your morale and your spirits are elevated. People look to you as an example; some ask you to share your feelings with them. People are generous to you, bestowing gifts. Love will not be absent—you'll say, "This is one Christmas I will never forget!"

Tuesday, December 26 (Moon in Pisces)   As the New Year approaches, you make resolutions. Today you will be independent, creative, dynamic, exuding sex appeal. The Aquarian moon highlights your ability to be in charge of your own destiny. Today's scenario highlights the stirring of creative juices, innovativeness, and originality. Have the courage of your convictions. Leo is involved.

Wednesday, December 27 (Moon in Pisces)   Lucky lottery: 2, 12, 7, 17, 25, 6. Attention revolves around family relationships, large household products, gifts, and preparation for a New Year's celebration. You'll rediscover a family member who recently faded from the picture. Cancer and Capricorn figure in today's dynamic scenario.

Thursday, December 28 (Moon in Pisces to Aries 2:06 a.m.)   Attention revolves around diversity, versatility, and the ability to make wishes come true. The Pisces moon in your eleventh house coincides with friends, hopes, and wishes. Use your charm and powers of persuasion. You'll make important contacts in connection with your business, personal life, and career.

Friday, December 29 (Moon in Aries)   The Aries moon coincides with secrets, clandestine arrangements, and the need to be discreet. Your invitation list will be revised—what appeared to be a loss will boomerang in your favor. You're actually on more solid ground both financially and emotionally—know it, and choose happiness instead of being depressed.

Saturday, December 30 (Moon in Aries to Taurus 10:21 a.m.)   You felt for some time, "I wish I had somebody to talk to, to confide in." By 5 p.m., your wish will be fulfilled. You'll experience the euphoria that coincides with freedom of expression. A dynamic Gemini in your life today could have a name with these letters: E, N, W. Your lucky number is 5.

Sunday, December 31 (Moon in Taurus)   New Year's Eve—with the moon in your sign, you'll be at the right place. You'll love and be loved. Both numerical and astrological cycles indicate it would be best for you to stay close to home, so entertaining in your home would be an excellent idea. Focus on music and romance! Happy New Year!

ABOUT THIS SERIES

This is one of a series of
twelve Day-by-Day Astrological Guides
for the signs in 1995
by Sydney Omarr

ABOUT THE AUTHOR

Born on August 5, 1926, in Philadelphia, Omarr was the only person ever given full-time duty in the U.S. Army as an astrologer. He also is regarded as the most erudite astrologer of our time and the best known, through his syndicated column (300 newspapers) and his radio and television programs (he is Merv Griffin's "resident astrologer"). Omarr has been called the most "knowledgeable astrologer since Evangeline Adams." His forecasts of Nixon's downfall, the end of World War II in mid-August of 1945, the assassination of John F. Kennedy, Roosevelt's election to the fourth term and his death in office ... these and many others are on record and quoted enough to be considered "legendary."

The Most Important Money/Power/Romantic-Love Discovery Since The Industrial Revolution

© 1994

Receive Free — The valuable, 8000-word Neo-Tech Information Package

An entire new field of knowledge has been discovered by Dr. Frank R. Wallace, a former Senior Research Chemist for E.I. du Pont de Nemours & Co. For over a decade, Dr. Wallace researched Psychous Advantages to uncover a powerful array of new knowledge called Neo-Tech. That new knowledge allows any person to prosper monetarily, personally, romantically, and financially anywhere in the world, even during personal or financial hard times, inflation, boom times, recession, depression, war.

Neo-Tech is a new, scientific method for capturing major financial and personal advantages everywhere. Neo-Tech is a new knowledge that has nothing to do with positive thinking, religion, or anything mystical. Once a person is exposed to Neo-Tech, he can quietly profit from anyone — anywhere, anytime. He can prosper almost anywhere on earth and succeed under almost any economic or political condition. Combined with Psychous Advantages, Neo-Tech applies to all money and power gathering techniques — to all situations involving the transfer of money, power, or love.

Neo-Tech has its roots in the constant financial pressures and incentives to develop the easiest, most profitable methods of gaining advantages. Over the decades, all successful salesmen, businessmen, politicians, writers, lawyers, entrepreneurs, investors, speculators, gamers and Casanovas have secretly searched for shortcuts that require little skill yet contain the invisible effectiveness of the most advanced techniques. Dr. Wallace identified those shortcuts and honed them into practical formats called Neo-Tech. Those never-before-known formats transfer money, power, and prestige from the uninformed to the informed. Those informed can automatically take control of most situations involving money and power.

Who is The Neo-Tech Man? He is a man of quiet power — a man who cannot lose. He can extract money at will. He can control anyone unknowledgeable about Neo-Tech — man or woman.

The Neo-Tech man has the power to render others helpless, even wipe them out, but he wisely chooses to use just enough of his power to give himself unbeatable casino-like advantages in all his endeavors for maximum long-range profits. His Neo-Tech maneuvers are so subtle that they can be executed with casual confidence. His hidden techniques let him win consistently and comfortably — year after year, decade after decade. Eventually, Neo-Tech men and women will quietly rule everywhere.

The Neo-Tech man can easily and safely beat any opponent. He can quickly impoverish anyone he chooses. He can immediately and consistently acquire large amounts of money. He has the power to make more money in a week than most people without Neo-Tech make in a full year. He commands profits and respect. He controls business deals and emotional situations to acquire money and power...and to command love. He can regain lost love. He can subjugate a business or personal adversary. He wins any lover at will. He can predict stock prices — even gold and silver prices. He quietly rules all.

Within a week, an ordinary person can become a professional Neo-Tech practitioner. As people gain this knowledge, they will immediately begin using its techniques because they are irresistibly easy and overwhelmingly potent. Within days after gaining this knowledge, a person can safely bankrupt opponents — or slowly profit from them, week after week. He can benefit from business and investment endeavors — from dealing with the boss to the biggest oil deal. He can also benefit from any relationship — from gaining the respect of peers to inducing love from a partner or regaining lost love from an ex-partner. He will gain easy money and power in business, investments, the professions, politics, and personal life.

Indeed, with Neo-Tech, a person not only captures unbeatable advantages over others, but commands shortcuts to profits, power, and romance. The ordinary person can quickly become a Clark Kent — a quiet superman — taking command of all. He can financially and emotionally control whomever he deals with. He becomes the man-on-the-hill, now. He is armed with an unbeatable weapon. All will yield to the new-breed Neo-Tech man, the no-limit man. ...All except the Neo-Tech man will die unfulfilled...without ever knowing wealth, power, and romantic love.

ARE YOU DESTINED FOR TRUE LOVE?
ASK ME ABOUT LOVE FAME FORTUNE
"I CAN TELL YOU WHAT THE FUTURE HOLDS"
DISCOVER YOUR SECRET DESTINY!
CALL NOW!
Talk LIVE with America's leading professional Psychics and Astrologers.
1-800-693-SEER
(7337)
Call anytime. Open 24 hours! $3.99 per minute.
Must be 18+. For entertainment purposes only.

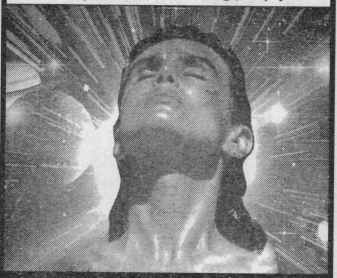